Teaching on Solid Ground

Knowledge Foundations for the Teacher of English

Thomas M. McCann
John V. Knapp

Foreword by Carol D. Lee

THE GUILFORD PRESS
New York　　London

Copyright © 2019 The Guilford Press
A Division of Guilford Publications, Inc.
370 Seventh Avenue, Suite 1200, New York, NY 10001
www.guilford.com

Printed in the United States of America

This book is printed on acid-free paper.

Last digit is print number: 9 8 7 6 5 4 3 2 1

Library of Congress Cataloging-in-Publication Data is available from
the publisher.

ISBN 978-1-4625-3762-4 (paperback) — ISBN 978-1-4625-3763-1 (hardcover)

About the Authors

Thomas M. McCann, PhD, is Professor of English at Northern Illinois University, where he contributes to the teacher licensure program. He taught English in high schools for 25 years, including 7 years working in an alternative high school. The author or coauthor of numerous books, Dr. McCann has served on the Secondary Section Steering Committee of the National Council of Teachers of English (NCTE) and on the Executive Committee of NCTE's Conference on English Education, from which he received the Richard A. Meade Award. Dr. McCann has provided inservice professional development to schools and districts in the Chicago area and nationally.

John V. Knapp, PhD, is Professor Emeritus of English at Northern Illinois University. He is the author or editor of several books and over 50 articles and reviews on literature, family systems psychology, literary criticism, and literature instruction. Since 2007, he has been editor of the literary journal *Style*. As an English teacher and later a professor, Dr. Knapp has educated students at every level, from middle school to doctoral seminars.

Foreword

An Homage to George Hillocks, Jr.

This project was originally conceptualized as a collaboration between Tom McCann and George Hillocks, Jr., who passed away in 2014. The project then evolved into a partnership between Tom McCann and John Knapp, both professors at Northern Illinois University. There are interesting parallels in the relationships out of which this important book was born. Tom was a student of John's as an undergraduate, and then a PhD student of George Hillocks' at the University of Chicago. Rhetorically, each chapter in the book is organized as a third-person narrative, while explicitly naming, comparing, and contrasting points of view on key issues between Tom and John. At the same time, the "metavoice" informing virtually every chapter is that of George Hillocks.

I should note that I, too, am a student of George Hillocks'. I received my PhD in 1991 at the University of Chicago under George's tutelage. I also had the wonderful opportunity of working alongside George in his MAT program. In many respects, many of the underlying arguments in this book are informed both by George's research and his groundbreaking MAT program. Students who worked with George as master's and/ or doctoral students have for many years sponsored a Hillocks listserv, which functions as a community-building and community-sustaining vehicle where those of us trained by George are able to post questions, share research and practice, and push forward new ideas. It is a testament to George that his students, over the decades, have been socialized to sustain inquiry as part of our identities, whether as practitioners and/ or researchers, working in the K–12 system or in university contexts. A pivotal foundation of George's training of his MAT students was that studying their own practice is always part and parcel of learning. After students took classes from George at Judd Hall, they would then walk down the street to Ray School, a public elementary school in the Hyde Park community in Chicago with a diverse student population, to try out lessons they had designed based on the foundational principles around how middle and high school students learn to engage in literary reasoning and to write both arguments and narratives. I point this out because one important feature of the structure of *Teaching on Solid Ground* is to introduce readers to foundational research around the topic in question, and then ask readers to interrogate their own understandings and engage in reflective practice. McCann and Knapp argue, as Hillocks consistently did, that a core pillar of teaching is systematic reflection on practice. It is interesting to note how many of George's MAT students working in the K–12 system are also published researchers on their practice. One can only imagine the impact on the quality of teaching in public education in the United States if teachers-as-researchers was indeed the model and the norm, rather than the exception.

Teaching on Solid Ground is expansive in the breadth of topics and targets of teacher knowledge it addresses. Each chapter synthesizes research that informs the broad knowledge needed by teachers of the English language arts (ELA). An important feature is how McCann and Knapp review and discuss competing research-based explanations and situate the discussions in terms of their historical contexts. For example, in the chapter on the teaching of writing, they contrast what have been longstanding competing models of writing instruction—process approaches and inquiry-based approaches. Hillocks' voice emerges in these comparisons, as he was a strong proponent of inquiry-based approaches. The authors do a careful job of comparing the empirical bases underlying claims for *both* approaches, and in so doing invite readers to employ a social science epistemological framing in evaluating the pros and cons of each approach. They then go on to focus explicitly on points of convergence and divergence in the two approaches.

George Hillocks' presence in this volume is evident in many ways, although the authors are clearly expansive in the range of research on which they draw in introducing each key area of knowledge that ELA teachers need. If we look at the range of research conducted by those of us who were trained by Hillocks, we find common themes. The fact is that many of the studies discussed in this volume were written by George's students. One of the rhetorical techniques I find particularly interesting is the implied dialogue between Tom and John that the authors employ across chapters. This reminds me of the explicit dialogue between Peter

Rabinowitz and Michael Smith (1997) in *Authorizing Readers*. As is the case with Tom and John, Peter Rabinowitz represents the formal world of literary criticism, while Michael Smith represents those who train K–12 teachers to teach literature. Metaphorically, George Hillocks integrated these disciplinary worlds. For example, his approach to the teaching of literature sought to apprentice novice readers in middle and high school to use the formal, intellective tools employed by expert readers of literature, including tools from the world of literary criticism, to support meaning making of complex literary texts. Pedagogically, he called for the design of introductory activities that help prepare students—ahead of being assigned formal literary texts—to, for example, develop criteria for making judgments about characters and theme. George (Hillocks & Ludlow, 1984) developed a powerful taxonomy of questions for examining fiction. The two most challenging categories were what he called questions of author generalization (e.g., having to do with issues of theme and characterization, or what the text implies about the world beyond the text itself) and questions of structural generalization (e.g., interrogating the import of structural and rhetorical choices made by the author, connected to what Rabinowitz [1987/1998] calls an authorial reading). A really important focus of this work for George involved helping students develop both conceptual and procedural knowledge of literary analysis. A lack of attention to such knowledge continues to plague the field, as such knowledge is typically addressed neither in commercial curriculum and textbooks, nor in the Common Core curriculum standards (Lee, 2011, 2014). George's student Michael Smith (1989, 1991), drawing on literary critical work by Wayne Booth (1974, 1983), extended this work by addressing conceptual and procedural knowledge for detecting irony (as Rabinowitz would argue in what he calls *rules of notice*—discussed in this book) and problems of irony and unreliable narration. I (Lee, 2007) have continued this line of work, addressing the noticing of problems of symbolism and satire and identifying strategies for reconstructing warrantable implied significance.

This volume is a tribute to George Hillocks both in how it synthesizes his groundbreaking research in response to literature and composition and, equally important, in how it introduces readers to the breadth of complementary research that informs what ELA teachers need to know and be able to do. This "problem space" is complex, including content knowledge (literature, composition, language), pedagogical knowledge, and knowledge from a human-development perspective on students' cognitive, social, and emotional needs. This complexity results not only from its many dimensions but also from the ways in which these kinds of knowledge are interrelated and must be integrated in dynamic ecological spaces. McCann and Knapp contribute substantively to the field of teacher education, in discipline-specific ways, with this important book.

CAROL D. LEE, PhD
Edwina S. Tarry Professor of Education and Social Policy
Northwestern University

REFERENCES

Booth, W. (1974). *A rhetoric of irony.* Chicago: University of Chicago Press.

Booth, W. (1983). *A rhetoric of fiction.* Chicago: University of Chicago Press.

Hillocks, G., Jr., & Ludlow, L. H. (1984). A taxonomy of skills in reading and interpreting fiction. *American Educational Research Journal, 21,* 7–24.

Lee, C. D. (2007). *Culture, literacy and learning: Taking bloom in the midst of the whirlwind.* New York: Teachers College Press.

Lee, C. D. (2011). Education and the study of literature. *Scientific Study of Literature, 1*(1), 49–58.

Lee, C. D. (2014). Reading gaps and complications of scientific studies of learning. In S. Harper (Ed.), *The elusive quest for civil rights in education: Evidence-based perspectives from leading scholars on the 50th anniversary of the Civil Rights Act.* Philadelphia: Center for the Study of Race and Equity in Education, University of Pennsylvania.

Rabinowitz, P. (1998). *Before reading: Narrative conventions and the politics of interpretation.* Ithaca, NY: Cornell University Press. (Original work published 1987)

Rabinowitz, P. J., & Smith, M. W. (1997). *Authorizing readers: Resistance and respect in the teaching of literature.* New York: Teachers College Press.

Smith, M. (1989). Teaching the interpretation of irony in poetry. *Research in the Teaching of English, 23,* 254–272.

Smith, M. (1991). *Understanding unreliable narrators: Reading between the lines in the literature classroom.* Urbana, IL: National Council of Teachers of English.

Acknowledgments

As we report in the opening pages of this book, George Hillocks, Jr., was working on the early stages of a version of this project at the time of his death in 2014. We are grateful to George for his vision for the project and for his encouragement to see it through to completion. We also appreciate the support of George's daughter, Marjorie Hillocks, and his son, Mac Hillocks, both of whom have encouraged our efforts to complete a book about pedagogical content knowledge, even when the book was quite different from George's original plan. We also appreciate Carol D. Lee's contribution to the book. We value Professor Lee's previous discussions about pedagogical content knowledge and are grateful for her insightful Foreword to the current book.

As we planned and composed this text, we had extensive conversations with colleagues at Northern Illinois University (NIU). We are especially grateful to Gulsat Aygen for her insights and guidance in discussing what English teachers need to know about language. We have long depended on our frequent conversations with such knowledgeable and congenial colleagues as Judith Pokorny, Laura Bird, Elizabeth Kahn, and Carolyn Walter, all of whom have helped us think about what English teachers should know and how teachers might teach in a principled way. We are also indebted to NIU English Department Chair Kathleen Renk and Directors Brad Peters and Jessica Reyman for their steady support in advancing our scholarship.

We thank Professors Bryan McCann and Ashley Mack from Louisiana State University for their extensive help in the development of Chapter 5, "The Territory of Oral Discourse." Bryan's and Ashley's insights helped us to think about the possibilities and responsibilities for teaching oral communication in the English language arts classroom.

Over many years, several high school teachers have been generous in discussing with us the challenges of teaching English in the contemporary classroom. In many instances, these teachers have invited us into their classroom or have collaborated with us in developing models for inquiry-based learning activities. We are especially grateful to Andrew Bouque, Joe Flanagan, Dawn Forde, and Nicole Boudreau Smith. We acknowledge also the generous consultation with school leaders Andrea Cobbett, Mary Howard, and Patricia Santella.

We appreciate the connections and dialogues with our hundreds of students across decades of teaching. We cite Patti Dalton by name in the Introduction, but we could easily list scores of other students who have expanded our thinking and prompted our reflections on what is especially important to know about our discipline and about the processes for teaching the content of our field.

John is grateful for the invitation of his long-ago former student, now colleague and coauthor, Tom McCann, to contribute to his memorial for George Hillocks. Tom is grateful for John Knapp's willingness to tackle a daunting task with energy and good humor. We found our conversations and disagreements as stimulating as they were productive, discovering that what we believed in common far exceeded our oppositional ideas. John particularly wants to thank some of his former students, now colleagues and friends, whose insights into effective mentoring, good teaching, and pedagogical literary scholarship have enlarged his mind and improved his thinking: Christine Drew, Gillian Lachanski, Beth McFarland-Wilson, and Ken Womack. John appreciates friends both close and far away: his late colleague Gustaaf van Cromphout and the lively William Baker for many illuminating conversations over a career's worth of literary and historical debate. Finally, John wants to mention two scholars whose ideas about reading literature have informed so much of his own, and our, work in this book and in the journal *Style*: Peter Rabinowitz and James Phelan.

Taking on a book-length project inevitably, but temporarily, draws our attention away from family. We must acknowledge the patience, support, and encouragement of our families. John sends love to his daughters, Margaret Anne Knapp, Lara Maria Cantuti (and husband, Eric), Joanna Eve Haskin (and fiancé, Mitch), and Jennifer Joy Schmeiser (and husband, Brian). Affectionate mention also goes to his grandchildren: Stephane Cantuti, Jack Saltzberg and Hailey Horacek, and Abi Joy and Emily Joy Schmeiser. He also lovingly thanks his wife, friend, and traveling companion, Joan I. Schwarz. Tom appreciates especially the steady support of his daughter, Katie Carlson (and her bibliophile husband, Alex), and his dear wife, Pam, who listens patiently to plans, reads drafts closely, and offers candid advice.

We are indebted to Craig Thomas, Senior Editor at The Guilford Press, for recognizing the merit in this project and encouraging us through the production process. We are also grateful to Judith Grauman, Anna Brackett, and other members of the Guilford production team who have guided us in moving a rough effort into a more refined final product.

Contents

Introduction

The Importance of Pedagogical Content for the Teaching of English

At the time of his death in November 2014, George Hillocks, Jr., was preparing a book with the working title *Pedagogical Content Knowledge That Teachers of Literacy Need for Grades 6–12*. In George's grand plan, a glimpse of which appears in a 2016 article, he would identify and discuss what every English teacher needs to know in order to teach English effectively, in a way that is exhilarating for both students and teacher. He knew that the teaching of English, or the teaching of any discipline for that matter, requires more than knowing some generic strategies for setting objectives, managing a class, assessing progress, and suppressing disagreeable behavior. George insisted that teachers needed to command deep and extensive knowledge of their discipline—the kind of knowledge that allows them to recognize the broad concepts and "essential questions" that organize the content and allow the student and scholar to see the subject of inquiry as a unified whole. This deep knowledge of a subject informs teachers' judgments about what to teach and how to teach it. We do not presume to execute George's grand plan, at least not in the scope that he had envisioned. Rather, we discuss "what every English teacher needs to know," but in a way that is a bit different from what George had in mind. Our intent is not to report about what George Hillocks envisioned for the teaching of English, although we do cite his work in chapters of this book.

We have had a long history together in the field of English studies. Tom McCann was a student in John Knapp's literature and English methods classes as an undergraduate. Tom went on to a long career in teaching, primarily in high schools, but also with extensive work in fifth grade and in college. Along the way, he earned graduate degrees and published articles and books while John continued to teach literature, advance his scholarship, and prepare a long line of middle school and high school English teachers. The paths of the student and the professor converged again when Tom returned to teach at the university and joined his mentor, John, in preparing others to become English teachers. In the process of this effort, we have talked frequently about what should be taught in English language arts, and how it should be taught. Sometimes these conversations became debates, in the best sense of a give-and-take about areas of doubt and disagreement. We offer this book as an extended conversation, and through this modest effort, we explore what George Hillocks had in mind in proposing the pedagogical content knowledge that every English teacher should command.

Of course, part of the difficulty in the presumption of noting what every English teacher needs to know is the likelihood that any 10 authorities will offer 10 distinct visions, and definitive visions at that. In fact, when we, and George Hillocks in an earlier iteration, ran the idea of the book by some well-regarded colleagues, they cautioned us that it was far too presumptuous to suggest what others need to know in order to be prepared to teach in our profession. But if our presumption is provocative, we see that provocation as a healthy thing. It is likely that the reader will find much in our conversation to disagree with, and we judge those disagreements serve as aids in helping the practitioner to define what is necessary to know in order to teach English well.

Part of our discussions over the years has revealed many differences of opinion. We can attribute some disagreements to contrasting preparation in English studies and our personal experiences working in schools. Differences have also emerged because of varied influences on our literary, composition, and language studies. But, for all of these differences, we have found many more points of convergence. For example, we may disagree about specifying which works of literature every English teacher should know well, but we agree that every English teacher should have read a great deal of significant literature, representing various genres, modes of literature, literary movements, and cultural perspectives. It is these points of convergence we want to explore as the perennial substance—the pedagogical content knowledge—that all English teachers need to know if they are going to teach in a way that Smagorinsky (2001, 2007, 2009) calls *principled*. The conversations, including elements of debate, are likely to represent the kind of exchanges that reflective English teachers engage in—sometimes as interior dialogues, sometimes as deliberations with colleagues, and sometimes as imagined interchanges with the scholars they read. We hope that we provoke the reader both to reflect and to debate, perhaps with us in a virtual way and with colleagues as part of a healthy professional dialogue.

As George Hillocks would have it, these conversations explore the territories of English: the literature we should know, the literature we should teach, how we should teach literature, how we should approach writing instruction, how we can engage learners in sustained dialogues that have everyone speaking and listening, and how we infuse everything with the close examination of language. During these exchanges, through our references, several significant figures in our discipline will voice their opinions, including Wayne Booth, Gerald Graff, Northrop Frye, Peter Rabinowitz, Louise Rosenblatt, James Britton, Sheridan Blau, and Stanley Fish. Through other attributions, George Hillocks, Mina Shaughnessy, Constance Weaver, Janet Emig, James Moffett, Donald Graves, Nancie Atwell, and others will enter the conversation. We anticipate that many readers will react strongly to our positions and to our basic presumption in saying what every English teacher needs to know, and we hope that these reactions will prompt further discussions and debates, which we deem necessary to keep instruction in our discipline current, lively, and rigorous.

In writing this book, we have had three groups in mind: fellow English educators who are preparing future teachers, preservice English teachers preparing for work in middle school and high school, and current English teachers looking to refine how they envision the whole endeavor of teaching English language arts. While this is not a methods book, it certainly offers a vision of what an emerging English teacher should be preparing to teach and how to teach the subject, including examples of instructional activities, especially in the appendices, that run counter to the practices in many schools. As every English teacher knows these days, just getting students to read anything more than a couple of pages has become more and more problematic in the age of social media, hyper-texts packed with millions of facts, and instantaneous exchanges of information and images generally. However, as N. Katherine Hayles (2012) says:

> The problem, as I see it, lies not in hyper attention and hyper reading as such but rather in the challenges the situation presents for parents and educators to ensure that deep attention and close reading continue to be vibrant components of our reading cultures and interact synergistically with the kind of web and hyper readings in which our young people are increasingly immersed. (p. 69)

PEDAGOGICAL CONTENT KNOWLEDGE

Former U.S. Department of Education Secretary Rod Paige (U.S. Department of Education, 2002) summed up what he judged to be the key elements in teacher proficiency in noting that "the only measurable teacher attributes that relate directly to improved student achievement are high verbal ability and solid content knowledge" (p. 39). Politicians, policymakers, and even school leaders have repeated this simple formula for effective teachers: They need to know their subject deeply and they need to be articulate enough to convey the substance of this deep knowledge to young learners. We judge this view too simplistic to represent the complexity of what good teachers know and what they are capable of doing. The view is also misguided in suggesting that teaching is a matter of *conveying* and learning is a matter of *receiving*. As Elizabeth B. Moje (2015) argues:

> Although it is tempting to default to the idea that to teach disciplinary literacy well one needs either deep disciplinary knowledge or deep knowledge of literacy skills, neither is true. In fact, the unavoidable truth is that *both* are needed. . . . [However, that] knowledge-in-practice is what teachers need for disciplinary literacy instruction, and these practices are rarely taught in university content courses. (p. 270; cf. Knapp, 2000, p. 662)

We agree that to teach English in a principled way, a teacher needs both extensive content knowledge and the pedagogical knowledge that is required to frame the questions for inquiry and to plan and facilitate the learning experiences that will advance students' knowledge.

By analogy, one could argue that all that physicians need to know is the human body in its many manifestations and, armed with such information, they should be articulate enough to explain it to a patient. But anyone headed for a physical might object. Don't "they" need to know more than that? What about chemicals in the air and water, radiation from natural sources, diseases that come from animals, bugs, and plants? What about the assessment of patients' complaints and conditions? What about the skills necessary in applying knowledge to design a course of treatment and to direct a patient's wellness efforts? Our analogy is not really that far-fetched. Anyone working in a hospital could immediately point to a dozen limitations in our original definition of physicians' attributes. Likewise, anyone who has walked back into a school as an adult would note that the place is smaller than he or she remembers and the teachers look like human beings trying to do a good job for their charges and not merely disciplinarians; but the new math, the new sciences, the new humanities are very different from when he or she attended school as a child. What do these teachers need to know to teach our children? What exactly IS solid content knowledge in this day of speedy cultural and scientific change? What does a teacher's "articulate" voice mean in a room full of very busy teenagers all talking at once? Should that articulate teacher's voice be the one that dominates the classroom?

Secretary Paige's view does not begin to represent how a deep knowledge of a discipline serves a teacher in organizing learning experiences so that students can begin to construct knowledge of a subject. Over long careers, we have each known brilliant scholars who seemed oblivious about ways to connect with learners and about ways to scaffold sequences of experiences to deepen students' understanding as they interacted with each other. We have also met experienced teachers who could devise, borrow, and invent a variety of tasks and tests for students to accomplish, while knowing the subject of English language arts only superficially. We understand that any teacher of English needs to know her discipline deeply. But teaching is not a simple matter of *telling* what one knows—of conveying, transmitting, or otherwise "transfusing" knowledge to the presumed empty vessels under the teacher's charge. The art and science of teaching English is neither the telling of what one knows nor is it merely a repertoire of pedagogical tricks without substantive content.

In our more desolate moments of reflection, we can sometimes imagine teachers who assign students tasks and masterfully keep the learners on task, assess their progress in completing any given task, and measure growth on similar tasks over time. These same teachers might regularly apprise parents of the learners' progress, maintain dazzling bulletin boards, participate enthusiastically in committee meetings, meet all of the administrative deadlines, complete necessary reports, attend professional development activities, and remain emotionally attuned to every student in the room each day. At the same time, these teachers might have completed relatively few upper-level literature, language, or composition courses at the university and profess many misconceptions about the discipline of literature and language study.

Hence, deep knowledge of a subject is indeed necessary, but there must be something more. If teaching and learning involve simply the transmission of knowledge from expert to novice, the logical consequence in a digital age in a highly technological society is, for us, a nightmare. While we judge that we know more than most high school and middle school teachers about literature, writing, and language, we also know others who are more expert than we. If teaching is a matter of transmitting knowledge, we humbly invite learners to attend to the most knowledgeable literature, rhetoric, and language scholars in the world, always available via the Internet. Certainly, their lectures and writings can be broadcast, saved, and viewed repeatedly. If transmission of knowledge were as simple as binge-watching any television series, there would be no reason to come to a cold auditorium or attend a stuffy classroom on campus to have a lecture poured into a receptive brain: students could stay home in their pajamas and receive transmission on the sofa; the professor could transmit from the home office or from the kitchen while pouring a second cup of coffee.

In contrast to these disturbing scenarios, we can recall dynamic classrooms where students actively engaged in learning, talked to each other and to the teacher, assessed their learning, set goals, made plans for subsequent learning, and reflected on learning. As Patti Dalton, one of our former students, once said, "Don't teach a lesson that you could just as well teach with no students present." Patti's idea, one that we embrace, is that little learning takes place if students are assumed to be passive receptacles into which an expert pours knowledge. Learning simply doesn't work that way (Freire, 1993; Hattie, 2012). Instead, learners need to be involved in their learning in order to construct understandings and to practice procedures of which they can be consciously aware. Toward this end, a middle school or high school teacher needs deep knowledge of the discipline of English and command of the procedures for planning, facilitating, and assessing learning experiences to promote students' deep understanding.

In Appendix A (see pp. 156–162), we offer a set of descriptions of English teachers at work and invite the reader to judge the extent to which any of the descriptions aligns with your vision of the teaching of English language arts. You might find it useful to discuss the scenarios with other teachers. You might also find that none of the descriptions accurately represents the way you view the job. The point of the effort is to have your own firm sense of what the endeavor of teaching English is all about.

Shulman (1987) offered the idea of pedagogical content knowledge as "that special amalgam of content and pedagogy that is uniquely the province of teachers" (1987, p. 8). Shulman points out that at the time of his writing, most of the research on teaching investigated teacher practices without regard to the subject matter at the core of that teaching. Referring to his contemporaries' body of research about teachers' practices, Shulman (1987) observes that "[in] their necessary simplification of the complexities of classroom teaching, investigators ignored one central aspect of classroom life: the subject matter" (p. 6). He comments further on the neglect of acknowledging content knowledge as a necessary element in strong teaching:

Policymakers read the research on teaching literature and find it replete with references to direct instruction, time on task, wait time, ordered turns, lower-order questions, and the like. They find little or no references to subject matter, so the resulting standards or mandates lack any reference to content dimensions of teaching. Similarly, even in the research community, the importance of content has been forgotten. Research programs that arose in response to the dominance of process-product work accepted its definition of the problem and continued to treat teaching more or less generically, or at least as if the content of instruction were relatively unimportant. Even those who studied teacher cognition, a decidedly non-process/product perspective, investigated teacher planning or interactive decision making with little concern for the organization of content knowledge in the minds of teachers. (p. 6)

The deep knowledge of English as a subject—knowledge about literature, writing, speaking, and listening—guides teachers in planning instruction, and in recognizing the problems or essential questions that distinguish the discipline (Sosnoski, 1994; Wilson, 1983). These include deciding how to initiate and organize lines of inquiry related to compelling problems or questions, devising sequenced learning experiences to foster student learning, providing for the variety of assessments to track development in order to know how to pace instruction and intervene in processes, and deciding from episode to episode and moment to moment within a lesson whether the planned learning activities actually foster students' understanding of concepts and procedures at the heart of the discipline.

As Grossman (1989), Grossman, Smagorinsky, and Valencia (1999), and Stodolsky and Grossman (1995) note, teachers are not interchangeable: teachers in various disciplines think differently about the nature of teaching, influenced of course by their understanding about the content they teach. In part, this is what often makes efforts at "reform" misguided, with proposals for sweeping changes failing to take into account the specifics about the content and the context for teaching. Grossman and Shulman (1994) note, "Nonetheless, no organization can overcome fundamental deficits of content and pedagogy in preparation of its teachers" (p. 12).

VISIONS OF ENGLISH AS A DISCIPLINE

Other authors, as part of their larger purpose or ancillary to their purpose, have taken up an expression of the central endeavor in teaching English. Burke (2012), Christenbury (2006), Christenbury and Lindblom

(2016), and Gallagher (2015) primarily address the high school English teacher. In *The English Teachers Companion,* Burke offers his view of "what English is—and is not." He cites three "traditions" that explain the purpose of the discipline of English and ends with a vision most closely aligned with Langer (2004) in her expanded vision of what allows schools to "beat the odds," but dependent in many ways on the specific group of learners and their needs and characteristics. Similarly, in her narrative of an attempt to return to the high school classroom and experience its realities, Christenbury (2006) suggests the kind of disciplinary knowledge she assumed she needed in going into the assignment and reports the many ways this knowledge failed her in working with adolescents from day to day. She focuses most attention on the teaching of literature and calls literature "The Heart of Language Arts" (p. 124), depicting the study of literature from a distinctly reader-response perspective. While Christenbury knew much about literature, she admits that she knew much less about her learners and how to frame inquiry into the literature in ways that the teens would find compelling. Gallagher (2015) envisions "what works" in teaching adolescents how to read, write, speak, and listen well. While he expresses some reservations about the Common Core State Standards, he offers his book as a resource for teaching toward the standards in a way that he judges "works" and "serves the best interest" of learners. Gallagher largely reflects on his own substantial experience in the classroom to emphasize the power of modeling reading and writing processes and relying on models (i.e., "mentor texts") to guide production. His examples imply the knowledge of procedures for close reading and composing that every English teacher should know, without specifying the body of literature and the concepts of language that a teacher should know well enough to design instructional experiences and units.

While Scholes (1999) discusses the state of English, especially the study of literature, as a discipline in higher education, he explores some of the same territory that we do. His discussion of what English is as a discipline asks if the endeavor to study literature is a matter of narrating the story of the development of literature, or a matter of experiencing and appreciating some selected "great works" of literature, or an effort at commanding the procedures necessary to read complex texts closely and talk about that reading in mature ways. These are considerations for middle school and high school English language arts teachers as well, as they decide to plow their way through an anthology; handpick students' literary experiences; or empower learners to follow their own inclinations to pursue their own literary enthusiasms, if they have any.

Rabinowitz and Smith (1997) focus particularly on the interactions among the reader, text, and author. Their extended conversation reveals the extent to which readers depend on their knowledge of the conventions of genres, especially of narratives, to recognize patterns and conventions in order to see the hand of the author at work. Whereas many teachers tend to consider primarily the thematic patterns in literary works, Rabinowitz and Smith also explore how teaching selected formal patterns in literature gives students a means of learning to read more independently by applying the requirements of certain genres to newly experienced literature. Their "rules" suggest that teachers must help students to learn how to comprehend literary works that combine formalized learning pathways (e.g., authors get readers to "notice" imagery patterns and then expect them to connect those images to something significant) and, by following those several important and significant ideas, such readers build and configure them to increasingly larger patterns. Only then will any reader be able to speak of the largest and most important ideas or themes in a piece of literature, ideas that, woven together, offer the reader a sense of overall "coherence" in the aesthetic communications between writer and reader. Nonetheless, Rabinowitz and Bancroft (2014) also caution teachers against stressing the "thematic leap," the almost obsessive "search for overarching themes," which encourages "students to see the discovery of easy-to-formulate tags as the end of reading, thus stressing 'meaning' over experience." Secondly, it "erases the differences among texts, reducing their individuality, often with the effect of softening their moral and political impart" (p. 19). Certainly, a teacher of English will need to be familiar with a discipline for reading literary texts, or "rules" for the reading and interpretation of literature, in order to plan for the experiences that will allow students to become sensitive about what to notice and note, as Beers and Probst (2013) suggest.

We offer these examples from the study of literature to illustrate teachers' "special" knowledge—the knowledge about the content of their discipline as that knowledge impacts how they plan and facilitate instruction and interact with learners. We suggest that teachers will also need "special" knowledge as part of their preparation for teaching writing, speaking and listening, and the study of language.

ORGANIZATION OF THE BOOK

In this introduction, we have attempted to define *pedagogical content knowledge* and to make the case for the necessity of command of this knowledge as a teacher of English language arts. In the pages that follow, we offer an extended conversation about what English teachers need to know about their subject in order to teach English language arts in a principled way. Instead of representing the conversation as a script, we refer to the speakers (i.e., Tom or John) in the third person until we reach our points of convergence and speak as the unified *we*. We hope this format helps the reader to distinguish the contrasting perspectives.

In the following chapters, we tackle first the "territory of literature," to use Hillocks's (2016) phrase. We discuss the competing perspectives on what literature a teacher of English should have read, and what literature teachers should introduce to their learners. An accompanying chapter describes some choices in *how* to teach the reading of complex texts, including examples related to the teaching of specific genres. The next broad category is the pedagogical content knowledge for the teaching of writing. The conversation moves into the competing approaches to the teaching of composition, with illustrations of instructional activities that allow learners to develop a repertoire of processes for writing in various genres. While our conversations in this book trace shifts in instructional emphases over time and reveal areas of disagreement, we intersect at a decidedly constructivist approach that values process and supports students' efforts to write in meaningful ways about literature, about their experiences, and about issues critical to their lives.

While many schools address the goals related to public speaking through a one-semester speech course, we see speaking and listening as common and necessary elements in every class meeting. In contrast to common practices supported in schools where teachers dominate the classroom discourse, we agree with Britton (1983) that "reading and writing float on a sea of talk" (p. 11) and encourage extensive classroom conversations as important experiences for formulating and practicing the procedures that are part of reading, writing, and critical thinking. The related chapter discusses the complexities of oral communication and illustrates the many ways that purposeful peer interactions and more formal public speaking experiences help students to prepare for reading, analyzing, and reflecting on literature, and to practice the procedures that transfer to writing.

We recognize that close reading and clear expression require knowledge about how language works. The related chapter discourages a prescriptive approach to teaching grammar, usage, and the conventions of language. We also tread carefully through the territory of "correctness" and "standard" English. We discuss what we see as some high-priority concepts that an English teacher should know and be able to teach to adolescents. A deep understanding of these concepts leads to what Williams and Bizup (2013) and Williams and Columb (2010) call "clarity and grace" in written expression and serve the reader in critical transactions with literature.

Throughout the book, we discuss efforts to teach digital literacies and other "new literacies." This discussion explores the changing nature of the way in which readers often experience texts and what they recognize as "texts," including films and graphic novels. We readily admit our limitations in regard to knowing how to combine and synthesize these relatively new fields of scholarship with the more traditional forms of literary and compositional theories gracefully, but also understand the difficulties of constructing any synthesis whose new and old elements remain in motion. Thus, we discuss the reality of the changing literacy landscape and note the procedures for close reading and clear expression, whether the experience is with a traditional print text or other forms of media. We insist that teachers need to be aware of the shifting conceptions of texts and the expansion of forms of literary expression.

We conclude with a chapter about the common threads of knowledge that we see across fields of pedagogy, cognition, linguistics, literature, and composition studies. While this list represents vast intellectual territory, we insist that thinkers from various disciplines use different language to represent what are essentially the same concepts, revealing some core principles for English language arts instruction that require deep knowledge in the substance of what we teach.

Of necessity, we have separated elements of English language arts into separate chapters, but we recognize the reciprocal nature of various language activities and we envision that the enacted curriculum in a middle school or high school would integrate the many elements into coherent conceptual units, along the lines suggested by Hillocks, McCabe, and McCampbell (1971), Langer (2001), Smagorinsky (2001, 2007), Smith, Appleman, and Wilhelm (2014), and Stern (1995).

Throughout the chapters, we include text boxes that examine implications for teacher development and offer recommended resources to support this learning. Each chapter ends with a section that invites "Your Thoughts" by posing questions for self-reflection and discussion with your peers. At the end of the book, Appendices A through H provide a variety of examples of classroom practices that illustrate the application of pedagogical content knowledge.

1

Knowing the Territory of Literature

At the university where we teach, posted on the bulletin board for students in the teacher licensure program is a "Strongly Recommended Reading List." An introduction emphasizes the teacher candidate's need to build substantial knowledge of significant literary texts before entering into the methods courses, and exhorts the candidates to read the recommended texts and track progress toward completing the list. The list includes the following titles: *The Odyssey, The Iliad,* the Old Testament, *The Aeneid, The Metamorphoses* of Ovid, selected plays by Aristophanes and Sophocles, Plato's *Republic* and *Meno,* Aristotle's *Poetics,* and translations of *The Divine Comedy* and *Beowulf.* A major implication of the list is that teaching literature requires a developing level of expertise, one that begins at minimum with a basic understanding of the building blocks, the texts of the discipline, constituting such expert knowledge and practice. Consequently, the authors of "the list" assumed that novice teachers of English in middle schools and high schools should be familiar with classic literature, even if they never engage their own students with these texts.

As two professors in the same teacher preparation program, we have disagreed about the list—both the specific titles and the idea of a list of "strongly recommended" texts. In fact, we disagree about several issues about preparing candidates, although we converge about some core principles. As we share our disagreements and convergences on these pages, we invite readers to reflect on their own positions, perhaps taking the opportunity to refine thinking about what English teachers need to know in order to teach English in a principled way in middle school and high school.

According to John, the thinking behind the recommended reading is consistent for those who consider the teaching of literature as an acquired expertise, one that begins early in life with the pleasures of reading stories and then, over time, also includes noticing that story patterns develop in the ways tales are both told and received. Some readers appear naturally to gravitate toward stories that reflect their own time, situations in life, and familiar people, while others prefer literary experiences that take them out of their own world and into domains and lives very different from their own. The central issue confronting all teachers of literature is to achieve a balance between these two tendencies: encourage those students looking primarily for confirmation about the already familiar to explore other times, cultures, and varieties of characters, human or otherwise. David Lowenthal insists, "The past remains integral to us all, individually and collectively. We must concede the ancients their place. . . . But their place is not simply back there, in a separate and foreign country; it is assimilated in ourselves and resurrected into an ever-changing present" (p. 412; quoted in Santirocco, 2016, p. 5). Conversely, some teachers urge those who want primarily imaginative versions of unknown people and places to look more closely at what they believe to be seemingly familiar. In a diverse classroom, selecting texts that convince some reluctant readers to expand their reading is a real challenge for many teachers.

One way to attack the problems just mentioned is prescriptive, and a well-known example may be seen with Hirsch's argument for cultural literacy. In his influential text, Hirsch (1988) reviews research literature about reading and accurately notes that a reader's prior reading experience will influence, and perhaps facilitate, the current reading experience. As a general precept, the more one has read, the easier it is to read other texts for understanding and appreciation: prior learning influences current learning. Few educators disagree with this part of Hirsch's argument, but he has had his critics for other reasons. Part of the controversy focuses on Hirsch's prescription for what constitutes appropriate background knowledge in a diverse cultural context; critics claim that his text choices come from a literary tradition that is primarily white and Western, and that they are too narrow to represent a "shared" cultural experience. Those refuting Hirsch's lists argue that every student brings a fund of knowledge to the variety of literacy experiences required in schools, although that knowledge base may not align with the texts that Hirsch values. And what was arguable in 1988—the presumption of a monolithic and stable social culture—has been settled in the face of an undeniably diverse population in the 21st century. If our culture were stable—à la British literature of the later 19th century—it would be considerably easier to catalog what one should have read as a teacher prepared to introduce other learners to the world of quality literature. John argues, however, that cultural diversity is only one part of the problem even though some have made it the central issue in literary education.

Over the years we have heard preservice teachers complain about the expectations that they should be familiar with the works appearing on the "Strongly Recommended" list. In some instances, the teacher candidates recall that their early enthusiasm for reading, especially for reading popular fiction and various series targeting adolescent readers, influenced their decision to pursue a license to teach English. These reading enthusiasts rarely recall having read anything on the "Strongly Recommended" list, making it difficult for them to see the necessity for an English teacher to be familiar with these texts from a traditional literature canon: they had never met these texts along their path to the university and saw no imperative to introduce younger readers to them. Other skeptics among the prospective teachers are those who have experienced clinical placements in middle schools where they have encountered some readers reading at a third- or fourth-grade level. The preservice teachers question how their familiarity with Dante, Homer, Aeschylus, or even Shakespeare will help them as they work with reluctant and struggling readers.

While we appreciate that our university students are sometimes skeptical of the course of study that requires them to read some difficult texts, and we understand that many of the preservice teachers will never have an opportunity to teach *The Aeneid, The Republic,* or even *Romeo and Juliet,* we do see a need for emerging English teachers to have a strong background in literature. We recognize with Shulman (1987) that teachers need to have substantial pedagogical content knowledge. Such knowledge marks a major difference between one's own growth as an adolescent or early adult reader—for whom the pleasures of the text are paramount—versus an expert teacher who must know how and why some texts are effortlessly able to pull in the reader into its story world. Coplan (2004), a well-known literary critic, mentions that research in narrative study "all points in one direction, namely, that people—or stand-ins for people—are the primary vehicles by which we make sense of stories. Readers typically adapt their point of view to one or another of the story's characters, usually the protagonist, and make their way through the narrative by tracking that character's actions" (p. 142; quoted in Vermeule, 2010, p. 41). Hence, the expert literature teacher also understands why others require the help of someone more knowledgeable to guide the emerging reader in understanding characters they may not automatically like, especially those from an unknown and relatively alien universe. Even the teacher working with the struggling sixth-grade reader needs to know much about the way literary texts work and should be able to help students distinguish between quality literature that challenges their minds and emotions from predictable and gratuitous pulp.

The tension for us, as university faculty charged with preparing new teachers, comes in defining what would consist of adequate pedagogical content knowledge in the territory of literature. What do middle school and high school teachers of English need to know about imaginative literature? We are resolute in arguing that literature teaching, just as any of the STEM disciplines, requires a level of domain expertise for the instructor to teach effectively in any of the grades or ability levels, from middle through high school and beyond. Such expertise includes some ordinary technical knowledge, for example, of poetic enjambment and line integrity, fictional narrative differences, and dramatic scenic contrasts in tragedies. Expertise also requires the teacher to have experienced a broad and diverse range of literary reading: readings from multiple genres, time periods, and even languages (in translation); and knowledge of the political, cultural, and scientific history into which many of such works are set; as the novice teacher grows in his or her knowledge of the primary works, we also believe it will be useful to develop some understanding of the previous conversations (criticism) about the literature being taught.

TEACHING LITERATURE THEN AND NOW

As we explain in our Introduction, our approach to thinking about what an English teacher needs to know about literature (and writing and language in other chapters) is dialogic, taking the form of a conversation—between author and reader certainly, but also among readers, both in the classroom and across printed reactions and assessments and online responses. Applebee (1996), in his influential *Curriculum as Conversation*, says,

> A considerable part of teachers' tacit knowledge of the academic tradition and of pedagogy is expressed in the conventions they establish for discourse within their classrooms. In my studies of the ways curriculum emerges over time in individual classrooms, the presence of such a set of tacit conventions of discourse has been one of the most consistent features of accomplished teaching and learning. These conventions provide the essential backdrop against which everything else takes place. (p. 105)

These conventions include, of course, the "form and content of discussion and interaction." They also include "what topics and issues are considered appropriate as part of the English language arts in general and literature in particular (ranging from textual analysis to issues in contemporary life)" (Applebee, 1996, p. 105). So, in thinking about the pedagogical content knowledge for the teaching of literature, it is impossible to separate the text selections (and who gets to select them) from the mode of discourse that distinguishes the class that encounters the texts. *How* a group of learners and their teacher talk about a text and *what* they talk about sets the priorities and reveals a teacher's conception of how students learn about literature. We will say more about modes of discourse in Chapters 2 and 5.

Long ago, Tom was a student in John's literature and methods classes at the university. We both recall the perspective about what was important to know *then,* some of which remains important, and more that has evolved or changed. We also appreciate recent demands to reform or at least expand that perspective *now* in a contemporary teaching world. We re-create our ongoing dialogue with a certain tongue-in-cheek style, and do so because we believe that one can better describe and more clearly evaluate what one believes in (or used to) with some emotion rather than merely mentioning philosophical stances in a relatively intellectual and detached way. We acknowledge areas of disagreement, but, at the end of each chapter, we emphasize what we still have in common and analyze what we can agree needs change or reconsideration. Although many changes in contemporary education have been for the better, not everything in the contemporary classroom is necessarily an improvement over past practices and attitudes. We judge that many changes have been merely cosmetic, with the core practices remaining essentially the same as they were 50 years ago. As with cultural and academic changes generally, there are trade-offs, past and present, and we think those are worth exploring.

John had much to do with the "Strongly Recommended List," and he ruffled some feathers in the department when he posted the document to guide the preservice teachers. His insistence on the necessity of being familiar with the works on the list centers on the idea of "expertise." Although it seems obvious that one cannot study, much less teach, advanced chemistry or physics without some attention to calculus and the languages of mathematics generally, some teacher-trainees, nonliterary humanists, and even a few English teachers do not typically consider their subject domain as a craft requiring expert knowledge—among other things, via mastery of classical literature. Many writers, past and present, do, however, and one only need consider one of Toni Morrison's

novels to become struck by how much of the Bible she employs, both
thematically and imagistically, in her novels and how much such "background knowledge" of it the reader must acquire to comprehend her
writing even at a basic level. Other examples of needed background
knowledge abound as one considers the influence, for example, of
Thomas More's *Utopia* in comprehending more recent attempts at creating ideal societies in such diverse story worlds as Francis Harper's *Iola
Leroy,* Orwell's *1984,* or the film series *The Matrix.*

Whether the reader learns about older ideal societies, or biblical stories, sayings, and images through lectures, TED Talks, or book reading,
the reader who has developed some expertise in biblical lore will very
likely find Morrison's novels deeper and richer than those who have not.
The narrative voice of Morpheus in *The Matrix* would then not appear
quite so unworldly to those who are familiar with Winston Smith's tor-
mentor O'Brien in *1984,* or Raphael Hythloday's in More's *Utopia.*
The inside jokes would be funnier as well, if Neo doesn't know that
the lecturer, Morpheus, is the god both of dreams but also sleep; that
Smith, the quintessential Englishman, has an inquisitor with an Irish
name; and More's Hythloday means "talker of nonsense" in Greek. So
"appropriate" background knowledge means paying some attention to
the originator of a given book's conversation, the author, and investigating what he or she expects or at least hopes that the reader will bring
to the conversation. Rabinowitz and Smith (1997) call those who fulfill
such expectations as joining or becoming members of the "authorial
audience" (p. 5), the audiences of his or her time a given author assumes
would understand the cultural context of his work. In the literature written in the English language, that audience contains an evolving group of
members for over a thousand years. John poses these questions: Who are
we to dismiss hundreds of other minds who have lived over tens of centuries and who have considered many, if not most, of the same reading
problems we now face? Do we not owe it to them to at least think about
the issues they have raised many times in the past? Do we really want
our students and offspring to live only in an eternal present?

Hence, much that is involved in the act of reading literary texts
requires a familiarity with the bodies of literature to which authors
refer. Such allusions are powerful symbols that call up whole narratives
and histories. Conventions of modes of literature and specific genres
become conventions because there is a tradition that a contemporary
writer might repeat or reject; but an understanding and respect for the
tradition or the significance of its violation will depend on knowing
what the tradition has been. The poetry theorist Reuven Tsur (2010)
refers to several of these older traditions as cognitive fossils, saying that
many "cultural and poetic conventions are verbal constructs that reflect

active cognitive . . . processes and constraints that become fossilized in time. . . . The use of such verbal devices may remain sporadic . . . [but, with] the sporadic, sometimes ingenious inventions of creative individuals may become generally accepted conventions—sometimes even in unrelated cultures" (pp. 496–497). As has been mentioned many times before, familiarity with earlier literatures and/or allusions to them requires a joint responsibility of both author and reader. Allusiveness only works for readers if they notice both the allusion and the reason why it has been employed. Authors refer ideally to works they can assume the average reader in their authorial audience knows or should know, and readers, ideally, have consumed enough cultural material to comprehend those references that go beyond the relative provinciality of everyday adolescent life.

In addition, we believe that literature itself offers an invaluable mode of thinking, one that seems typically buried to many in our scientific age. We try to teach our students to explore their own pulses as they read. As Philip Davis (2013) points out, just as a spectrograph printout shows readers their out-loud verbalizations, so too the idea "that silent readers might see something of the internal motions they intuitively feel inside themselves seems to offer another possible stage of learning" (p. 23). Indeed, he argues that literature "will go disregarded as a deep form of thinking if only visible and material evidence can seem sufficient against post-humanist skepticism" (p. 23). Later, Davis concludes that for "those who wish to use thinking to get above themselves whilst *still* remaining within themselves, it is reading that serves as the trigger for such reflection and as a space for such contemplation" (p. 25). Therein lies the chicken-and-egg problem for teachers: how to motivate adolescent readers to experience works that they might not likely or willingly read on their own, while at the same time encouraging them to also read a wide body of literature with enthusiasm, depends both on a teacher's knowing students well and knowing a considerable body and range of literature. Likewise, we propose that students must acquire the thinking processes we associate with literary reading, and as with learning at any level of expertise, such acquisition requires wide-ranging textual experiences and ongoing practice in reading and thinking.

To help with this task, students should be given opportunities to converse and socialize with each other in the context of literary analysis. As Moje (2015) describes, students need "explicit conversations around how language is used and how it functions to construct meaning" (p. 268). Students' conversations with one another, initially organized and properly supervised by the teacher, break the one-way traffic between only the single learner and his or her teacher. As Gary Weissman (2016) points out:

In literature courses there is typically just one person who learns from engaging with and responding to multiple written responses to an assigned work of literature, and that person, the great beneficiary of the students' work, is the teacher. The teacher has a uniquely enriched perspective, an understanding expanded not only through rereading literature he or she has taught but also through exposure to myriad students' writings on that literature. (p. 2)

We agree with his wisdom when Weissman vows to "open up and broaden this perspective by involving its readers [the students] as participants . . . in collaboration with others who have read and written on it" (p. 2).

EXPANDING THE TERRITORY OF LITERATURE

In some ways, many schools have not changed very much since the late 1960s and early 1970s. For all of the political and social upheaval that we associate with that time, schools have remained relatively conservative places, culturally, and while some of the literature curriculum has been discarded, a substantial number of works taught over the years remains largely intact (Applebee, 1993; Stotsky, 2010). Few English departments now require students to read, for example, the staple texts of the schools of the 1950s and 1960s, like George Eliot's *Silas Marner,* but Harper Lee's *To Kill a Mockingbird* survived the civil rights revolution of the 1960s and 1970s. So while school curricula have remained relatively stable in that one sense, the populations making up the school environment have been evolving dramatically and creating many cultural changes in their wake.

Perhaps the biggest drivers of cultural evolution in the schools have been the triple results of the civil rights movement since the 1960s, where John dates the beginning of his teaching career; the renewed rise and continued development of feminism; and the immigration of millions of people from all over the world into North America, thus making the school-age population not only more multicultural but more multilingual as well. In the 1980s, Tom taught in a public high school where dozens of different languages were the first language spoken in the homes of the students; since then, this variety of languages and the cultures they represent has become more common. A recognition of the changing demographics in schools has prompted many teachers to question the appropriateness of the "traditional literature canon" on at least two grounds: (1) the texts commonly assigned as required reading in schools

Considerations for Professional Development

We have noted some debates that have occupied teachers of literature for at least 60 years. We can trace the debates since the time when we entered the profession in the 1960s. The points of contention in professional conversations have focused on the literature that teachers should have read in order to prepare students to become enthusiastic and skillful readers of literature. Wherever you stand in these debates, know that the National Council of Teachers of English has set standards that expect emerging teachers to be "knowledgeable about texts—print and non-print texts, media texts, classic texts and contemporary texts, including young adult—that represent a range of world literatures, historical traditions, genres, and the experiences of different genders, ethnicities, and social classes" (NCTE, 2012, Standard 1). Of course, substantial knowledge of all of these different categories of literature and forms of texts is a tall order, and we know that few teacher candidates have read such a variety of literature with depth. But any teacher of English is likely to be working throughout a career to expand her knowledge through a personal program of reading.

We do not dare to list specific titles that teachers should have read before entering the classroom. Instead, we list here some categories of literature for the teacher's consideration. As we have done throughout our careers, you might note the categories with which you are less familiar and seek to improve your literary knowledge in this area. We love to read texts in areas that we already know well and that represent our enthusiasms; but just as we encourage adolescent learners to venture outside of their comfort zone for reading, we recommend that teachers continue to venture into less familiar literary territory, especially to be prepared to meet students at various literature crossroads. Here is a general outline to guide the expansion of literature knowledge:

• *Traditional canon.* What are some works from a traditional literature canon that you have intended to read and that can deepen your knowledge about specific authors, genres, movements, and literature development?

• *Multicultural voices and underrepresented authors.* Beyond the voices represented in a traditional high school canon, teachers should be familiar with some authors who offer new cultural, economic, and social perspectives, especially authors who might represent language, situations, and issues that are close to the lives of their students.

• *Young adult literature.* Of course, the broad category of young adult literature crosses into other categories, such as multicultural literature. Many English teachers come out of college after studying Shakespeare, Chaucer, Milton, Austen, and Dickens and enter schools where they are asked to teach *The Outsiders* or *Monster.* If you have avoided literature intended for a young adult audience, it is time to discover some of the more significant works in this field and read some of the texts that are likely to resonate with the learners in your classes.

• *Identity and therapy.* We know that adolescents often come to school in crisis, in part because their sense of self and their place in the world are emerging.

(continued)

Several texts help students to explore many conflicts and complications in a simulated world that allows the reader to safely explore. Teachers can look to read texts that allow students to see themselves and constructively contend with many issues that complicate their lives.

• *Thematic explorations.* As we have noted in this chapter, sometimes the esthetic value of a text is less important than its ability to support inquiry into compelling themes. Certainly, many students face life-or-death issues with violence, poverty, justice, and equity. A teacher would do well to become familiar with compelling texts that invite inquiry into any one of these difficult issues.

• *Graphic narratives and digital platforms.* In many schools, teachers recognize that in most instances graphic novels are not simply long comic books. We encourage teachers to discover high-quality graphic literature. We also recognize that students often read on digital platforms, which allow the reader to navigate text in ways that are different from turning the page and highlighting a print text. Teachers should distinguish a digital reading experience from a conventional print-text reading experience in order to help students take advantage of features in each platform.

---

rarely represent the diverse cultural, experiential, and social issues associated with the lives of many of the students who are expected to read the texts; and (2) the relatively narrow scope of the literature constrains students from witnessing the rich variety of human experiences and recognizing the diversity of responses to those experiences. We intend to address both of these claims below.

In visiting a high school for an accreditation review, Tom observed a tenth-grade class in which students were assigned to work in teams to pick out a scene from Lerner and Loewe's *My Fair Lady,* the adaptation of Shaw's *Pygmalion.* This seems like a conventional and perhaps reasonable assignment. But all of the students in the class were African American, and it seemed a shame, from Tom's point of view, not to offer the works of Lorraine Hansberry, August Wilson, Amiri Baraka, Ntozake Shange, or other African American writers who depict experiences that might offer a greater probability to resonate with the students. These authors offer high school students opportunities for rich oral interpretations of the experiences of African Americans in the 20th century, at least as compared to figuring out characters from contrasting upper class social strata in late 19th-century London. Alfred Tatum (2009) and others (e.g., Colby & Lyon, 2004; Harris & Willis, 2003; Hunt & Hunt, 2005) argue for a familiarity with multicultural literature and the necessity of respecting learners' needs to see their lives represented in the literature that they share with peers. We invite prospective teachers to join Tom and John in what has now been a century-long debate over textual selection and appropriateness for adolescent readers.

John agrees, in part, with Tom's arguments about being responsive to the needs and interests of the students in the middle school and high school classrooms. One can easily see the cultural gaps between the concerns of contemporary students struggling with ordinary daily issues about safety, economic stability, health, and legal matters versus their possible interests in a literary work revealing what appears to be the problems of a late 19th-century upper-class British academic. However, this particular textual choice might elicit a further question: Why choose a pop-musical textual version of George Bernard Shaw's more serious work *Pygmalion* (1916/1994), where the issues were exactly the problems of highly stratified social classes; lack of women's career mobility; and the insensitivities of upper-class, educated males, issues that a group of students in a contemporary classroom might have been struggling with daily? Hence, one could suggest that the teacher's knowledge of Shaw's original play, and insistence and demonstration that his issues were indeed relevant, might have stretched that class conversation.

John also suggests that the names of the African American playwrights listed above and references to their texts bring us to the heart of the matter: identity and cultural politics have driven school curricular choices for several years now, but those choosing texts for inclusion in school curricula perhaps have paid less attention to the artistic quality of identity-based choices. And the idea of "quality," John argues, is based on such verities as character complexity, verbal skills, and debatable ideas, and more than simple solutions to issues set up in the plot. Without removing the likes of Shakespeare, Chaucer, Homer, the Brontës, Austen, and Dickens from the curriculum entirely, the rich diversity of our society (represented by the populations in public schools), suggests the importance of exposing students to a wide variety of texts, depicting diverse experiences and cultures and competing perspectives on values, problems, and human experience.

STUDYING LITERATURE
TO MAKE A BETTER WORLD

Both of us agree that a second demand for a change in thinking about preparing to teach literature is an increased sensitivity to the issues of social justice. In recent years, the faculty in some middle schools and high schools have been less concerned with exposing students to culturally and artistically significant works of literature and more concerned with the shared examination of texts that depict the plight of oppressed people, fostering reflections and action plans for moving communities closer to a sense of justice for all. Tom recalls reading Elie Wiesel's *Night* and other literature about the Holocaust with his ninth graders. During this experience, he thought that nothing could be more important than to use the literature to witness events of the Holocaust and to identify the conditions in society and in human dispositions that would give rise to a program of oppression and genocide, especially so that nothing remotely similar could happen again. In other words, it seemed far less important to have consumed the great works of literature represented by some scholar's endorsed list or some anthology's canonization and more important to engage in literacy experiences for the purpose of fighting back against oppression, even at a local and seemingly simple level.

Other teachers in other schools, witnessing the devastating effects of poverty and violence and seeing the real threats of deportation that cause children to live in constant fear, select literature that will directly or indirectly allow learners to see the sources of their fears graphically portrayed and immerse young readers in processes of evaluating how harmful conditions emerge and how characters cope with situations that seem hopeless. Teachers experience similar empathic responses for students who, because of an unconventional or unpopular sense of identity, face rejection and persecution at home and at school. Under such circumstances, teachers care less about the enduring artistic merits of a work of literature and see other merits in the fact that the literature can help students to cope or take action against oppressive conditions.

In a similar vein, Bieler and Burns (2017) and Miller et al. (2015) insist that an effort to advance social justice and to examine texts and other content through the critical lenses related to oppression, equity, poverty, and identity precedes attention to learning about specific literary titles, movements, and procedures for interpretation and assessment. Smagorinsky, Clayton, and Johnson (2015) emphasize the need for preservice teachers to shape the ways that they are going to teach English in a culturally responsive way. Bieler and Burns (2017) address the primacy of the NCTE teacher-preparation standard for teaching English to advance the causes of equity and justice: "[English educators] must reject traditional conceptualizations of scaffolding and approach equity and social justice knowledge as the *first* domain taught to future teachers rather than the last" (p. 152).

The dangers of assuming oppressive positions persist. As far back as 1971, a psychologist named Philip Zimbardo developed a "game" by randomly assigning Stanford undergraduates to act either as prison inmates or guards. Rather quickly, he had to cancel the experiment because most of these young people took up their "roles" so intensely and quickly that several were traumatized. Similarly, the now infamous experiments of Stanley Milgram (1973) illustrate the "perils of obedience" and the potential for seemingly decent people to do great harm to others. Such explorations through related literature connect to events on a local level, inviting students to puzzle over how some of their peers could justify tormenting some fellow students because they see them as different and thereby inferior. In thinking about pedagogical content knowledge to prepare for these kinds of inquiries, a candidate would be inclined to read a body of literature that documents many instances of injustice, oppression, subjugation, and even atrocities, as ugly as these reports are, in order to sound an alarm and awaken an empathic response toward the oppressed, whether in the local middle school or halfway around the world.

LITERATURE STUDY AS THERAPY
AND PROBLEM SOLVING

Tom suggests that another element of the literature curriculum relating to social justice would see some middle school and high school students especially benefiting from a teacher who is familiar with literature that offers some promise to sensitize classmates about those who are differently abled or suffering through rocky episodes of adolescence. Many students contend with trauma, loss, and disappointment—perhaps the death of a family member, the struggle with serious illness or identity formation, the rejection from another, or loss in competition. If literature serves a "bibliotherapeutic" function, then perhaps an English teacher needs to be familiar with a range of literature intended for adolescents, especially narratives that depict various conflicts, traumas, challenges, disappointments, threats, and obstacles, dramatizing the situations that worry the students and offering hope that an average adolescent can cope with, and perhaps overcome, the difficulties. The familiarity with a body of young adult literature portraying various issues that might impact the lives of students will guide a teacher in making these texts available and revealing something about their content rather than assigning the reading and plodding laboriously through each text as a class.

John grudgingly accepts some of Tom's points here, but he disagrees about others. The issues surrounding "the canon," that is, the body of texts that one should teach at the university AND at the secondary level (grades 7 to 12), have had a long history of debate (Arnold, 1869/2008, 1969; Graff, 1989; Guillory, 1993; Showalter, 2003). And conversations about *why* we teach a given work of literature—are we building our students' critical faculties and literary skills, illustrating examples of social (in)justice, or enhancing their empathetic qualities—have all been noted as indicating relative importance stemming from our textual selections. Showalter (2003) lists, for example, about a dozen competencies and skills literature students should develop, ranging from recognizing "subtle and complex differences in language use" to "making connections between the literary work and one's own life" (pp. 26–27). Her catalog is merely one example of listings that are dependent upon the opinions of a given teacher or coterie of teachers and offered as empirical evidence and settled critical theories.

In another example, Carol D. Lee (2007) speaks of the "limitations of [teachers'] knowledge base and assumptions about language, culture, cognition, motivation, and most of all, the social/emotional realities of urban students" (p. 182). In obvious ways, the canon cannot easily be separated from the teacher's audience to whom the canon is being taught. As every teacher knows, pretaught students (those already familiar with the school, the books used, and the interplay of ideas in the classroom) have a much easier time learning than those with none of the above advantages (Blum, 2012). While we do not want to force upon students a set of texts that they find impossible to read or care about, we also do not want to underestimate what students know and are capable of achieving.

Lee "found that she needed to know how people learned [English]— what distinguishes a novice reader from an expert" (quoted in Green, 2014, p. 225). And as with any athlete in training, one begins at a lower proficiency level and gradually intensifies the experience so that novice readers are not limited only to reflections of a world they already know, but are strongly encouraged—when ready—to view worlds they have never seen and dialects or languages they might struggle to master. John thinks that the small percentage of teachers who limit their classes to "No-Fear Shakespeare" and justify their choices by blaming their charges (and Shakespeare) for students' inability to read blank verse will not likely be able to see them finish the Bard's verbal games; their students tend to remain on the bench, so to speak, and in their comfort zone rather than getting up and playing, because training for participation is a struggle.

In the context of recent debate, many have tried to argue that text selection and debates about particular novels, plays, and poems should be changed because of curricular thinking from over a century ago. In the 19th century, educational proponents sought to stabilize Western culture by looking backward and "using an assumed set of distinguishing literary characteristics until a hypothetical continuum based on generally uniform and aesthetic and moral standards was clear enough in the minds of students to enable them to use the apparatus to think the discipline forward once again" (Court, 1992, p. 156). This was the thinking Michel Foucault reacted to in the heyday of theory with his idea of power/knowledge, but now John would argue that he was 100 years too late (1972, pp. 1–31). Once one recalls that vernacular literature did not become a common school subject until a few decades before World War I (Court, 1992; Graff, 2003), one sees clearly that what might have been arguably a cultural truism 130 years ago has been shaken up by two world wars; the rapid circulation of populations, languages, and literary vernacular writings across the globe; as well as the near-universal spread of electronic and social media.

JUDGING THE ESTHETIC VALUE OF LITERATURE

Our problem now is to consider teachers who are no longer struggling against those ossified cultural conditions just mentioned, but rather coping with the bewildering vertigo one gets trying to keep track of contemporary cultural fragmentation and splintering. Too many choices and too many options have led some either to retreat to unthinking conventionality (e.g., deifying Jane Austen and her late 18th-century novels of manners) or to pursue an ever-receding cultural event horizon. Fans of the latter seem ready to burst into song at any "new thing" (massive open online courses; 20-minute TED Talks, Twitter, etc.) and so insist that it will prove that reading is dying and that culture appears to be whatever these fans and I say it is today (but don't hold us to that tomorrow).

While John and Tom agree with many of the arguments the proponents of multicultural reading employ, John worries that the idea of—indeed the tenuousness of, even the fact of—textual quality seems to have been given only modest consideration. Questions about what makes a good novel (or poem or play) for classroom use, or ordinary esthetic enlightenment, as contrasted with one that illustrates the values or beliefs proposed by some segment of that school's social group have been given scant attention for many preservice teachers. John argues that some teachers have, unfortunately, taken to heart Foucault's dogmatic assertion that cultural choices derive primarily from a power and gender nexus and a given elite's control over their educational population (Foucault, 1972, p. 25). As a consequence, the literary past apparently belongs to these members of the dominant culture only and the best way to assert one's independence from it and them is to reject much of it wholesale.

Still others work around issues of quality and the advising role of teacher's expertise in pedagogical content knowledge by advocating "free voluntary reading," also the title of a book by Stephen Krashen (2011). Krashen argues that "self-selected recreational reading . . . is the major source of our ability to read, to write with an acceptable writing style, to develop vocabulary and spelling abilities, and to handle complex grammatical constructions" (p. 23). Similarly, Wilhelm and Smith (2014) encourage teachers and parents to allow adolescents to read what they want to read, for various pleasures and benefits: "Another implication would be to work to expand the range of texts in which students can take pleasure, taking care as we do so to teach in a way that engages students in experiencing the pleasure of texts that they might not select on their own, while recognizing that this pleasure might not be easily forthcoming" (p. 181). One can agree with and applaud the influence Krashen has had on many teachers (and students) in the elementary grades, for English language learners and for those students whose school-sponsored readings have threatened to undermine any initial enthusiasm for literature. However, we know that adolescents can make choices that can also stifle their reading development. Almost by definition, many students tend to be comfortable, intellectually, with the familiar, given their experiential immaturity and growing development; and in their limited horizons, too many avoid literary works that would stretch their skill levels and humanistic growth. At some point, a well-prepared teacher must lead, either by example or by suasion. To do that, the teacher must have moved much earlier well beyond mere self-selection. So, the recommended reading list Tom and John speak of was initially intended as both a guide and, ultimately, as a defining statement about the expertise required of those who would claim the title and role of literature teacher.

However, setting aside for a moment the political expectations of those advocates of a given group's identity, these issues of multiple languages, ethnicities, and identities can be seen as yet another way of looking at what Tom has called "the traditional literary canon." As John has alluded to earlier, that "traditional" canon has existed inside a highly flexible mental universe because debates on what is appropriate, useful, and popular have continued now for over 100 years. During the formation of the vernacular literature classroom in the late 19th century, the emphasis by many scholars and teachers in English was to prove the value of and usefulness in education of the common tongue in contrast to an exclusive emphasis on the literature in Latin and Greek. They too struggled with promoting "a broader and more diverse comparative approach," in this instance as part of their ideas of "positivist philology" (Court, 1992, p. 157).

John recalls a real historic figure mentioned in Franklin Court's *Institutionalizing English Literature* (1992): Sir Walter Raleigh. This Raleigh (not Shakespeare's contemporary) began his teaching career in India in 1885, using what were then traditional methods in India; but he became disillusioned by "the reasoning techniques used to teach English literature" (p. 156). Returning to England, his views on teaching developed in ways quite familiar to NCTE writers over a century later: Raleigh "envisioned a personal receptiveness to literature that had nothing to do with class--an instinctual, mutual susceptibility that could form a bond between the academic profession and the general populace" (Court, 1992, p. 157). Via "omnivorous reading," he argued that "literary history and the reading of marginal, non-canonical works had a place if one hoped to assess accurately the role of the 'classics' in the history of civilization" (Court, 1992, p. 158). That eternal tug-of-war still remains today between those who value "a personal receptiveness" and who are now referred to as "postmodernist expansionists" versus those who consider such thinking as tantamount to dismantling the discipline in the name of diversity. A traditionalist like Frank Kermode warns:

> It is not really possible for me . . . to think that the values we give to (or, more boldly, that we *recognize* in) *Hamlet* or *Coriolanus* or the "Horatian Ode" . . . are the product simply of our own brainwashed responses. They are instances of literary value. It is true that the capacity to recognize such value is sometimes hard to distinguish from its shadow, the trained but vacuous response, the stock cultural okay. But that is far from being a reason for giving up faith in the real thing. To do so might entail the destruction of literature." (*Appetite for Poetry*, p. 45; quoted in Court, 1992, pp. 189–190)

EXPANDED NOTIONS OF LITERARY TEXTS

Tom's experience in schools has impressed upon him that another noteworthy change since we began teaching decades ago is the expansion of conceptions of literary texts to include graphic novels and digital, nonlinear representations of texts. These relatively new kinds of texts invite us to reconsider what we judge to be literature and to recognize the specific demands that each kind of text makes on readers. The teacher of English should be familiar with several kinds of texts, both print and nonprint, digital and analog. Many of the alternatives to traditional texts explore the same themes as their more conventional counterparts, yet they stand on their own artistic ground, and English teachers need to be aware of these possibilities. Perhaps it is a fairly short leap from reading popular comic books to reading Satrapi's *Persepolis* or Yang's *American Born Chinese*; but Ware's *Jimmy Corrigan: The Smartest Kid on Earth* presents other challenges, with pages of graphic images with no words, and other pages with the author/illustrator's own notes and diagrams. The story relies on flashbacks and parallel narratives. In the form that Ware constructs, he follows both the conventions of the genre

---

Resources for Teacher Development

The Company You Keep: People You Should Know

In preparation for the teaching of English language arts, teachers have likely completed several literature courses in which the professor expected the students to read several literary texts. Another element of preparation would include attention to commentators who note the place of literature study in schools and the competing perspectives about what texts to teach and how to teach students to engage with them. We can think of a long list of commentators, and any teacher of literature can probably offer a far different list; but as a beginning point, we offer a few possibilities for people you should know as you continue to build your knowledge about the teaching of literature:

Applebee, A. N. (1974). *Tradition and reform in the teaching of literature: A history.* Urbana, IL: National Council of Teachers of English.

Blau, S. D. (2003). *The literature workshop: Teaching texts and their readers.* Portsmouth, NH: Heinemann.

Edelstein, B. (2007). *Thinking Shakespeare.* New York: Spark.

Frye, N. (2000/1957). *Anatomy of criticism: Four essays.* Princeton, NJ: Princeton University Press.

Graff, G. (1989). *Professing literature: An institutional history.* Chicago: University of Chicago Press.

Hirshfield, J. (1998). *Nine gates: Entering the mind of poetry.* New York: Harper/Perennial.

Lee, C. D. (2007). *Culture, literacy, and learning: Taking bloom in the midst of the whirlwind.* New York: Teachers College Press.

Pritner, C., & Colaianni, L. (2001). *How to speak Shakespeare.* Santa Monica, CA: Santa Monica Press.

Rabinowitz, P., & Smith, M. W. (1997). *Authorizing readers: Resistance and respect in the teaching of literature.* New York: Teachers College Press.

Zunshine, L. (2006). *Why we read fiction: Theory of mind and the novel.* Columbus: Ohio State University Press.

---

and breaks with those conventions to expand what is possible in the medium. If students are going to read such a work for its esthetic values as well as its personal, economic, and political themes, then a teacher needs to know enough to teach adolescents how to read in this genre and not take for granted that buoyed by enthusiasm, they will figure it out.

But some teachers might ask, "What business does the teacher have in determining what texts a group of adolescents should read?" From this perspective, the teacher would claim that by allowing students to follow naturally their own inclinations and enthusiasms, students will inevitably read texts that they find useful and appealing (Daniels, 2002; Goodman & Goodman, 1979; Krashen, 2011; Wilhelm & Smith, 2014). The question of what an English teacher needs to know about literature becomes almost moot in this circumstance, since the learners would direct their own exploration of literature, following whatever program of study their intuition suggest. While this approach seems most democratic, Tom considers it unrealistic, especially in an age with increased calls for introducing learners to complex texts and increasing the level of rigor for the transactions with texts. Indeed, John agrees with Tom and adds that the very question appears to diminish a teacher's claim to expertise. Ask a physician what business she has in prescribing medication for an adolescent's acne and she would say that years of training, experience, and clinical insight give her the qualifications in question. Well-prepared and well-read teachers are no less qualified in their domain to render judgments about the steps toward literary complexity an adolescent would benefit from taking in order to become a better, more insightful reader.

John finds one interesting example of a teacher-orchestrated literary experience is the lesson found online in the controversial series of programs associated with EngageNY (2014), where the teacher is taking her students through a conversation about the differences between Horatian and Juvenalian satire. What seems like a fairly esoteric topic not only turns out to be stimulating for the students but also remains one of the building blocks for reading anything where the tonal choices of the author make comprehension initially difficult. This particular teacher connects the ideas of textual analysis with Common Core expectations on types of satire. She wants the learners not only to recognize satiric elements in an unusual graduation speech, but to specify why the language chosen by the speaker is directly connected to his larger intentions. By asking them to approach the whiteboard and write out their thinking, she insists on evidence-based reasoning, in a way that most students would be unlikely to experience (at first) on their own. Regardless of whether or not one embraces the controversial learning targets expressed in the Common Core State Standards, the teacher who dares to stretch learners into complex writings like Horace's needs to be familiar with the kind of texts that illustrate differences in mode, tone, and literary richness.

One reality of teaching any group of readers suggests that the teacher of literature should be willing to meet students where they are. While the authors we read are the company we keep, as Wayne Booth insists, and we want students to keep the best company, many students who struggle with reading are not immediately ready for encounters with

Spenser, Thackeray, Cervantes, Eliot, Morrison, or Achebe, as much as some teachers might be eager to share their enthusiasm for these authors. At the same time, Tom argues that while a teacher will want to meet students where they are at the moment, the same teacher will plan to extend students' reading beyond their current comfort level, or learning will inevitably be narrow. So the territory of literature for students might include the miles somewhere between *The Outsiders* and *Light in August,* requiring their teachers to have read this range of literature in order to plan for specific groups of students and foster enthusiasm for the reading. As we suggest in Chapter 2, teachers will also want to be familiar with a body of significant literature in order to recognize connections to support the scaffolding of learning and a sequence of inquiry that moves students from relatively simple to relatively complex texts, and expand thinking into the various complications and nuances that the inquiry demands.

When we were graduate students trying to strengthen our content knowledge about literature, the literary scholars that we admired—like Northrop Frye, Wayne Booth, Frank Kermode, Maynard Mack, and M. H. Abrams—seemed to have read everything ever written. For these scholars, their wide and varied experiences with literature allowed them to see patterns and connections. Frye warned against an inclination "not to find a conceptual framework for criticism within literature, but to attach criticism to one of a miscellany of frameworks outside it" (p. 6). In other words, he cautioned against looking outside the discipline of literary studies—like history, psychology, sociology—for a means of making sense of a body of literature. Instead, he looked within the body of literature for ways to represent it as a unified whole, offering the examples of modes, genres, symbols, or myths as ways to see coherence and contrasts among works. These giants of literary scholarship share the fact that they have read a vast store of literature. As with any line of scholarship, this familiarity with the field allows them to pose significant questions and frame appropriate problems that drive further inquiry into their discipline. Over the years, many scholars have argued about the necessity to see bodies of literature as unified wholes (e.g., genres or modes) and have continuously debated whether or not literature and storytelling may be treated as inexhaustible sets of autotelic cultural artifacts, or regarded as cultural elements existing inside permeable and dynamic human societies subject to regular upheaval and transformation. We do not pretend to have come to any profound conclusion, but what we do know is that teaching literature requires both knowledge of widely recognized masterpieces of literary art (e.g., *Hamlet*) and works transformed by the creativity of many artists into something new, transformative, and even unusual.

POINTS OF CONVERGENCE

Preparation for the teaching of literature has changed much since the 1960s, when John was an undergraduate and, later, in the early 1970s, when he was preparing Tom to be a teacher of English. But much endures. One thing that we agree on is that English teachers should have read a lot of literature. A list posted on a bulletin board at a university or the appendix of an E. D. Hirsch book may not define that reading experience, but an English teacher would be wise to know well many of the works listed and representing a traditional canon. In addition, we see a need to press cultural boundaries and to become familiar with some quality works of literature that seem to resonate with young adults. We recognize that authors deliver texts in many forms—graphic, digital, multimedia, and traditional print—and we need to be familiar both with these possibilities but and the unique demands and conventions, as well as the esthetic standards, of each form.

Tom recalls a literature professor in graduate school who scoffed, "I don't see how anyone who calls himself an English teacher can do his job without having read *The Faerie Queene* every year." Similarly, we can imagine a literature professor at an American university in the 19th century insisting that the conscientious English teacher would have to read and reread Ovid in the original Latin and Aeschylus in the original Greek in order to be properly prepared. While we can reject such pronouncements today, we judge that English teachers still need to have read a good deal of literature that represents a tradition of study in the discipline. The canon wars are as old as the teaching of vernacular literature, and few contemporary arguments add much that's brand new to these important debates. The tensions between traditionalists and reformers are healthy and represent conversations about an evolving cultural heritage and expanding cultural experience. But one cannot enter the debates and arrive at reasoned judgments without being familiar with some of the literature that the two sides embrace.

The wider the choices in reading selections and, to a point, the more complicated the texts, the better (ultimately) for the novice reader. Although literature teachers most often work with prose, dramatic texts, or poetry, the English teacher should not rule out film or graphic novels completely as a means of influencing students to invest in a story world. One point of convergence for us is the hope that teachers will invite learners to "enter the reading zone," as Atwell (2007) and Krashen (2011) suggest. We hope that teachers are prepared to cultivate an enthusiasm for reading and can orchestrate experiences in which learners lose themselves in the rush of a compelling narrative or drama. The trick is finding how to help students do so, requiring teachers to be familiar with a variety of texts, know how narratives, poetry, and drama work; and distinguish between predictable formulas and thought-provoking and sometimes lyrical explorations of human experience. Age-appropriate standards are not set in stone, but depend on the persuasiveness and skills of the teacher, the qualities of the text, and the willingness of the student to venture into unknown territory.

In the end, we agree that teachers should endeavor to expose students to literature of the highest quality that is age- and developmentally-appropriate. This assumes that English teachers have established solid conceptions of what constitutes quality literature. Identity-based text selections are merely one way of developing a literary curriculum, and, depending on the reasoning for such choices, may not always be the most advantageous for all of the students. Quality of style, the intelligence of the author, and, we insist, the expertise of the teacher are at least as important for students as group identification. In a classroom of multiple identities, it will be very difficult to please all of the students even most of the time. John argues that recent assumptions insisting upon the primacy for social and cultural congruency between author and audience need rethinking, with the focus as much on what diverse identity groups have in common in American culture as in the ways they differ. Tom suggests that teachers need to know their students well, pay attention to their responses to literature, and draw from their extensive experience with a variety of texts to invite learners into the rich and exciting territory of literature.

YOUR THOUGHTS

We expect that at some point in this chapter, positions and responses in our conversation have likely provoked you. We judge that if you are a current or aspiring teacher of English or if you are preparing candidates to become teachers of English, you should be able to say what you agree with and what you reject. You should be able to voice the basis for your support or disagreement. Here are some questions to spur your thinking:

- To what extent is it possible to say which works of literature are essential for the teacher of English to know?
- How might a teacher's expertise in literature serve students with their selection of literature to read and discuss?
- What business does any English teacher have in assigning texts to be read, instead of simply allowing students to select the texts that interest them?

- To what extent is it important that teachers expose students to texts that in some way reflect the students' own community and experience?
- Why might it be important for a teacher to select texts that will help students to be aware of critical problems in the world?
- When might it be important to expose learners to a range of texts that offer a variety of cultural views and experiences?
- To what extent is it important that a teacher introduce students to texts that might help them to cope with difficult situations or to understand challenges in their lives at the moment?

2

Teaching in the Territory of Literature

After modeling for our students how to construct literature-based lesson plans and units of instruction, we have asked these preservice teachers to produce their own lesson plans. We are always pleased to see our students follow the examples that we have set, and we expect that the preservice teachers will consult with their mentor teachers to devise lessons that make sense in the specific instructional context and fit in cohesively into the sequence of instruction that the experienced teacher had in mind. Sometimes, however, these novice lesson planners devise lessons that imitate what the beginners had experienced themselves as middle school and high school students, or they troll the Internet to find a convenient plan after which to model their own effort or to use as found. The result of their labors is sometimes an assortment of hits and misses. Occasionally, Freytag's pyramid raises its ugly head; or simplistic character charts; or worksheets that prompt learners to categorize characters as round or flat and conflicts as man versus man, man versus nature, or man versus self. We also occasionally see worksheets that prompt learners to record text-to-self, text-to-text, and text-to-world connections, as if these were free standing connections and the exhaustive representations of transactions with literature.

The more dubious lesson plans make us self-conscious about the apparent lack of impact of our methods instruction and worry us about a broad effort to discourage students from enjoying literature and developing a lifelong enthusiasm for reading (cf. Gallagher, 2009). Our skepticism is that these Thomas Gradgrind–style lessons reduce transactions with, and interpretations of, literature to monologic recitations of the "facts" of a text, as if the *conflict* can be pinpointed in a literary text, and an objective reader can decide if that conflict falls under one of only three categories. We sometimes stagger under the burden of teaching others to instruct adolescents in the complexities involved in simply following the plot of a narrative, making complex inferences that draw from a wealth of knowledge outside of the text, and critically judging the quality of the literature or the ideas that the author seems to promote. This type of reading is often called "close analysis" and in practice can range from a 12-year-old's memory of connecting repeated images to an 18-year-old's comprehension of an author's intentions spoken through the mouths of characters debating a conflict between themselves. Unfortunately, the experiential reduction of literary knowledge to a recitation of facts and teacher-endorsed choices seems to us to be a misunderstanding of what reading literature and its goals are all about, a collapse under the immense burden of imaginative story telling that is rich in complexity. We fear that in the worst circumstances, the teachers' pedagogical goal in this context seems to entail a mere simplification for all concerned. Examining such pedagogies, one could be forgiven for assuming at times the startling idea that literature in English is a discipline too forbidding to allow unprotected students to work out its problems on their own.

Of course, how a teacher teaches literature and what that teacher needs to know about the teaching of literature will be dependent on one's conception of what the teaching of literature, especially in middle school and high school, is all about (Scholes, 1999). When Tom was preparing to become a teacher, he was required by his university program to complete, among other things, several survey courses in American and English literature. The implication was that the study of literature involved telling the "story" of literature—which writer preceded another writer, how one writer and movement influenced the next, and how a historical and cultural milieu shaped authors' interests and shaped particular texts. Another implication was that certain works of literature were just not to be missed. Too often, some curriculum committees or an individual professor assumed that if the Norton anthology included an author, he or she must be important, suggesting that the study of literature amounted to student consumption of selected great works, works not always chosen for their reputed quality (Shesgreen, 2009). A third perspective suggests that the study of literature emphasizes the procedures involved in reading any text closely and critically and being aware of the processes that one follows in constructing meaning and forming judgments. We lean toward this third perspective, which requires the teacher to know a lot about the features of literary texts and the "rules" for reading them

(Rabinowitz, 1987/1998; Rabinowitz and Smith, 1997). In tracing the shifts in approaches to the teaching of reading literary texts, Downing, Harkin, and Sosnoski (1994) offer this loose summary: "The profession has moved from raising questions about texts, to raising questions about readers, to raising questions about the conditions of possibility for any reading, to raising questions about how we teach students to read" (p. 6). In this context, teaching students to *read* means more than focusing on word recognition, fluency, and basic comprehension; the endeavor requires instructors to teach the *discipline* of reading literary texts closely and critically, and, John insists, not try to substitute comic books, TV, and/or film viewing for the story as a convenient way to allow students to consume texts. Each of those visual domains is worthwhile studying in its own right and for its own values and goals, and we can partly assent to Robert Scholes's (2001) arguments about "how texts in various media, and their authors, moving from one world to another, one medium to another, [can make] a culture that is interesting—and teachable—on many levels" (p. 235). One should note that Scholes's claims are made by someone who already knows "how to read" and can readily branch out to media other than print with relative ease. Literary instruction in schools demands, however, that teachers know much about how highly literate people read complex texts and know how to organize and structure experiences so that learners can command procedures and be aware of how they made sense and judgments from the texts they have read. The goal of knowing *procedures* for reading, including analysis and critical judgment, emphasizes the generative knowledge that students carry with them from text to text, offering students more than a consumption of selected great works.

GETTING LOST IN OUR CLOSE READINGS

John has been teaching the study of literature for a long time, and he now hears common complaints from experienced English teachers: Most high school and college students don't want to read literature the way students used to back in the 1960s, 1970s, or even into the 1990s, as far as people are in a position to make such a judgment. We have both observed teachers who seem to have succumbed to students' resistance in reading any literature they judge too complex, too long, or too far removed from their adolescent experiences. One form of response is for the teacher to find texts that match students' comfort level in reading, that is, comfort both with vocabulary and syntax, while paying less attention to the literary quality of the work. We understand that complexity resides both in the features of the text and the critical and creative work involved in the readers' transactions with the text (Bailin & Grafstein, 2016), but we both cling to the idea that some literature is distinctive in its quality, including the insightful representation of human experience, the provocation of judgment and reflection, the inventiveness of its characters and pattern of narrative, and the precision and lyricism of language.

We have also witnessed some teachers get around the problem of students' reluctance to read complex literary texts by reading every word of a text aloud to students in class, as if pouring language into receptacles and hoping at least to give students a taste of the plot and maybe even motivating some to read on their own, as such nudges occasionally do. Another response is for teachers to assume a Rousseau-like stance by offering the garden of literature before a group of eager learners, allowing them to find their own way in the pleasures of the text. It is good to recall that Stephen Krashen, long an advocate of "free voluntary reading" (2011), also couples such freedom with what he calls "narrow reading," "focusing on one topic, author, or genre, according to the reader's interests, and gradually expanding the range of what is read over time . . . the opposite of the 'survey' approach" (p. 71). Krashen does not mention specifically how the novice reader is to learn about "topics, authors, and genres" without at least some modeling, even though Krashen would no doubt agree that most adolescent Emiles and Emilys could profit from some literary tutelage; the question remains: how, when, and why?

Perhaps the saddest and least productive set of coping mechanisms some teachers have adapted to some students' resistance to reading complex literary texts is to laden the learners with reading guides, graphic organizers, recitations, and objective quizzes, as if these conventional attempts at "accountability" should encourage students to read assigned texts. Gallagher (2009) and Kohn (2011) both warn against the dispiriting effects of such practices. Indeed, at our university, John has famously and frequently referred to such "worksheets" as "tools of the devil." Nonetheless, getting students to do the solitary task of reading is increasingly more difficult even in graduate literature courses, as witnessed by notable teacher-scholars such as N. Katherine Hayles (2013), who confesses that she "can't get [her] students to read whole books anymore" (p. 9). In John's classes, where a decade and a half ago, he could expect students to read seven or eight Shakespearean plays and two dozen sonnets in an average semester, now his default list includes merely four or five plays and a handful of 14-line sonnets—and students still complain that he is pushing them very hard.

What is needed for most English and humanities teachers is not a recitation of the problems they already know all too well, but instead a number of suggestions for useful solutions. What do English teachers need to know about how middle school and high school students learn to read literary texts closely? What must English teachers master in preparing adolescent readers to care about literature enough to read in ways that mature and highly literate adults read? As Nicholas Carr (2010) has discussed so persuasively, the texts we read and how we read them matters a great deal: "The use of intellectual technologies has shaped and reshaped the circuitry in our heads . . . [Any] repeated experience influences our [synapses]" (p. 49). The study of literature and the conversations about meanings found therein (referred to back in John's day as *literary criticism*) are activities explicitly connected to what Carr calls "deep reading skills": critical analyses of verbal statements, and a skeptical mind looking for and expecting evidence for assertions and demanding cognitive subtlety in critical thinking. Brottman (2011) has framed the challenge in this way: reading serious literature with "a full understanding demands individual reflection and private judgment, qualities that can be cultivated only through the practice of careful reading, a practice that demands solitude."

Many literature teachers, if honest with themselves, continue to ask questions about the future of our discipline: Will the skills we usually associate with the study of literature and of the humanities generally— deep reading—get relegated to a tiny minority of aficionados? Must the discipline of literary criticism and literary analysis go the way of the ancient classics in educational history (Court, 1992; Graff 1989, p. 31)? If preservice teachers are not setting out to shape all of their students into future English majors, why are they trying to get students to read and appreciate literary texts the way that they do? What are the procedures that these English teachers must know how to teach, not to produce English majors necessarily, but to promote a highly literate citizenry? To help answer such questions, we intend to discuss not only the problems that seem obvious to many but also some possible strategies to help our students and ourselves cope with this changing world and stay true to some enduring practices.

In preparing future English teachers, we hope to position these literature instructors to help their students work on at least two planes: First, we judge that all English teachers need to show their students how to immerse themselves in a text independently—to make their own judgments, to ponder their own questions, and to reflect on their own experiences with the text. On a different level, we want to prepare teachers to position their own students in engaging confidently and enthusiastically with others in deeper explorations of literature. In this later regard, Elaine Showalter (2003) mentions a technique not often admitted to students but well-known nonetheless by veteran teachers:

> All of us have had the experience of reading a book the night before class, just one breathless step ahead of the students, and

discovering that our teaching suddenly seems electric and the students are lit up with excitement. Teaching new material works, because we are teaching a way of reading, and modeling the way a trained professional thinks about understanding and analyzing literary texts. (p. 45)

Another way of considering Showalter's "discovery" is to state what most of us have believed for a long time: reading and then teaching literature is *both* a solitary act *and* a social engagement, activities that interpenetrate one another in dynamic and often unpredictable ways. We discuss each of these goals below.

PREPARING FOR READING LITERATURE

When Tom was preparing to be a teacher, and John was instructing his like in literature and methods classes at the university, the common instructional approach was to assign students to read a complex text and then explore the text together, assuming that students had read it. If students seemed negligent in their reading duties, the teacher relied on scheduled or pop quizzes to set a pace and prod learners to keep up. As of this writing, Tom still visits dozens of schools and sees the same model persist. However, by the 1970s and 1980s, advances in cognitive psychology and in reading research demonstrated that students understood their reading better and were to some extent motivated to read when teachers frontloaded reading with discussions and demonstrations that helped students to tap prior knowledge or construct relevant background knowledge before they read (Bransford & Johnson, 1972; Fisher, Frey, & Lapp, 2012; Smith & Swinney, 1992).

Tom quickly became a devotee of prereading activities. As he has written elsewhere (McCann, Johannessen, Kahn, & Flanagan, 2006; Smagorinsky, McCann, & Kern, 1987), Tom has found that well-designed prereading activities, especially those that are discussion-based, help students to follow the pattern of a narrative, respond empathically to characters, and assess critically the implications of a literary work. For example, a discussion about our obligations to fellow human beings (McCann, D'Angelo, Galas, & Greska, 2015), an exploration of concepts of *friendship,* or our feelings about putting to sleep a beloved pet (Smagorinsky, McCann, et al., 1987) are likely to position learners to follow the narrative about George and Lennie in *Of Mice and Men* and to think critically and empathically about their behavior and decisions, and with a little help, reflect on how they have arrived at their decisions and have inferred the author's sentiments about the core problems.

Of course, not all prereading activities are equal. First of all, we have to acknowledge with Shanahan (2013) that some prereading efforts hijack the reading experience from the learners. We can imagine this danger, mostly with readers in early grades, when a teacher previews the substance of a book, walks students through a text, and highlights a succinct expression of theme. We have both witnessed occasions when students were able to perform well on quizzes and tests without actually having read the target text because, as we witnessed in many prereading activities and many in-class discussions, the students knew generally what the book was about—at least as far as the main outline of the plot, the principal characters, and the teacher's sense of the themes explored. At the same time, as Beers and Probst (2013) point out, there is the danger that students will be unable to read a text or will read only superficially if the teacher does nothing to prepare the readers. We can imagine, for example, that without any preparation, students might find Orwell's *Animal Farm* an absurd fantasy about an improbable rebellion by talking farm animals. But if a teacher appropriately prepares students for their encounters with the text, there is a greater likelihood that they will consider the text a political allegory and be in a position to experience its pathos, judge its gravity, and ponder its current relevance.

So, a teacher who plans to introduce middle school or high school students to *Animal Farm* will, of course, need to know the text well, but will also need to know much about Stalin-era Soviet Union and the rest of Europe between two world wars. If teaching *Animal Farm* is an important undertaking in a middle school or high school, what must aspiring English teachers know in order to help learners make sense of a popular allegory when the target of those allegorical techniques has now passed into what is for students ancient history? Orwell could assume that his authorial audience would understand his novella in 1946 just by listening to the radio, reading the newspaper, or simply by listening to parents' dinnertime conversation. For the average teenager in the early 21st century, however, reading *Animal Farm*—or the *Beowulf* poet, or Shakespeare, or *Pride and Prejudice* or even *To Kill a Mockingbird*— requires a substantial exercise in the historical imagination before and during reading.

Still, we would regret seeing a teacher lecture high school students at length about Stalin, communism, and the Cold War; instead, many teachers devise some alternatives to helping students internalize appropriate information about the Russian Revolution, Trotsky's 5-year plans, the Stalinist purge trials, and so on (cf. Knapp, 1996). Similarly, we have to question the wisdom of introducing *Hamlet* or *Romeo and Juliet* by lecturing students about the life of Shakespeare and asking learners to make a papier-mâché model of the Globe Theater to help them learn how to read Shakespeare's early modern English. So, the question remains: How do we prepare students to learn necessary information about issues over which they have little or no direct experience while at the same time encourage them to remain awake and even excited? We both recognize limitations in trying merely to *transmit* relevant background information, bucket-style, that will support students' work with complex texts, and we realize the challenge in finding inductive means to help students to construct such knowledge themselves and together with peers.

Hence, Tom and John agree that the design of any good prereading activity should align with the needs of the students and help them to negotiate the challenges of a complex text. This means that a gateway into a rich literary text is likely to be the questions and interpretive problems that engage highly literate adults in exploring texts and sometimes losing themselves in them. Clearly, in preparing younger readers for their encounters with some difficult texts, an English teacher would need to know how to design prereading activities that introduce critical questions and prepare learners with the interpretive tools to be able to recognize and trace patterns, deconstruct symbols, and reflect on the questions that an author raises.

We know several helpful books that offer examples of the kinds of prereading or *gateway activities* (Hillocks, 1995, p. 149) that offer students a point of entry into an unfamiliar text, raise significant critical questions, and allow learners to anticipate the narrative arc of fiction or drama. We recommend Beers (2002); Beers and Probst (2013); Johannessen, Kahn, and Walter (2009); Smagorinsky, McCann, et al. (1987); and Smith and Wilhelm (2010) to see a variety of prereading activities. While these texts offer a wealth of examples for introducing students to significant works of literature, an English teacher will want to use the activities strategically and learn how to design such activities on his or her own. Gateway activities can be as simple as an anticipation guide, or as complicated as an extended simulation game. We offer two types below and explain their distinctions.

First, an English teacher might anticipate that adolescent readers might be puzzled by the behavior of a character in a work of literature from long ago and far away. The example below comes from a prereading sequence that prepares learners to look critically at characters introduced early in *King Lear* (McCann, 1991). By putting students in a contemporary position that asks them to judge characters and express advice, especially through exchanges with classmates, the prereading activity positions students to understand Cordelia's affection for Lear and her reluctance to participate in the flattery that offers her material gain.

The simple activity puts students in the position of an advice columnist responding to writers who seek help with family conflicts. A teacher could distribute three or four different letters across a class, so that a third or a fourth of the class each focuses on one problem that, according to a long critical tradition, has been associated with interpretations of the play. In sharing their responses to each letter, students invite critical judgments about their advice, stimulating some processes of judging the behavior of characters and evaluating alternative critical receptions. Here is an example of one letter:

Dear Ms. Mannerly,

My aging mother is very wealthy. Although she is in relatively good health, at eighty-two she is not likely to live very much longer. The thing that distresses me is that my two brothers-in-law are always flattering her and trying to win her favor in hopes of getting some of her fortune after she dies. Whenever Ben, my sister Ruby's husband (not their real names), sees Mother, he tells her how attractive her hairstyle is and how fashionably she is dressed. To tell the truth, Mother has changed neither her hair nor her style of clothes in the last thirty-five years. Warren, my sister Grace's husband (not their real names), tells Mother how "cute" her figure is and how young she looks. I love my mother, but she is at least thirty pounds overweight and she looks every bit her age. These two guys would make you sick if you could see them "buttering up" Mother. I've always been a very honest person, and I find it difficult to join in their game in order to gain my rightful inheritance. Should I try to level with my mother and reveal these two guys for the gold-diggers they are, or do you think I should follow their example?

—Dyspeptic in DeSoto

It is fairly easy to construct such letters to the advice columnist to generate discussion and activate prior knowledge about sibling rivalry, inheritance, in-laws, and rectitude. With the example above, we have witnessed extensive discussions that allowed students to recognize conflicts, judge the behavior of characters, and evaluate the judgments of their classmates. When students begin their work with *King Lear*, they still face the challenge of working with Shakespeare's language, but they have both the activated knowledge to allow them to anticipate actions and a critical position from which to judge the implications of the play.

A more complicated example of a prereading activity asks students to collaborate in writing their own narrative (Smagorinsky, Johannessen, Kahn, & McCann, 2012). The format here offers students the beginning and ending sentence for each in a series of episodes. For each episode, the two sentences present the challenge of connecting them by constructing the body of the episode that logically connects the beginning and the end. Again, it is fairly easy to construct a set of beginning and ending sentences for a sequence of episodes that make up a romance, comedy, or tragedy. The key is to offer the few details that will suggest what must happen in the body of the episode while allowing for variation and invention. The following set invites students to write a story that anticipates Steinbeck's *The Pearl*. For many middle school and high school students, their participation in constructing a narrative together offers insight into the craft of fiction and positions them to judge critically the behavior of characters.

Collaborative Story: What Do You Value Most?

Episode 1

- *Beginning sentence:* When Simón Garcia arrived home from work and learned that the hot water heater was broken and his son Rudolfo had a severe ear infection, he felt overwhelmed and desperate.

- *Ending sentence:* When Simón and his wife Esmeralda left the doctor's office, they felt angry and disappointed; they also worried about their son's health.

Episode 2

- *Beginning sentence:* On their way home from the doctor's office, Mr. and Mrs. Garcia stopped at the supermarket, where they bought some essentials and then spent their last dollar on a Lotto ticket.

- *Ending sentence:* As they looked at the Lotto ticket and waited for the winner to be announced, Simón and Esmeralda marveled at all the things they dreamed of doing with the money.

Episode 3

- *Beginning sentence:* Esmeralda and Simón slowly recovered from their astonishment and called their friends to tell them the good news.

- *Ending sentence:* Not only were they surprised by the doctor's visit to their home, but they also doubted whether the medicine that she left would be necessary.

Episode 4

- *Beginning sentence:* On the night of the day that Simón learned that he was the winner of 20 million dollars, he awoke from his slumber, sat up in bed, and listened again for the noise that disturbed his sleep.

• *Ending sentence:* Simón lifted himself from the kitchen floor and looked out the window to see if he could identify the intruder.

Episode 5

• *Beginning sentence:* It was clear to Simón and Esmeralda that someone had broken into their house in search of their winning lottery ticket, and they had to decide how they would protect it.

• *Ending sentence:* After this attack on the street, Simón realized that no place was safe for him; he looked at his bloody hands and saw that he was driven to do things he thought he was incapable of doing.

Episode 6

• *Beginning sentence:* When Simón returned home and told Esmeralda what had happened, she took the Lotto ticket from his hand and quickly walked to the fireplace.

• *Ending sentence:* As they recounted all their recent troubles, the young couple realized that what they had just done, as difficult as it was, would be the only solution to their problems.

These examples represent simple possibilities for *introducing* a work of literature. The form the prereading takes and its particular focus will depend on the needs of a particular group of learners and the demands a work of literature makes on those students. The planning for strategic prereading that offers students a point of entry into a text and does not supplant the learners' experience with the text requires teachers to know the literature well and know a good deal about how readers read texts—how they recall, how they infer, and how they construct critical judgments. See also Appendix B (pp. 163–168) for a sample learning activity to help students to define the concept of literary *tragedy,* when the definition will allow students to anticipate the configuration of the action of a play or narrative and to judge critically the behavior and fate of a central character.

KNOWING SOME "RULES" FOR READING LITERARY TEXTS

When Tom works with preservice teachers who have successfully completed several upper-level literature courses at the university, he reminds them that their students are going to see them as readers who are particularly adept at finding "hidden meaning," as Graff (1989, p. 83) suggests. A key for these future teachers of literature is to be aware of the processes they follow in deriving meaning from texts and judging them critically and to share these processes with their students. The process of constructing meaning should not seem a dark mystery to the adolescent reader, although much of the process may be obscure, even to the most reflective reader. One of the real challenges for secondary teachers is finding a process by which students can learn to comprehend works of literature more or less on their own. Reading and teaching literature are more heuristic processes than algorithmic procedures. Cognitive psychologists refer to the challenges of inferring meaning and instruction in literature analysis as ill formed. That is, there are multiple paths to any answers a student might give, there is rarely a fixed end point or final answer to complex literary works, and the conclusion cannot be learned by mastering a given formula.

Tom recalls high school students who insisted that a poem can "mean anything you want it to mean," which is a literary novice's broad way of saying that a text might be open to a wide variety of interpretations. But the students' claim overstates matters. At the same time, we do not want the experience with literature in an English classroom to be students' recitations of a teacher's representation of a text and judgment of its interpretation, even if the teacher claims to be able to conjure what the author *intended*. The narrative theorist Peter Rabinowitz (1987/1998) and his coauthors (Rabinowitz & Bancroft, 2014; Rabinowitz & Smith, 1997) offer another approach, and we think it appropriate here to discuss this work in some detail, because we judge Rabinowitz addresses the problem of revealing to others how highly literate readers read literary texts. If we agree that a text cannot mean simply anything we want it to mean, then we have to acknowledge that some intelligent and intentional human being designed the text in a way to guide us toward certain ideas and emotions and away from others. Experienced readers of literary texts recognize that the features of a literary work typically exhibit regularities and discontinuities that require us to understand and then apply "rules" for reading these features and making some sense of them. English teachers need to be aware of such rules in order to demonstrate how they apply to complex texts. We are suggesting here an approach that is neither *reader response* (although we recognize that personal connections will influence processing and recall) nor *new critical* (although we ask learners to pay close attention to features of the text). An alternative option begins with an *authorial reading* (Rabinowitz, 1987/1998; Rabinowitz & Smith, 1998) that invites learners to notice the features of the text (e.g., the title, the names of characters, repeated images, narrative arc) that the author consciously constructed with the expectation that an intended audience would recognize that these features carry significance. But pointing to features of a text is just a starting point since a reader will also need to be aware of how narratives (i.e., fiction, verse narrative, drama, and nonfiction narrative) work in order to say why the features are noteworthy and how they can construct meaning from them.

Unfortunately, there are few critical tools offering both reasoning processes and ways of noticing genre patterns available to most literature teachers who ply their craft at the secondary level. We recommend the work in narrative study of Peter Rabinowitz, whose ideas have helped our students with useful guides to reading fiction and some drama. Immediately below, we offer a highly simplified thumbnail sketch of Rabinowitz's "rules" for reading fiction, which is probably the most common literary form studied in middle school and high school. These are not cookbook recipes, but guideposts and helpful roadmaps in thinking about imaginative writings in fiction.

Rabinowitz begins his schema by including rules of (1) *notice*— what the author meant for us to see; (2) *signification*—what is important about those items or ideas we are meant to see; (3) *configuration*—how what is important begins to form patterns; and (4) *coherence* or *unity* of the whole work. In one sense, literary reading is, loosely speaking, rule-bound, because in the transactional exchange between author and reader, the author can assume certain ways that the reader will experience the text. Rabinowitz (1987/1998) offers a "system" for beginning a careful reading as a member of what he calls the authorial audience:

> Specifically, the system sets out *four types of rules* . . . [governing] operations or activities that, from the author's perspective, [are] appropriate for the reader to perform when transforming texts— and indeed, that it is even necessary for the reader to perform if he or she is to end up with the expected meaning. And they are [. . .] what readers implicitly call upon when they argue for or against a particular paraphrase of the text [. . . and] serve as a kind of *assumed contract between author and reader*—[specifying] the grounds on which the intended reading should take place. They are, of course, socially constructed—and they can vary with genre, culture, history, and text. (p. 43)

Rabinowitz then offers a major caveat: "But even when readers do not apply the specific rules the author had in mind, in our culture virtually all readers apply some rules in each of the four categories whenever they approach a text" (p. 43). Since these are "rules" most mature readers apply to texts, then English teachers should be familiar with them and develop ways to help novice literary learners to discover them, name them, and apply them. Rabinowitz goes so far as to judge that "the rules have to be learned before the reading begins" (p. 112). We agree: English teachers should engage learners in inductive processes of discovering rules for reading literary texts and exhibit a repertoire of approaches for learners to apply their discoveries.

Rabinowitz (1987/1998) reminds us that "anything in a text can be made to 'mean' by an ingenious reader" but "giving meaning is not the same as finding it or construing it, and to the degree that a novel is an attempt by a novelist to convey some more or less precise meaning, it is impossible for all features to bear weight" (p. 49). Most readers *notice*, for example, both the red rosebush and the pointed hats in the opening two pages of Hawthorne's *The Scarlet Letter* but soon discover that one detail is both imagistically and thematically very important, while the other is simply a visual detail.

It becomes crucial, therefore, that an English teacher knows how to plan learning experiences that help students to distinguish among (1) *authorial intentions* (where the reader can be sensitive to the assumptions that an author was likely making about an imagined audience); (2) *ingenious readings* (where the reader develops a coherent system of some sort and where we can argue as much with the system itself or its elements as with the author's exemplification of it or them); and (3) some relatively *randomized set(s) of associations* that make up an interpretive move. See Appendices C and D (pp. 169–181) for sample learning activities to help students discover and apply rules of notice and significance.

Once we know, through the rules of *notice,* what to attend to (e.g., what the author has engineered our attention toward seeing/hearing/feeling), we still have to face the problem of *how* to attend to it. To think of some part of the work (image, word[s], character, etc.) as *significant*, the reader "moves from what appears to be said to what is really said, or at least from one level (which, if not literal, is more immediate or closer at hand) to another which is more distant, more mediated," an activity Rabinowitz (1987/1998) calls *signification* (p. 77). He explains, "Rules of signification are vast in number, and teachers probably have more trouble teaching their students to understand them than other kinds of rules" (p. 79). For example, when King Lear has a map spread before him and designates how portions of the earth are to be distributed, the image reveals much about Lear—the political vulnerability of his actions, and the scale of his ultimate descent. Since Lear is not looking at a road map to plan a family vacation, students can note the image and conjecture about its significance. The idea here is to model how a reader notes certain details and ponders their significance, positioning students to practice the same efforts as they work through the play and other texts.

Once a text is finished, all rereaders contrast making sense of the work while in "the process of reading" versus the "retrospective interpretation of that process once it has been completed" (Rabinowitz, 1987/1998, p. 110). In *Authorizing Readers,* Rabinowitz and Smith (1997) call this distinction simply the difference between "reading and re-reading," and sometimes Rabinowitz speaks of "reading from memory" (p. 90). In Rabinowitz's model, "rules of *configuration* govern the activities by which readers determine probability," and "can be just as important to the reading experience when the outcomes it predicts turn out not to take place as when they do" (pp. 111–112).

The way in which a work of literature is *configured* prepares readers for what is to come and implies a certain worldview. Ruptures to the conventional structures also prompt reflection and imply challenges to artistic assumptions and other worldviews. Authors provide much guidance. In *Pride and Prejudice,* we can assume that Elizabeth is likely to change her mind, ultimately, about loving and marrying Darcy—not because of some *kismet* in represented reality but because the genre of the marriage plot suggests it. Our familiarity with specific modes and genres of literature allows us to anticipate two meta-rules: (1) "something will happen" (openness) or (2) "not anything can happen" (limits of possibility) (Rabinowtiz, pp. 117, 126). Rabinowitz notes: "Events have a predictive value in fiction that they do not have in life" (p. 118). See Appendix E (pp. 183–188) for a sample learning activity to help students discover some rules of configuration.

Finally, Rabinowitz speaks of the rules of *coherence* or *unity,* and we know from long experience that articulating this end point seems to be important to many teachers. We agree with its importance but suggest that students learning how to define this end point often lose sight of the journey and how they got there. The theme of a given work only makes sense—beyond articulating simple one-liners—when one knows the details of how that thematic end was achieved. Rabinowitz notes: "The majority of critical work done today still aims at setting out the basic coherence of literary works, their 'unity,' or 'basic pattern,' or 'overarching meaning'" (p. 141), what high school English teachers have always called the "theme" of a work. "For many writers, from Aristotle on, the coherence of art is what separates it from life" (Rabinowitz, 1987/1998, p. 144). This sentiment is best expressed by the detective character Philip Marlowe in *The Big Sleep,* who refers to a fictional problem thus: "It had the austere simplicity of fiction rather than the tangled woof of fact" (Chandler, 1950, p. 157). "Coherence, then, often serves as a vehicle by which ideological biases are smuggled into literary discussions disguised as objective aesthetic qualities" (Rabinowitz, 1987/1998, p. 144).

The varieties of coherence in many texts range from those essentially pre-assembled, or formulaic, "readerly texts" (e.g., Harlequin romances, vampire tales, or Horatio Alger novels) to their opposite, a few texts that are completely incoherent, to works that baffle or confuse us until we apply "the rules of coherence" to them. They may seem not unified but can be made so "through critical manipulation" (Rabinowitz, 1987/1998, p. 146). This activity puts the locus of coherence not in the text(s) so much as in the reader by assuming that "the work is coherent and that apparent flaws in its construction are intentional and meaning bearing" (p. 147).

It would seem obvious that digesting these rules cannot be done easily via a simple character or plot chart, or through a long lecture, but requires some sort of patterned experience and repetition to make them useful to teachers, much less secondary students. Just as teachers of science or math require mastering some of the tools of their trade, so too should English and literature teachers learn the techniques and processes associated with the close reading of literary texts as part of their training. John and Tom may differ on choices of texts that are the most useful for contemporary secondary students, but both still agree that the English teacher, no less than any practitioner of a complex set of tasks, must find or invent ways of taking the tools of the trade in adult text analysis, and by adjusting and modifying them, make them useful for their middle school or high school students as they read complex literary texts. Novice teachers soon learn that merely rereading a novel they are teaching certainly helps plot recall but does not by itself help the beginning teacher answer students' questions about character motivation or cultural puzzles that "feel" important but remain opaque to the first-time reader.

CONNECTING TEXTS

So far in this chapter, we have focused on what teachers need to know and can do to prepare students for reading individual works of literature. Tom's preference is to move beyond the examination of any given text as an isolated experience and plan a course of shared inquiry that would allow students to connect a series of texts. From this approach, it is less important to select individual works of literature as optimal esthetic experiences than it is to select literature that will extend and expand inquiry, whether that be into critical questions, particular genres or movements of literature, or individual authors. For teachers of literature in middle school or high school, there is an advantage to teaching coherent units of study rather than jumping from one text to another as

Getting "Lost" without Losing Our Way

As enthusiastic readers and teachers of literature, we want to help students discover an enthusiasm for reading and support their effort to become "lost" (in the sense of total immersion, not total confusion) in a compelling text. We have found it helpful to reflect on the conditions that allow us to immerse ourselves in reading and to note the efforts we make as readers to construct meaning as we enjoy our reading experience and as we share our experience with others.

• *Fostering enthusiasm.* English teachers typically can recall many experiences when they were "lost" in their reading of a text—by being swept away by the power of a narrative or drama, by the beauty of the language of a text, or by reflections about the implications suggested by a text. If you reflect on yourself as a reader, including your history of reading, perhaps you can identify the conditions that allowed you to become immersed in your reading in a kind of "flow" experience that removed you mentally from your immediate surroundings. It would be good to know the factors that fostered your immersion in a text, especially so that you can help students to find similar conditions, especially those that support students in their individual circumstances (Nell, 1988).

• *Recognizing "rules" for reading.* We have cited some "rules" for reading and interpreting literature, especially narratives, referring particularly to the work of Peter Rabinowitz. Don't let the idea of "rules" worry you. Rabinowitz and Corinne Bancroft (2014) specify that following such rules typically means "working with what our students already know—providing a framework and a vocabulary that allows them to express and build on that knowledge" (p. 2). So, as a mature reader, you have probably employed some "rules" yourself, such as paying special attention to the title of a work or to the names of characters. Mere ability to answer text-specific questions or to cite details from a text while formulating arguments about an interpretation isn't enough; you should also be able to cite some reasons, what Rabinowitz calls "rules," allowing you to explain the significance of the textual details. From your reading the reflections of other teachers of literature and from your reflections on your own reading processes, what rules can you identify? More importantly, how can you design experiences so that students can also discover rules for interpreting literature?

• *Noticing and interpreting.* Students sometimes express frustration that their English teachers can "find hidden meaning" in literary texts through a process that seems mysterious and baffling. While trying to describe an algorithm for interpretation is unproductive, teachers can do much to model the procedures that they follow in interpreting and evaluating a text. Certainly mature readers note the details that seem likely to be important, but they also apply rules and evaluate genre options. The image of a white rose in a poem, play, or story might serve as a symbol for love; but in historical genres the white rose might be an emblem of a political faction, and in another context, a symbol of death. A mature reader not only is sensitive to possible important images but also knows *how* to analyze those images to construct likely interpretations. Of course, reading such symbols

(continued)

in the work's context requires a reader to know something about their history and their significance in particular social and cultural milieus. We think it important for literature teachers to remain aware of their own processes for constructing meaning, while thus removing the veil of mystery by modeling for students the rational processes that allow readers to construct meaning.

• *Connecting texts.* As teachers and learners closely examine an individual work of literature, students also benefit from connecting a single work of literature to several other works. Judith Langer (2001) argues that students thrive when the curriculum is coherent and when teachers can make explicit connections across elements in the curriculum. This is basic to learning theory—connecting new information, concepts, and procedures to what we already know. Earlier, we noted that Northrop Frye (1957/2000) insisted that the discipline of literary study needed to be reformed, and claimed that students of literature can see a body of literature as a unified whole. He began by exploring particular genres, tracing a recurring theme, or interpreting a common archetype as elements in the universe of literature. One need not be a devotee of Frye to agree that one of the demands on a teacher, then, is to know a body of related literature and to know how to organize its study in a way that expands and complicates learners' experiences.

• *Introducing conflicts.* As teachers who have written about the literature we have enjoyed and have taught, we have also read what others have said about the same works. Inevitably, scholars typically disagree in their interpretations and assessments of literary works, in part because if every reader did agree, there would be little further to say other than the obvious. Interestingly, if we rely on teachers' guides and online supports for teaching such common high school choices as *Romeo and Juliet* and *To Kill a Mockingbird*, we may note that there is wide agreement about how to judge the central characters and evaluate themes. Yet even with such aids, there exists an extensive critical tradition revealing points of contention. While we are not at all advocating that teachers assign literary criticism to their students, we recommend that teachers be familiar with the surrounding debates so that they can frame authentic interpretive problems. The problems can set the context for discussions and written responses and, as Gerald Graff (1992) suggests, can even motivate students to grapple with a complex text.

---

if moving from one isolated experience to another. Teachers and learners are in a far better position if they can view a set of readings as a unified whole, with each text and its related discussions contributing to the investigation into some compelling questions or problems. For example, it will be a far different experience for students to read *Beowulf,* followed by an eclectic mix of poetry and then a contemporary American novel, than for learners to collaborate in probing what distinguishes a hero in a warrior culture as opposed to contemporary culture, why such a narrative endures across time and cultures, and how the archetype itself can function symbolically (Tsur, 2010). In the second instance, the teacher would need to know a great deal about the *romance* of the hero as a mode of literature and would need to follow some principles of curriculum development in order to support the purposeful investigation into several connected works of literature.

Burke (2010), Smagorinsky (2007), and Wiggins and McTighe (2005) lay out principles for designing coherent units of instruction. For the beginning English teacher especially, knowing how to develop an instructional plan that the teacher can convey to learners as purposeful, significant, and coherent would be an advantage for engaging learners and advancing their literacy learning. Smagorinsky is particularly useful, both with his *Teaching English by Design* (2007) and the sample units that he shares on his related website, Virtual Library of Conceptual Units. We recognize that some schools adopt a curriculum, and the teacher serves as the technician to execute someone else's plans. If, however, a teacher has a hand in constructing a curriculum that integrates various elements of literary and language instruction and is responsive to the needs and interests of a particular group of students, the teacher would do well to be familiar with the principles that guide the development of the curriculum. Although one could profitably read Smagorinsky (2007) for detailed guidance, we can specify here that the English teacher who has an opportunity to develop curriculum, either alone or in collaboration with colleagues, would need to know how to do the following:

- Identify a rich concept that can engage learners through sustained inquiry into literary experience, whether that inquiry concerns themes, genres, modes, movements, or authors.
- Represent the concept as a critical problem that can drive inquiry over a period of weeks.
- Explain the significance of the overarching concept, discuss its many aspects and complications, and justify the inquiry and the use of selected texts as appropriate for a given group of learners.
- Express specific learning targets in ways that learners can understand and in sufficient detail to be able to assess evidence of student learning.
- Design authentic assessments to monitor development and measure growth in students' various proficiencies in their work with literary texts.
- Identify, assemble, and connect instructional materials, especially the literary texts that support the inquiry into the central concepts.
- Integrate various language experiences and critical thinking activities to support learning and promote engagement.

A rich literature curriculum will take time to develop, but these basic components suggest what a teacher should know in order to design a coherent course of study that students can enjoy and learn from. Familiarity with a rich store of literature from many genres will allow a teacher to select appropriately the texts that will support inquiry. This conception perhaps turns conventional approaches to curriculum development upside down: Instead of thinking of the curriculum as the literary texts that a class "covers" (as in "I'm teaching *Romeo and Juliet* this year."), we recommend that the teacher's focus emphasize students' learning the *procedures* for reading complex texts closely and connecting them as part of a rich investigation into some significant concept or compelling problem. Inquiry into matters that resonate with learners establishes purpose and drives the close reading and the effort to persevere and remain flexible.

COLLISIONS OF ADVERSE VIEWS

Tom would like to add one more matter for teachers to consider for their secondary classes by reiterating Gerald Graff's (1992, 2003) assertions that secondary students could be helped enormously by the teacher finding some way to introduce into classroom discourse a similar sort of thinking and arguing that adults do in literary criticism (2003, pp. 173–189).

Although experienced middle school and high school teachers might judge that introducing adolescent readers to literary criticism and literary theory is preposterous, Graff notes simply that "we need to recognize that criticism is what we inevitably do when we talk about a work of art" (2003, p. 175). He, too, rejects assigning adult-level literary criticism in the secondary classroom, granting that assigning such "criticism will probably backfire if a way is not found to bridge the gap between critical discourse and student discourse" (2003, p. 174). To that end, Graff recalls how his own adolescent attention elevated to a complex literary text when he recognized that adult readers disagreed about how to read and value a text. Graff (2008) warns that a student who writes about a literary text as if the learner was the first to have read the text, will ultimately offer something insignificant. In thinking about the university student in particular, Graff (2008) suggests that a teacher needs to introduce the surrounding critical responses as well as the literary text itself: "Students need that conversation not only as a prompt for generating their own critical response but also as a model of what critical response to literature looks like" (p. 4). Tom suggests that middle school and high school students in their own way need to engage in similar kinds of conversations that have them sort through various responses to literature and, in a way, negotiate the meaning that they construct.

Resources for Teacher Development

The Company You Keep: People You Should Know

In preparing candidates to become teachers of English language arts, the faculty at colleges and universities design programs that have students taking many literature courses. That's what English majors typically do. But the special knowledge that teachers have includes attention to how to help learners become skillful and critical readers of literature. While it is common for teachers to learn how to teach through trial and error, we can also draw from the trials and errors of others to see several options for approaching the task of helping adolescents to read literature with care and reflection. Again, as we suggest in Chapter 1, it is likely that ten different English professors will identify ten different lists of authorities in the field, but we have found the scholars and the works listed below to be both helpful and provocative. In looking for help and in attempting to expand conceptions of reading and teaching literary texts, we judge that the following list is a good place to start:

Appleman, D. (2014). *Critical encounters in secondary English: Teaching literary theory to adolescents* (3rd ed.). New York: Teachers College Press.
Beers, K., & Probst, R. E. (2013). *Notice and note: Strategies for close reading.* Portsmouth, NH: Heinemann.
Gallagher, K. (2009). *Readicide: How schools are killing reading and what you can do about it.* Portland, ME: Stenhouse.
Graff, G. (1992). *Beyond the culture wars: How teaching the conflicts can revitalize American education.* New York: Norton.
Rabinowitz, P. (1988). *Before reading: Narrative conventions and the politics of interpretation.* Ithaca, NY: Cornell University Press.
Smagorinsky, P. (2007). *Teaching English by design: How to create and carry out instructional units.* Portsmouth, NH: Heinemann.
Smith, M. W., & Wilhelm, J. D. (2013). *Fresh takes on teaching literary elements: How to teach what really matters about character, setting, point of view, and theme.* New York: Scholastic.
Tatum, A. (2009). *Reading for their life: (Re)building the textual lineages of African American adolescent males.* Portsmouth, NH: Heinemann.

John and Tom agree that for students in middle school and high school, it would be impractical to introduce articles of literary criticism that in many instances would baffle the learners and discourage the reading of the text under examination. But in another way, it is crucial that a teacher frame interpretive and evaluative problems as ways to examine a text and discuss it in a meaningful way. This is not to say that the teacher needs to scan the breadth of literary criticism before introducing middle school learners to *The Outsiders*. The idea is not to scour the literary criticism to have the last word about how to read and value the novel. Instead, familiarity with the literary criticism, sometimes in the form of book reviews and popular commentary, alerts the teacher about the remaining areas of doubt, even with chestnuts such as *To Kill a Mockingbird* and *Lord of the Flies.*

Consider a ninth grader assigned to read *To Kill a Mockingbird* by a teacher who proclaims that the novel has long been his favorite and he has hoped to model himself after Atticus Finch. Before cracking the book open, the shrewd ninth grader would know that she should share the teacher's endorsement of the novel as a great book and should speak admiringly about Atticus Finch. In contrast, another teacher might introduce the reading of the novel by saying something like this: "You know, I used to admire the character of Atticus Finch in this story, but I am not sure what to make of him now that Lee's new second novel shows a different side of him. Some recent critics have characterized him as complacent about injustice and slow to press for reforms in 1930s Alabama. Perhaps it's unfair to judge him by today's standards, but even Harper Lee might be critical of him. I am interested in knowing what you think of him." This approach is what Nystrand (1997) calls making a "dialogic bid," in that the teacher is announcing that judgments about Atticus and the novel as a whole are a genuine invitation to discuss assessments with others, instead of reciting the teacher's endorsement.

If it is not practical to direct students to the literary criticism surrounding a work of literature, an alternative is to orchestrate experiences that put students in positions to look at texts through a variety of lenses. Tom suggests Appleman's work (2014), which offers an approach that teaches students about critical theory. John worries that in her effort to make ideas of critical theory accessible to secondary students, she has watered them down to near-unrecognizability. In a less formal way, McCann and Flanagan (2002) suggest ways to position students to experience the conflicts that surround a significant text like *The Tempest.* Perhaps it is a stretch to ask students to delve into deconstruction, family systems, and poststructural views of literature; but experience tells us that students enjoy considering a single text from gendered, political, psychological, historical, and biographical views when the consideration of those views awakens the learners to new possibilities and puts them in a position to explain their interpretations in the face of contrasting assessments and mistaken assumptions (Knapp, 1996, p. 195).

POINTS OF CONVERGENCE

Tom and John agree that certain older techniques such as memorizing literary terminology and applying them to simplified texts are counterproductive in inspiring joyful and independent readers. We hope teachers

have some basic understanding about the processes involved in reading and making meaning from complex texts. As we have pointed out,
sometimes this effort to foster the construction of meaning requires the
teacher to work strategically to activate relevant prior knowledge or to
help learners to construct the background knowledge necessary to infer
meaning. We also advocate for teachers to move away from presentation and recitation as the dominant mode of discourse and move instead
toward richer strategies that help adolescents continue reading through
increasingly complicated literary works. Doing so requires mastering literary analysis techniques like Rabinowitz's, and considering other readers' ways of experiencing a text, as Graff suggests, so that students learn
more about other minds, the world in general, and about literature. Our
ultimate goal is for adolescent readers to learn how, ultimately, adult
readers use their experiences both in life and in reading to make sense of
texts requiring both intellectual engagement and emotional sensitivity.
While the chicken-and-egg problem always exists for those adolescent
readers—develop maturity first and then learn to read well versus learning to read to become more mature via the expansiveness of a literary
education—our hope is to alert the teachers about the body of knowledge that will serve them well in planning rich literary experiences for
their students.

YOUR THOUGHTS

Too often we have seen teachers simply assign reading and then, through
recitation or quizzes, assess whether or not students have read and
understood a text to the extent that the teacher deems sufficient. In this
chapter we have offered alternatives, but we trust that the reader has
participated in learning activities that have helped students to become
more mature readers of literary texts. What is your assessment of our
proposed practices, and what other options seem reasonable? Here are
some questions that you might reflect on, or discuss, with peers:

- To what extent is it necessary to prepare students for their encounters with literary texts?
- How, if at all, might an insistence on recognizing "signposts" or
  learning "rules" of reading undermine a learner's creative reading
  of a text?
- How might a learner's struggle with a text ultimately equip him
  or her to become aware of the procedures to follow in constructing meaning?

- To what extent is it possible for a teacher to *show* less expert readers how to construct meaning and interrogate a text?
- How is it possible for a teacher to model reading and interpreting processes and then transfer responsibility for these processes to the learners in a scaffolded, strategic way?

3

The Territory of Writing

What Makes for Good Writing?

If any English teacher in middle school or high school is going to prompt students to write and then judge the quality of that writing, the teacher should have a keen sense of what good writing is in order to set the learning goals that guide instructional planning and to identify a target for the developing learners. In other words, if a teacher is going to help students to become better writers, then she should have a clear idea of what good writing is. Without a firm vision of what good writing looks like and sounds like, the teacher is presenting learners with a moving target or no target at all.

We can imagine that some teachers are extremely confident about judging the qualities that distinguish good writing. We also know that many English teachers lack confidence in their own writing skills. Some teachers have an intuitive sense of differences between good or strong writing and weak or ineffective writing, although they find it difficult to express what they find appealing about the writing that they prefer. And we appreciate that teachers typically follow a process of continuous refinement in defining for themselves and their students what features distinguish good writing.

It is easy to check off traits that we appreciate about good writing—clarity, logic, precision, thorough treatment, graceful expression—but each of these desirable elements is in itself elusive. Throughout this chapter we explore the difficulty in nailing down a reliable conception of good writing. At the same time, we expect that teachers charged with teaching young people to write better, presumably moving them closer and closer to a standard, should have thought about their own conception of good writing and recognized the limitations of rubrics and style guides as the standards to satisfy. We recognize that the conventions and expectations for specific genres and specific communities of readers will shape context- and community-bound standards, and we hope that teachers have broad experience with various kinds of writing and discourse communities to be flexible enough to look beyond rigid rubrics and formulas in judging, commenting, and planning.

SEARCHING FOR A STANDARD

In 1971, when Tom was an undergraduate in John's Introduction to Fiction class, he had some choices for writing about the assigned reading, Arthur Koestler's *Darkness at Noon* (2006). As Tom recalls, in class John had referred to Raymond Williams's *Modern Tragedy* (1966), noting that Williams challenged the reader to think of a new conception of tragedy and John posed that the students might apply this new conception to their assessment of the character of Rubashov in Koestler's novel. Tom was a novice at writing about literature at the university, but he knew that if the professor had expressed some interest in, or regard for, a critical work that applied to the current reading, it would be wise to take a look at this work and connect it to the writing assignment. Tom's thinking at the time involved a bit of measuring the likelihood of earning a good grade by tackling a more challenging writing task and deferring to the professor's interest in a particular literary critic. John recalls that as a student, Tom was hardly unusual when, having been given a standard for writing quality, as suggested by the writing prompt, he measured a good style by what might earn him a good grade in the eyes of the professor wielding the grade book.

John had a requirement for each writing assignment—that each student meet with him for a conference about the writing. The idea of the conference was not to move the current composition from a draft to a more refined version, but to review what had already been written and graded in order to learn how to improve on the next attempt. Over time, John refined his approaches to conferencing, coaching, and evaluating technique, with admittedly mixed success (Knapp, 1976). Students were to present drafts of papers as well as finished writings at weekly conferences, and they then read the papers out loud back to John (or he would scaffold writing sentences and paragraphs as students and teacher read paragraphs alternatively). The emphasis on these emerging writers was two-fold: developing ordinary readability and fluency, and second, fixing usage and copyediting problems that compromised clarity. Their papers were never graded traditionally (A, B, C, D) during conferences, but instead were judged "acceptable" by the teacher (or not), and if not, they took their draft away to work toward greater refinement. Students could rewrite these drafts as often as they or John had the energy and time to rewrite and reread them again, usually two to four drafts per assignment. This process suggests a negotiated and reflective attempt to find a standard for good writing of the sort that professors required at the university.

Tom judges that John was probably a bit ahead of his time in actually consulting with students about their writing, instead of simply assigning a grade or writing editorial comments. At the same time, the experience of writing about literature was probably a common experience among English majors decades ago and remains a common experience in colleges and secondary schools for all students in English classes. Of course, the dynamic of the teacher prompting writing, the student calculating the standard for performance, and the teacher and student consulting about what the written product should be and how to realize it is an effort toward conveying a vision of what good writing should be and an endeavor to produce something that lives up to that vision. This seems like a long and perhaps haphazard inductive process of gaining a conception of what constitutes good writing, and perhaps there is a more explicit way to elevate a viable standard.

It is likely that an inductive process toward embracing a standard is inevitable. At the time when Tom labored in John's classes, John's model for good writing came from what is now an old chestnut: George Orwell's "Politics and the English Language" (1954). John had completed a dissertation a few months earlier on Orwell and so had internalized his ideas associated with good writing, expecting students like Tom to try to craft "prose like a window pane," and to avoid the types of solecisms found in the writings of someone "not unlike" Harold Laski, or authors "playing ducks and drakes" with their style, like the proverbial Professor Lancelot Hogben—names now lost in the miasmas of maleficent "collocations of vocables" (pp. 163–164).

About the time when John was sending Tom off to teach high school, Paul Diederich (1974) reported on studies in the assessment of writing. Diederich observed that when a team of readers judged a sample of papers from first-year composition classes, there was wide variation in the assessment of quality: "Out of 300 essays graded, 101 received every grade from 1 to 9; 94 percent received either seven, eight, or nine different grades; and no essay received less than five different grades from these fifty-three readers" (p. 6). Under such conditions, students enter into a kind of grading lottery system, where the luck of the draw of teacher can make all the difference in whether one is deemed a strong writer or a struggling writer. Many students suspect that this is the case and complain, with good reason, about the lack of consistency. We know from testimonials from our students that when they have been judged at some point as "struggling writers," they are convinced of an almost insurmountable and innate limitation, like height, athleticism, or vocal range.

Of course, prospective English teachers often report that they come to their university preparation with an appreciation for reading literature. They note that they admire good writing, but the kind of writing that they admire is neither the kind of writing they are expected to do themselves nor that they will prompt their own students to produce. Even within the category of literary writing, English teachers have their personal favorites and their aversions, with some enthusiasts for Stephen King and J. K. Rowling and some admirers of Melville and Shakespeare. Perhaps all of the admired literary texts can be considered exemplary in their genre and have qualities that cut across genres. But rarely are these the qualities that middle school and high school English teachers expect their students to produce. While teachers might admire Virginia Woolf and William Faulkner, it is unlikely they would encourage their students to write like them to produce various kinds of academic essays. At least we hope not.

Such contradictions situate English teachers in the curious position of admiring some types of writing and then prompting students to produce another kind of writing. In fact, English teachers typically attempt to influence students to admire literary texts but then write in ways that are quite different from the writing the students are supposed to admire. We begin here an attempt at identifying the pedagogical content knowledge for the teaching of writing—that academic writing might have some features in common with the writing of Woolf and Faulkner and Shakespeare and Melville, but it is a distinct category. Furthermore, if teachers are going to help learners to be confident and capable writers, the teachers will provide students with a wealth of experience with a variety of writing, including the use of writing as a tool for understanding complex concepts and solving challenging problems.

THE IDEA OF "CORRECTNESS" AND "CORRECTING" PAPERS

When Tom was in graduate school and teaching first-year composition for the first time, he followed a prescribed syllabus that emphasized structure and correctness as the desirable elements in students' writing. It seemed to make intuitive sense that university faculty would want the neophyte university students to organize their discussions, develop thoughts, and produce complete sentences. Tom felt compelled to follow the example of other instructors who referred to Follett's (1966/1998) *Modern American Usage* and Fowler's *Modern English Usage* (2015) as the holy writ of "proper" usage. In those days, decades ago, it would be unlikely that a student would protest receiving a failing grade because he or she had dared to use a sentence fragment, intentionally or unintentionally. Instructors read students' work carefully, in search of errors that they could point out with checks, squiggles, carets, editing notations, and exclamation points. One assumption behind all this marking and the references to Follett and Fowler was that good writing involved precision and correctness, like distinguishing the proper use of the verb *consider* when we are inclined to substitute *regard,* as defined by the authority of the desk reference.

This preoccupation with correctness supports the stereotype of the English teacher as the pedant who corrects others' usage even during social occasions, as the obsessive–compulsive who would rather parse than eat, as Joos (1967) and Mencken (1988) would say. Of course, this stance of equating good writing with "correct" expression has problems on many levels. First of all, we have both read much academic writing that is precisely "correct," at least according to Follett or Fowler, yet obscure, meandering, overblown, and tedious. We also have known the English instructors who have corrected their students' usage errors and then waxed admiringly about Joyce, Faulkner, Woolf, or others who have defied the rules. As Joe Williams (2010) points out, the idea of correctness is a bit slippery as a standard for good writing. He reminds us that many of the authorities who insist on adherence to rules of grammar and usage often violate their own rules. And George Orwell famously reminds us at the end of his "prescription" for good prose to "break any of these rules sooner than say anything outright barbarous" (1954, p. 176).

We are not claiming that written expression is rule-free. But English teachers would do well to know that simple adherence to a set of rules of usage or "correctness" does not in itself distinguish good writing. Perhaps there are different categories of "rules," including the practices that promote clarity and occasional eloquence versus the practices that merely comply with prescriptions. In this second category are the "rules" that simply represent an agreement among the influential members of a power majority. We say much more about concepts of grammar and usage rules and conventions of language in Chapter 6.

DEFERENCE TO AUTHORITY

We know that for years teachers and students have looked for help in their development as writers from such authorities as William Strunk,

Jr. and E. B. White (1999) and William Zinsser (2006), as well as from Stephen King (2010) and John Gardner (1991). These writers deserve a position as authorities because they are accomplished writers, even though the enthusiastic readers of John Gardner might dismiss the work of Stephen King, which makes an understanding of good writing again seem like a moving target. And, if as teachers of English we are not focused on cultivating writers of fiction, perhaps King and Gardner do not offer great insight into a standard for writing about *To Kill a Mockingbird, Lord of the Flies,* or *Romeo and Juliet,* as is common in schools.

Strunk and White (1999) begin again with attention to "rules," but offer practical advice about voice, unity, focus, development, concision, and coherence. Zinsser (2006) discusses the process of writing, but suggests a standard for good writing that includes attention to precise word choice; the careful crafting and revising of sentences to promote concision and clarity; and simple and direct prose, as opposed to bloated and esoteric expression.

Joe Williams (1999) in his many editions of *Style,* emphasizes positive lessons to learn about writing, rather than pitfalls to avoid. Teachers of English would do well to read Joe Williams carefully for his candor, rigor, and insight. We judge that he offers practical and straightforward advice about practices that distinguish accomplished writers and promote "clarity and grace." If we are talking especially about the kind of academic writing forms that middle school and high school teachers set out to teach their students, we can point to some features of good writing that Williams promotes, and that Strunk, White, Zinsser, King, and Gardner would likely embrace. We suggest that good academic writing is distinguished by clarity, focus, cohesion, concision, completeness, logic, and precision, which would include attention to the stylistic expectations of an intended audience. In his own way, Orwell paid attention both to the average person's and the politically sophisticated reader's middle ground as he promoted these same features and included invention and novelty, while discouraging the esoteric and exotic. We will say more about these writing traits at the end of the chapter.

LEARNING BAD HABITS AND SUPPRESSING THEM

Now we want to move from a general understanding of good writing to specific problems encountered by relatively inexperienced teachers or writing teacher trainees, and perhaps the same ones that could also be familiar to more experienced educators. In our methods classes we have puzzled over preservice teachers' lesson plans designed to teach middle school and high school students to begin a composition with an "attention-getter," develop the composition according to a five-paragraph essay structure, and finish with a "clincher." We have puzzled over the persistence of these types of lessons, since the preservice teachers never heard about these practices from us. Johnson, Thompson, Smagorinsky, and Fry (2003) have studied the tenacity of the five-paragraph essay, which seems to be a sponsored form in many schools, offered as the desired structure for state assessments. Hillocks (2002, 2005) has noted that those who score state assessments of writing reward the five-paragraph response. It is likely that the novice teachers have learned from their own classroom experiences as students and from the mentorship of some cooperating teachers that these formulaic structural patterns constitute acceptable writing at a certain developmental level. We know that the formulas (or perhaps *formulae*), as with any algorithmic thinking, are fairly easy to teach and hard to break free from; they remain vice-like, even when teachers encourage alternatives.

At least one influential team of writing teachers, Graff, Birkenstein, and Durst (2009), actively promotes the use of certain types of formulas, what they call "templates," because they have a "generative quality, prompting students to make moves in their writing that they might not otherwise make or even know that they should make" (p. xv). Graff et al. note how many writing instructors may have understandable reservations about using templates, especially since they are often associated with the "kinds of rote instruction that have indeed encouraged passivity and drained writing of its creativity and dynamic relation to the social world" (p. xvii). Nonetheless, Graff et al. argue that templates have "a long and rich history" and were commonly employed by "public orators from ancient Greece and Rome through the European Renaissance" as they "studied rhetorical topoi" or "commonplaces." These were "model passages and formulas that represented the different strategies" for speakers and writers, and Graff et al. believe that their templates "echo this classical rhetorical tradition of imitating established models" (p. xvii).

Following some of Graff et al.'s thinking, we do not necessarily reject model imitation per se, but prefer, as Graff et al. do, those practices that are generative, learned through daily oral discourse (as we discuss in Chapter 5), and closely tied to communication practices of the 21st century. We have questioned preservice teachers' lesson plans that clearly promote formulaic writing. These plans trouble us not only because we have never promoted such practices, but also because we don't recognize these practices as anything that literate adults would actually do in business or politics or academia or for any purposeful messaging. In the days when middle school and high school teachers are supposed to be preparing learners for college and career readiness, we hardly think that beginning an essay with the "attention-getter" will quite fit the bill. When students matriculate to the university, we hope that we don't see such paragraphs as this:

> Did you ever wonder how you would respond if you suspected that your uncle had killed your father, but you didn't really have proof? Well, that's the situation that Hamlet faces in Shakespeare's *The Tragedy of Hamlet.* Hamlet fails to act immediately because he lacks definitive proof, he hesitates to kill a king, and he still respects his mother.

While the definition of good writing might be as nebulous as King Hamlet's ghost, we feel confident in saying that the paragraph above is not an example of good academic writing, even though there is an "attention-getter," a narrowing to a focused thesis, and a forecast of the subsequent development. What these three sentences signal to the attentive reader is this: "Beware! Imitative and amateur criticism ahead." As Williams (2004) emphasizes, academics do not read multiple paragraphs of analysis because the writer has offered a provocative question or cited a pithy quotation. Instead, academic writers are skilled at framing the kind of problems that convince us to invest the cognitive energy required to read on. Even in considering no more than the introduction to a piece of writing, we would like to see that the writer has framed a significant issue by identifying an area still in doubt, whether this be a policy question, a dispute about the merits of something, or the interpretation of a text.

In a search of online essays about *To Kill a Mockingbird*, we came across the following introductory paragraph offered as an enticement to buy the complete essay:

> Throughout their lives, individuals learn many valuable lessons that help them to grow and mature as human beings. This is evident numerous times throughout Harper Lee's fictional novel *To Kill a Mockingbird.* Individuals in this novel learn these amazing lessons through Atticus Finch's extraordinary teachings of morals. Atticus goes on to further teach valuable lessons of courage. Lastly, Atticus continues to teach valuable lessons, about sacrifice. Throughout the novel *To Kill a Mockingbird,* Atticus Finch is portrayed as an extraordinary character who teaches valuable life lessons about morals, courage, and sacrifice.

The website that displayed this paragraph offered the remainder of the essay for $19.95 and categorized the composition as "strong." While it is not easy to say exactly what good writing is, we are confident that the introduction above and the rest of the essay that would follow is not it; and we judge that a well-prepared English teacher would also see that this kind of writing is not the target to urge learners toward.

ERRORS AND ELOQUENCE

Shaughnessy (1979) cautions against seeing supposed "errors" in writing as evidence of ignorance and hopelessness; instead, she urges the teacher to consider what the "errors" reveal about the writer. Shaughnessy has helped teachers of writing to move away from bemoaning how ill-prepared students are to tackle current composition tasks and has encouraged a more empathic response to students' expression. On the one hand, the supposed "errors" may not be errors at all, but forms of vernacular expression that the writers consciously command. Shaughnessy notes, however, that a teacher's attention to patterns of errors across a group or exhibited by an individual writer might reveal a difficulty in navigating into new modes of writing and managing the diction appropriate for a given audience and purpose. The pattern of perceived errors could also reveal the writer's intentions, suggesting ways for the teacher to support those intentions. Shaughnessy (1979) encourages in teachers "a readiness to look at these problems in a way that does not ignore the linguistic sophistication of the students nor yet underestimate the complexity of the task they face as they set about learning to write for college" (p. 13).

A danger in categorizing some "basic writers" as prone to "errors" is that the students who come from communities where the language and patterns of discourse are different from the dominant language among those in power at the university will be identified as "struggling," "underprepared," or even "flawed." Elbow (2012), Kynard (2013), and others note the flaw in this characterization and encourage vernacular expression. Elbow and Kynard both point to the famous example of Fannie Lou Hamer, who, through the power of her vernacular speech, had more influence on the Credentials Committee at the Democratic National Committee and caused more trepidation with Lyndon Johnson and Hubert Humphrey than did the more famously eloquent and well-schooled Dr. Martin Luther King, Jr.

English teachers need to be aware of the complex nature of written language that derives from vernacular speech, appreciating the qualities that are there rather than the shortcomings as measured against a conception of "standard" or "proper" associated with a power elite. Elbow (2012) reminds us: "Part of the miracle of speech is *complexity*: Every human who learns a language from infancy possesses a rich, intricate, and complex native language. When any child talks without planning, his or her words obey complex rules—an intricate set of grammatical bells and whistles comparable to (though not the same as) every other human language" (p. 61). And the English teacher who naively endeavors to move or switch from the conventions of one discourse community to the conventions of another should heed James Paul Gee's (2001) reminder of how closely language is tied to identity. An insistence on suppression of certain vernacular forms in favor of perceived "standard" forms challenges the writer to deny identity or shrug off a comfortable identity in favor of an objectionable identity, even an identity associated with an oppressor.

Nonetheless, good writing—whether "expressive" or "transactional"—requires some experimentation and play by the novice writer. Asking middle or high school students to take a stand, to write upon a topic that *they* find important, can be a powerful inducement to energize learners into actually engaging with his or her peers in written exploration or debate. In *Transforming Talk into Text* (2014), Tom has detailed many such examples from middle school level, high school, and college, so we need not repeat them here. John does want to mention, however, that Tom's previous work is reinforced theoretically by some broader research, looking at human learning across world cultures. Rogoff (1990) stated some years ago that the teacher who employs the "metaphor of apprenticeship stresses the children's active role in learning the lessons of their culture, through guided participation with more skilled companions" (p. 192). For contemporary school culture, students learning to negotiate with one's peers inside a context where an expert teacher or more advanced peer is available for guidance and feedback is one of the most productive ways to recognize a standard for writing well.

GENRE AND VARIATION

Of course, a conception of good writing may depend on the circumstances for writing and the kind of writing that the writer intends to produce. The many occasions for writing and the many forms that the writing can take complicate matters for the teacher of English, if she encourages broad experience with a variety of writing situations and modes of expression. Deborah Dean (2008a) and Tom Romano (2000, 2007) warn us to check the school curricula and our own course syllabi for "genre hegemony" (Romano, 2007, p. 174). Dean argues that too often a single genre dominates in a school, and such domination suggests the idea of *genre* as a static form. This stasis implies that academic writing consists of one universally recognized form, and that the audience and situation for writing remain more or less constant. Dean and

Romano remind us of some complications in attempts to define good writing, because "good" will depend on a complex of elements, including the purpose for the writing, the intended audience, and the social and intellectual communities in which the writer operates. Beyond recognizing distinctions across drama, poetry, fiction, and nonfiction, a teacher needs to know that there are various possibilities represented by the combination of elements. Dean (2008b) mentions several combinations of texts and social actions, including "texts" as genres and evidence of social action, as documents, and as text-types, and "genres" as actions, as documents; and, to complicate matters even further, she suggests "macro-genres," in two broad-based categories: "exposition and narration" (pp. 98–99). An obvious implication is that a teacher needs to recognize multiple distinct standards associated with various genres.

Similarly, DeStigter (2015) argues against the "overemphasis" of argument as the primary mode of written response in schools. If the only kind of writing valued in school were argument or some common form of academic writing, it would be relatively easy to define a standard for one narrow form. But, if one expands the possibilities to help students to extend their repertoires as writers and problem solvers and to allow students to combine genres, then the teacher will need to be aware of standards for good writing that might cross genres or that might be distinct to particular genres.

State writing assessments and their accompanying preparation materials narrow conceptions of acceptable genres and a quality standard for writing in schools. Reliance on rubrics as a representation of quality and as a guide for students' performance has long been popular in schools. Culham (2003) insists that an awareness of a set of desirable traits (i.e., six or seven) will propel students to produce strong writing that exhibits these traits. The subtitle of Culham's book promises: "Everything you need to teach and assess student writing with this powerful model." Culham notes that her approach to writing instruction is "trait-based." That is to say, her approach encourages teachers and students alike to become familiar with the traits and the descriptors that distinguish the writer who is "not yet" there from the writer who attains the lofty "wow" state of exceeding expectations.

Culham cites George Hillocks, Jr., to support her claim that it is important for students to be familiar with criteria for defining or judging a quality piece of writing. Although Culham (2003) does not cite the specific source for her quote from Hillocks (p. 19), one can infer that the insight comes from Hillocks's influential meta-analysis of experimental treatment studies in the teaching of writing (1984, 1986). Perhaps Culham was thinking specifically of Hillocks's attention to the Sager study (1973), although she does not say. Sager worked with sixth graders in an inner-city school, and she trained students to use sets of scoring criteria for analyzing sample compositions. The criteria emphasized the importance of organization, elaboration, vocabulary, and coherence. For each feature, the teacher specified characteristics for papers rated 0, 1, 2, and 3. After the teacher led students in a discussion of the presence or absence of a particular feature of writing in a sample composition, the students worked in small groups and individually to rate sample compositions. But the students in the study did more than rate the compositions: they worked in small groups to speculate about how to improve the compositions, which moved the activity from judging someone else's composition to generating possibilities for revising.

Tom worked with a high school teacher who had developed a complex rubric with a list of 20 separate traits that he expected to find in students' writing. The teacher structured a peer-review activity during which partners judged whether or not the targeted traits appeared in each other's compositions. We confess to the difficulty we each have in keeping as many as five considerations in mind at one time, let alone 20. So we are glad we had more understanding teachers to foster our writing development. The example of this one teacher emphasizes that an understanding of what constitutes good writing is something more than the sum of the constituent parts. The elevation of a rubric to set the standard for writing in school fails to help students know how to generate their own writing. Alfie Kohn (2006) reminds us, "The fatal flaw in this logic is revealed by a line of research in educational psychology showing that students whose attention is relentlessly focused on how well they're doing often become less engaged with what they're doing" (p. 13). In addition, we are reminded by Barbara Rogoff's (1990) influential book on human development that "active thinking and development assumes multiple directions of development rather than accepting the premise of a unique ideal endpoint" (p. 56). This assumption is true because many "other theories focus on an ideal endpoint for development, and few theorists have escaped putting their own valued characteristics at the pinnacle" (p. 56).

THE INTEGRITY STANDARD

While George Hillocks was collecting data for a study that would be published as *The Testing Trap: How State Writing Assessments Control Learning* (2002), he observed in classrooms as teachers were preparing students for their state writing assessment. Hillocks reports that the standard for writing was defined not only by the scoring rubric but also by the sample compositions that teachers offered as exemplars of the

Implications for Teacher Development

What Is Good Writing?

We have published enough to know that the writing that we thought was both crystal clear and bordering on eloquence has struck readers as lacking in substance, style, and precision. When we have submitted writing for publication, we have subjected it to many critical readers—reviewers, acquisition editor, managing editor, copyeditors—and we have found that each has questions, critical comments, and suggestions. The process is quite humbling and sometimes makes us doubt that we can write anything with clarity. How then can we promote the development of the writing skills of our students when our writing suffers from grievous flaws? We also marvel at committees on which we have served, for when a review of a document or the judgments about a paper submitted for an award varied widely, it seemed as if it were impossible to find a consistent standard. How, then, can a teacher hold students accountable for meeting a standard for quality writing? Here are some questions and issues that we have pondered in this chapter and in our practice as teachers of writing:

• If there are scholars and practitioners to whom we can point as experts about writing, can we look to them for help in defining the characteristics of quality writing? If we could find such experts, what do they have to say about the features that distinguish good writing? How do we adjudicate among experts who disagree? Is there a consensus about quality writing and, if so, where do you find the consensus?

• We hope that good writing means more than the avoidance of errors, but we know intuitively that some written expression is just wrong—mired in confusing syntax, unclear references, misuse of words, and so on. At the same time, we appreciate that powerful and persuasive communication takes many written forms, and many of the accomplished writers whom we admire often flaunt "rules." If we allow for some flexibility, what standards are there for "correctness" and convention? Do these standards change or modify from one discipline or one audience to the next? If belief in such modifications represents a consensus among expert writers, does English as represented in a class at a university serve as the model to which we should aspire?

• Many common practices that we have observed in middle schools and high schools—for example, beginning compositions with an "attention-getter" or supporting a generalization with three reasons—seem to have taken on an institutionalized persistence, even though they hardly represent what mature writers actually do. We encourage teachers to scrutinize the easy and popular practices in schools, with an empathic response toward the learners, and distinguish between schoolish practices and the actual work of accomplished writers.

• As mentioned above, part of the challenge to define a quality standard for writing is that the standard can vary from context to context and genre to genre. We know from experience that the editor from one journal can reject our article while the editor from another journal enthusiastically accepts it. The seeming

(continued)

inconsistency might follow from the more inclusive way that conscientious editors understand, better than the average writer, the mission of the journal, the interests of its readership, and the preferred style for the publication. This realization for writers and teachers of writing—that there is no universal standard, but multiple standards—forces those wishing to publish for a particular journal, or for a particular publishing house, or for the school board one day and for an old friend another, to remain aware of the standard in context. Most students learn this intuitively when they face shifting standards from teacher to teacher and genre to genre.

• Commonly, teachers review in class the concept of plagiarism and threaten severe penalties for offenders. That is certainly the pejorative view of academic integrity—that some practices are clear offenses and punishable. Beyond urging an effort to avoid such transgressions, we judge that a teacher will want students to honor a standard for writing that emphasizes an obligation to be honest in the broadest sense—expressing ideas as clearly as possible, representing opposing views accurately and respectfully, developing arguments fully, and helping readers to navigate through the complexities of a discussion. We know that we are often frustrated by writers who take shortcuts and by those who make easy writing difficult reading. We even become angry at apparent attempts to manipulate and obfuscate. We suggest that as part of a quality standard for writing, teachers and students need to include a quality standard for integrity in written expression.

• We appreciate creativity and invention and know these elements when we see them. But we have some difficulty in defining creativity as a feature of good writing. We have witnessed teachers who have urged learners to "be creative" in their responses or who have offered "extra credit" for creativity. When teachers imply a creativity standard and offer to reward attainment, it is only fair to define what teachers believe that standard is, or, better still, to help students to construct a standard.

• As we have noted in our discussion of genres, the standard for writing quality can shift from one context to another; and the shift might be most evident when writing is in a digital mode. The conventions and standards for composing for web pages and blogs can share some features with conventional print texts, but these genres have additional standards, unique to the context. If students are asked to write in a digital age, teachers have an obligation to learn the many conventions and standards established for the various contexts.

---

form the students were expected to produce. Hillocks reports that while students by and large conformed to the model, they produced writing that most English teachers are likely to discourage. In regard to the models provided to students, Hillocks notes: "However, in every paper provided, the support and elaboration is irrelevant, facetious, inaccurate, or sometimes false. When teachers use these papers as models of good writing, irrelevancy, facetiousness, inaccuracy, and falsehood become the standards for good writing" (p. 77).

The rubrics accompanying state writing assessments encourage students to produce elaborated responses to prompts. We appreciate *elaboration* as an appropriate standard. Too often we have read students' compositions that were regrettably underdeveloped, whether the writing was a narrative or some form of exposition. We like to see that the writer has developed ideas thoroughly enough to allow the reader to well imagine the events and emotions portrayed in a narrative, or has supported a general proposition or ancillary claim through careful analysis that includes citation and interpretation of relevant data. But we want that elaboration to be something of substance. We recoil when we see our preservice teachers design writing assignments that direct students to produce "three reasons" or "three pieces of evidence" to support a thesis. Or, the novice teacher might insist that their students develop each paragraph with five sentences. On the surface, such a prompt might seem reasonable as a way to promote elaboration and development, but learners often read these directions as license to supply any reasons or any "evidence," with no attention to the substance of the development. Long ago, Ken Macrorie (1970/1996) called the offering of shallow, predictable, and voiceless development as "Engfish": "bloated, pretentious language . . . in the students' themes, in the textbooks on writing, in the professors' and administrators' communications to each other. It is feel-nothing, say-nothing language, dead like Latin, devoid of the rhythms of contemporary speech" (p. 18). Similarly, Hillocks (2002, 2003) cites his Scottish grandmother, who referred to unsubstantial talk as "blether" (p. 17). Too often, writing prompts and their accompanying scoring rubrics emphasize the forms or trappings of writing (Hillocks, 2005), with little consideration of the substance of that writing—that the content includes relevant data, judiciously selected details, accurate information, and keen reasoning.

As bad as it is that teachers preparing learners for state assessments encouraged students to follow questionable models, intentional falsehood is worse. As Hillocks witnessed students laboring on practice compositions in preparation for the state writing assessment, he was impressed that some students seemed to have a command of data that few people would know. When a teacher prompted students to take a position about a proposed increase in the age for eligibility for obtaining a driver's license, some students supported claims by citing the number of traffic violations per age group, the number of accidents per age group, the number of injuries and fatalities per age group, and so forth. When Hillocks expressed his surprise that the students could readily cite such detailed statistics, they admitted that they had made it all up: they fabricated data to support claims. The scoring rubric would not account for this subversion, since the students were able to produce the traits listed in a scoring guide, which called for *support* and *elaboration* and did not require accuracy or integrity.

This preparation episode underscores for us another important feature of good writing—that it is honest. Honesty means more than not fabricating evidence to support a position and not plagiarizing. Good writing has an essential integrity—that the writer makes an honest effort to be truthful, and to attempt to clarify rather than obfuscate or manipulate. Perhaps some marketing experts and political strategists judge certain advertisements and propaganda as "good" as long as the expression achieves its desired end. But Williams (2010) reminds us of the writer's ethical responsibility: "What is at stake is the ethical foundations of a literate society" (p. 194). He notes that "we write ethically when as a matter of principle, we would trade places with our intended readers and experience the consequences they do after they read our writing" (p. 194). The obligation, and the feature of good writing, is the intention to be clear, supportive, and honest, as opposed to confusing, callous, and deceptive. Of course, sometimes our best efforts can still make for expression that is difficult to comprehend. Tom recalls a university professor characterizing his essay about a Shakespeare play as "easy writing making for hard reading." Although Tom was not intending to deceive, he was perhaps careless enough of the task of the reader to interfere with clarity of analysis. Perhaps his reading of Shakespeare was confused enough to make clear analysis impossible. In the end, the ethical obligation and the associated feature of good writing is the element of integrity, which is a product of the empathy that the writer has for the reader.

PURSUING CREATIVITY AND INVENTION

We have marveled from time to time at the task of the creative writing teacher who is in a position to judge the extent to which writing is creative and shows signs of invention. Even in a conventional middle school or high school class, an English teacher might include in her assessment of students' writing some consideration of the novelty and freshness of ideas. While various thinkers (e.g., Brookhart, 2013; Csikszentmihalyi, 1996; Wiggins, 2012) insist that teachers can measure creativity and offer rubrics to help in the effort, the language of their rubrics (e.g., "highly effective," "sophisticated," "new," "interesting") still leaves the vision of creativity as a quality of good writing as an ineffable abstraction.

We will allow that creativity and invention are qualities often apparent in good writing, but we also expect that the teacher who assesses students on the basis of the creativity in their writing will be able to convey to the learners what *creativity* is, or, better yet, engage students in a process of defining for themselves what *creativity* is. If invention is more than waiting for the visit from a muse and is something that can be measured, then the teacher who holds students accountable for being inventive should be able to show students how to invent.

WRITING STANDARDS FOR A DIGITAL AGE

Hicks (2013), Turner and Hicks (2016), and Richardson (2013) note that contemporary students live for the most part in a digital world, communicating most often through text messages and various forms of social media. They are also consumers of various forms of texts, such as web pages, podcasts, wikis, and blogs. If teachers are going to prepare learners to produce various digital expressions, including videos and podcasts, they will need to be familiar with standards for each form. Teachers should also be familiar with the processes involved in composing and collaborating within these digital environments. At the same time, we judge that writing is writing, even though the writing task might become complicated by issues of design and by the technical matters of supporting links and embedding sound and images into more conventional texts. Even though text might appear on a web page or accompany sound and images to be shared across various communities, we would hope that the writing supports understanding, through its logic, clarity, coherence, and precision.

POINTS OF CONVERGENCE

Tom and John agree that many state examinations offer relatively mechanical models as examples of "good writing," whether for teachers to hold students to "high standards," or for students who mistakenly think that if the state says so, and since they have the power of the grade or assessment, then this type of writing is what one must do. Yet, we know that "good writing" is judged differently by different disciplines and different audiences (Diederich, 1974; Williams, 2010). We agree that at the sentence and paragraph level, there may be much more agreement than not for most types of "good writing." The major differences appear at the organizational and structural level and in the technical language and the assumptions about shared knowledge across the intended audience.

We judge that English teachers should reflect on what qualities resonate with them when they read the writing that they like. That's a starting point. But whenever we are inclined to insist on some rules of good writing, some gifted writer will dazzle us by rupturing these rules. In addition, various genres and various discourse communities and literacy environments have their own conventions and standards, making it difficult to insist on a rigid set of criteria. We judge that teachers should recognize that writing in its various forms, occasions, environments, and combinations requires some expansiveness, openness, and flexibility in defining what makes writing "good."

Our experience of at least half a century of reading academic writing and students' attempts at producing academic writing has shaped what we value when we read and judge the writing of others. We agree with George Orwell's well-known comment that "the great enemy of clear language is insincerity. When there is a gap between one's real and declared aims, one turns as it were instinctively to long words and exhausted idioms, like a cuttlefish squirting out ink" (1954, p. 173). We encourage students to write in a way that is clear, coherent, complete, and careful. If a student proceeds with integrity and sincerity, she will endeavor to write clearly and coherently. If the writer cares enough about the reader, she will develop ideas thoroughly and logically. A sense of integrity will also guide the writer to be fair-minded in representing and evaluating various perspectives. We appreciate writers who take sufficient care to respect the conventions of a particular mode of writing, whether the writing is in a digital form or a more conventional form. We appreciate creativity, innovation, and invention, although we struggle to define these qualities and therefore hesitate to set these as a standard for students.

Our list of desirable traits is short and cuts across various forms and expressions. As we explore in the next chapter, we distrust attempts to transmit a list of desirable writing qualities to learners and expect instead to design experiences that help learners to discover and express for themselves some standards for good writing. But teachers cannot design such experiences unless they have thought thoroughly for themselves what good writing is all about.

YOUR THOUGHTS

We offer as common sense that if a teacher is to teach students how to craft something—whether a birdhouse, a symphony, or an academic essay—the teacher ought to have in mind a quality standard, especially one that is broadly shared and not one that is idiosyncratic and esoteric. For the craft of writing, we have dismissed formulaic and dishonest expressions, and we caution against slavish attention to the strictures of rules, especially when the "rules" have dubious authority. That leaves a vast territory for viable and commendable writing, and we invite the reader to express a standard that can guide instruction and serve the needs of students.

- What is good writing? To what extent is there a universal standard?
- How should a teacher respond to vernacular expressions that do not align with conventional school-based and assessment-based standards?
- To what extent is it possible for students to *discover* or *negotiate* a standard for good writing?
- How can rubrics represent a standard for good writing?
- What function does the expression of a standard of good writing serve in the overall process of teaching students to write well?
- How much attention can the average teacher pay to beginning students' awareness of the social, cultural, and political roles that good writing entails?

4

The Territory of Writing

How Can We Facilitate Growth?

So far, we have explored knowledge foundations for the study of literature and for planning instruction in written composition. We have revealed where we disagree, and we have emphasized points of convergence. In the previous chapter, we discussed the challenges in defining what good writing should be. In this chapter, we examine what an English teacher needs to know about approaches to teaching writing. We understand that each teacher has particular strengths and limitations and preferred ways of operating in the classroom, and we understand that an approach to instruction should align with the particular context for learning. We acknowledge that there are many ways that teachers have approached the teaching of writing, but we also understand that some approaches are more promising and supportive than others. In this chapter, we describe popular approaches to the teaching of writing, discuss the assumptions that these approaches make about learners and learning, and review ways to think about the relative efficacy of the various approaches and the impact that instructional approaches can have on learners. In the end, we urge English teachers to know the distinctions among the approaches to writing instruction so that the experiences in their own classrooms represent "principled practice," and not comfortable intuition, indiscriminate imitation, or a confused hybrid.

We appreciate that many of the preservice teachers with whom we have worked attempt to combine elements of competing approaches. This might make good sense if the approaches are not at odds with each other. But if a teacher sees herself or himself as a constructivist and then has students completing grammar worksheets one day, taking notes on organizational techniques the next, and then "free writing" on a third day, these practices are inconsistent and probably work against the teacher's projected targets for learning.

While we might disagree in our assessments of many pedagogical practices, together we hold firm to an understanding that an assign-and-assess approach to writing instruction doesn't help students very much. First, the approach assumes that students already know how to write, and instruction is a simple matter of prompting learners to produce texts. In a few instances, this might be the case; but we have known hundreds of classes in which students needed a good deal of preparation to help them to know how to produce a piece of writing and to learn flexible and generative processes for writing under many circumstances. The second shortcoming to an assign-and-assess approach is that the emphasis is on the comments that teachers offer *after* students have already produced something. The implication is that students will have subsequent opportunities to write and that they will apply any of the teacher's suggestions for improvement during the next attempt. We have reason to believe that this hope is seldom realized, unless the teacher and learners follow the kind of supportive assessment approaches that Heller (2015) describes to give students an opportunity to build on their earlier efforts and work toward refinement.

We also agree about the limitations of teaching formulas like the five-paragraph essay. The form stubbornly persists in schools, seems to be rewarded on state assessments, and confines students as they move from high school and meet new academic and written expression demands in colleges and universities. We say more about this persistent structure later in the chapter.

These two popular approaches to writing instruction—assigning-and-assessing and prescribing the five-paragraph essay—emphasize the final product, the writing that a teacher sees after the student independently produces it and the writing that conforms to a preconceived structure. Of course, if a teacher is going to *teach* writing instead of merely *assigning* and *assessing* writing, she will need to know something about the processes involved in composing any text and the procedures that students will have to learn in order to generate their own texts. An English teacher will benefit from being aware of the evolving thinking in composition studies and from knowing the research that informs the theory that directs instruction. We shy from claims about "best practices" in the teaching of writing, but we judge that there is such a thing as "principled practice," with classroom learning activities and structures aligning with carefully conceived theory and viable research.

COMING A LONG WAY TO A PROCESS ORIENTATION

In the same year that Tom entered John's Introduction to Fiction class, Janet Emig published her influential *The Composing Processes of Twelfth Graders* (1971). Certainly, there were several influential voices in composition studies at that time, but Emig clearly influenced many teachers to recognize that it makes good sense to teach writing as a multi-stage process. In fact, in preparing our teacher candidates for job interviews, we suggest that an appropriate answer to a question about the teaching of writing is to say, "I teach writing as a process." This seems obvious, but an instructional approach that emphasizes models or "mentor texts" (e.g., Gallagher, 2011, 2014) or rubrics (e.g., Culham, 2003, 2010) places an emphasis on the finished product and does little to reveal the thinking, problem-solving, or decision-making procedures that a writer follows in order to generate texts.

In revealing elements in a composing process, Emig draws from science inquiry to suggest distinct stages in the process of writing: exploring, planning, drafting, and refining. Perhaps through Emig's influence or as a result of their own reflections and discoveries, Murray (1972/2003b) and Graves (1980, 1983) suggest a similar process: prewriting, writing, and rewriting, or visioning, planning, drafting, and revisioning, or some similar variation. Graves particularly influenced his student Lucy McCormick Calkins and other like-minded practitioners like Atwell (1998) and Daniels and Zemelman (1988). Calkins and Graves (1980) describe their research agenda and their instructional approach in this way: "We are building a tentative map of how children change composing, penmanship and spelling behaviors during the writing process" (p. 208). Calkins offers this variation: "We need to build a tentative developmental map of how children change as writers before we can raise questions and form hypotheses. We must identify and describe the what of children's writing before we can attempt to explain the why" (p. 331).

The apparent belief behind this research interest was that, à la Piaget, keen observers could watch students at work as they wrote, and the observers would note the stages in the learners' development. From this perspective, the teacher's role is to observe and facilitate the natural development of the learners and not to interfere with it.

For Graves, his friend and mentor Murray, and Calkins, the greatest threat to students' developing as authentic writers and not reciters of "Engfish," as Macrorie calls flaccid academic writing, was for the teacher to impose writing tasks, suggest universal ways for developing writing, or otherwise interfere with a natural developmental process. Their preferred approach places a great deal of emphasis on allowing learners time to write and protecting students' autonomy to choose what to write about and the forms that writing should take. Interactions with the teacher involve supportive conferences that do not take away decision-making from the writer, but reveal an effect on a reader and give rise to reflection about the development of the writing. This teaching of "the writing process" is often characterized as a "workshop approach," during which students explore ideas and episodes through writing and sharing their work with others, especially the teacher, to discover how the writing impacts an audience and to evaluate options for the further development of the writing.

Atwell (1987/1998, 2014) is another champion of a workshop approach; like Graves and Calkins, she relies on careful observation of her own students and reflection on their growth and development as her mode of research to affirm that her instructional approach supports students' learning. She describes in detail her workshop and process-oriented approach in her popular *In the Middle*. Again, Atwell eschews instructional approaches that might influence students to write in predictable and artificial ways and hopes to facilitate natural development and authentic voice: "when students believe that what they have to say is important, both within their lives and beyond them, they care about how their words go down on the page" (1987/1998, p. 250). Here Atwell reveals a belief that if unimpeded and allowed to pursue the topics that interest them, students develop naturally as writers. Like Emig and Murray before her, Atwell's workshop approach involves a process of development; depends on students' choosing their own topics and modes of expression; and relies on the teacher as careful and sympathetic reader and responder, a "mentor of writing, a mediator of writing strategies, and a model of a writer at work" (Atwell, 1987/1998, p. 25).

We offer some caution here. While we believe that writing is a process and the teaching of writing is a process, we also understand that the process might change from one writing task to another and from one writer to another. We also understand that a tidy representation of a process with distinct stages does not adequately represent what writers actually do. First, Smagorinsky and Smith's (1992) review of writing process literature reveals that there are many writing processes, rather than one generic writing process. Processes might be task-specific, context-specific, and "community-specific." The various occasions for writing can shift the writer's composing processes, requiring in the end that the teacher teach and the learner learn a repertoire of problem-solving and composing strategies. In addition, Flower and Hayes (1981) report that instead of a process unfolding according to distinct stages, writing is recursive, with the writer continually reviewing and revising, and with the immediate written output as powerful as the writer's original plan in guiding subsequent output. Instead of the writer laying out a static plan and carrying it through in a draft before reviewing and revising, Flower and Hayes report that "the sub-processes of revising and evaluating, along with generating, share the special distinction of being able to interrupt any other process and occur at any time in the act of writing" (p. 374). While a conception of a writing process with distinct stages for planning, drafting, and reviewing might be convenient and tidy for the teacher, in actual practice, the process is more complicated, and within each stage, the process might vary from learner to learner.

It is hard to generalize about a writing process also because it appears that the composing processes vary as much as the individual writer. In *Working Days: The Journals of The Grapes of Wrath,* Robert DeMott (1989) reports that even though Steinbeck thought about the subject of his novel for years and wrestled with how to tell the narrative, he wrote hundreds of pages long-hand in a ledger book, with no apparent revisions: "in the entire 200,000-word manuscript the number of deletions and emendations is proportionally so few and infrequent as to be nearly nonexistent" (p. 12). This flow of productivity defies conventional conceptions of the tortured novelist devising detailed plans and laboring over every word. At the same time, we know writers who make complex plans before embarking on a writing project and collaborative writers, like us, who know the general plan but meander a bit in a process of discovery through their writing. We suggest that teachers need to be aware of the cognitive complexities involved in composing and the idiosyncratic nature of the processes that writers follow to produce various kinds of texts. While there might be some pedagogical convenience to urging a neat multi-stage process, an English teacher would be wise to recognize that a multi-stage process model is only a rough approximation of what some writers do, and to allow for a good deal of flexibility for individual students.

PROCESS AND THE DEVELOPMENT OF "VOICE"

Many influential teachers of writing have long bemoaned that common approaches to teaching writing (e.g., assign-and-assess, five-paragraph essay, grammar drills) have influenced students to obsess about error avoidance and to write in the kind of artificial voice that Macrorie called "Engfish." A reaction against the kind of stultifying instruction that produces artificial and predictable responses has been the developmental and student-centered approaches advocated by Macrorie, Murray, Graves, Calkins, Atwell, Daniels, and Zemelman. Taken together as a community of like-minded thinkers about writing instruction, these theorists share an emphasis on free writing and journal writing, student choice in subject and modes of expressions, conferences with and among writers, and the development of authentic voice. These teachers of writing share a presumption that students will inevitably develop as writers if teachers do not interfere with the natural processes of development and allow students choice and ownership of their writing. These presumptions lead them to prefer case study methodologies of research to demonstrate how learners develop as writers and how teachers might support that development.

When Tom began teaching composition in a high school, Macrorie had a particular influence. The appeal touched two values—student choice and authenticity. Intuitively, it seemed sensible that students would write authentically and with effort and commitment if they were allowed to choose the focus of their writing and encouraged to develop that writing in ways that fostered an authentic written voice. Journal writing and free writing appealed to progressive instincts, especially when the competing alternative was the imposition of the five-paragraph essay, perhaps represented most stridently in Sidney Moss's *Composition by Logic*.

At an early stage of his teaching career, Tom turned away from the apparent formulaic and artificial spirit inherent in teaching the five-paragraph essay. The alternative championed by Macrorie, Murray, Graves, and Zemelman offered some promise of honoring learners' autonomy and helping students to write authentically. One could add Calkins, Atwell, and Daniels to the company of thinkers who value free writing, journaling, conferences, and workshops. Inherent in their approaches is the belief that students are inclined to develop naturally and authentically as writers when they function in a literacy-rich environment and the teacher does not interfere with development by imposing onerous and artificial tasks and valuing correctness above fluency and authentic expression. A common sentiment among these theorists is that students thrive when they have choice of topic and modes of expression. The theorists' tendency, at least as suggested from the case studies they feature, is to value personal narrative as a rich source of substance for writing and as a path for necessary identity formation and self-actualization. The teacher's role is facilitator of a natural process of discovery and development. Calkins (1986) asserts: "Topic choice is part of it, but the larger issue is that, when we invite children to choose their form, voice, and audience as well as their subject, we give them ownership and responsibility for their writing. This transforms writing from an assigned task into a personal project" (p. 6). When learners are autonomous agents pursuing their own writing agenda, the teacher does not devise specific learning experiences to prepare students for writing.

Instead, instruction features journal writing, workshop-style sharing and feedback, conferencing, and mini-lessons on selected features of writing and conventions of language.

The workshop and free writing approaches presume that students will be naturally inclined to pursue their own interests, and the approaches put a premium on the teacher's sensitive and supportive feedback and apply both in early grades and throughout middle school and high school. John recognizes that the work of Peter Elbow has long had an influence on compositionists at the university and in turn influenced some high school teachers. Elbow (2007) is particularly concerned with review and response to what has been written. He asks, "What makes writing audible?" while claiming that this question remains "a theoretical mystery" (p. 177). For someone placing such emphasis on students' learning to establish their "voice" in a writing class, the exchange of question-response remains crucial, yet frustratingly incomplete. Furthermore, Elbow admits that in discussing "resonance," one element of voice, his "hypothesis here is completely speculative" (p. 179). In his retrospective, Elbow reminds us that "voice formulation is a personal *subjective* projection—and it implies a subjective guess about how others will react and even about the mind and feel of the writer" (p. 178). Elbow cannot be faulted for the limitations of knowledge about the continued development of research in an adjacent area of composition studies, but other work suggests some interesting answers to his questions and to the difficulties of students establishing their voices inside the confines of a one- or two-semester writing program. John suggests that the ultimate goal itself has merit—"read the text aloud so that listeners without a text will really understand it"—but the question of how and why needs further development and analysis to be useful in the classroom (Elbow, 2007, p. 179).

Elbow and his like-minded developmentalists value that students develop an authentic voice in their writing. We certainly don't want students to be automatons and write in a predictable and artificial way, but the concept of what constitutes an "authentic" voice seems a bit slippery to us—both as teachers and as researchers. Perhaps authenticity has, as the French say, a certain *je ne sais quoi,* a quality that only those with attuned sensibilities can recognize, which makes it rather difficult to teach emerging writers. While we share Elbow's appreciation of the connection between spoken and written language, and the value of conversation as a path to written language, we find that he does not make clear in his writings how a middle school or high school student *learns* to understand "voice" as she or he wrestles with clarifying both differences and continuities between objective description and subjective projection.

Implications for Teacher Development

A conversation in a teacher preparation class or among members of an English department in a middle school or high school will reveal a wide variety of assumptions about teaching writing, including some assertions that writing can't be taught. As Bob Tremmel (2001) has revealed, candidates in teacher preparation programs see themselves primarily as teachers of literature and reading, and most candidates have little preparation to teach writing. If that trend holds true today, most teachers face their responsibility to teach writing without a well-established theory of instruction. We fear that the lack of preparation will position newcomers to adopt whatever seems to be the dominant practice in a local school, with uncertain results. We suggest that teachers need to know much about the varied and sometimes competing approaches to writing instruction in schools. We hope that teachers' classroom practices follow from knowing what viable approaches teachers have followed and the theory and research behind the practices. In other words, we hope that, as Smagorinsky (2007) and N. Boudreau Smith (2017) endorse, teachers follow principled practices. To that end, we invite teachers to consider the following possibilities, perhaps through reading, consultation with colleagues, and reflection on the impact on learners.

• If a teacher is going to plan instruction for writing, the teacher assumes that writing can be taught. That is a central stance. Otherwise, a teacher should have a clear sense of how someone learns to write without the benefit of instruction.

• It seems almost passé now to say that you "teach writing as a process." What are the alternatives? If you are taking a "process approach," what does that mean? Are there distinct stages? What is the teacher's role throughout the stages?

• As we have represented the field in this chapter, some teachers try to get out of the way of the learners' development, while others judge that learning precedes development. From what you know about learners and how any human being develops, what is your position about this balance between natural development and a teacher's intervention?

• We described some broad categories of instruction, with emphases on various components of writing instruction: for example, the use of models and rubrics, assessment and feedback, repeated practice, engagement in inquiry and discussion. If you emphasize any one of these components, how have you decided that this is an important part of writing instruction? If you believe that you combine these various components, what knowledge drives your decisions about emphasis and sequence?

• You may find that you can reflect on your own development as a writer to generalize about the experiences and interventions that should help any emerging writer. What practices did you find especially helpful, and why should these practices help other writers?

STRUCTURED PROCESS APPROACHES

While John labored at the university and Tom in high schools to achieve the ends the process approach promised, they found in actual practice that the freewriting, workshop, conferencing, and coaching approach to the teaching of writing was frustrating both to the teacher and to the students. For example, when Tom worked with very troubled students in an alternative school program within a public high school, he found students reluctant to write anything at all when they were liberated to write about what pleased them and in any form they liked. The workshop methods that apparently served Atwell so well in Maine and Graves and Calkins so well in New Hampshire were less impressive in a school where daily attendance was in itself a triumph. The most carefully crafted lesson plan ever written is not useful when the audience isn't there, or doesn't care, or acts in opposition to the teacher's enthusiasm. With an almost religious-like zealotry, the heroic teachers just named above may win over their charges by the force of their own personalities, but personality rarely scales to the average teacher trainee in an average classroom. Just as the average vocalist cannot merely try to imitate Beyoncé and expect huge audiences and record contracts, neither can the average teacher trainee faithfully follow Atwell and Elbow and frequently, much less always, expect similar results. Emerging teachers, too, have to "develop their own voice," and reading this book will, we intend, help.

Of course, many teachers will recognize that there has been much research that contrasts both in method and implications to the approaches inspired mostly by Murray and Graves. This alternative body of research has influenced our practices as teachers of writing and as English educators charged with preparing others to teach writing. We portray the contrast in research and instruction approaches below.

Daniels and Bizar (1998) see themselves as "long-term thinking coaches" (p. 159). They promote an instructional approach that features writing conferences and note that in "the best of conferences, the teacher does not step in to solve student problems, or make their decisions, but guides them through the process of deciding for themselves, making their own choices, and living out the consequences" (p. 158). This image of the hands-off teacher respecting the learner's autonomy places faith and value in students' natural development. An obvious alternative to this developmental view is an understanding that adults and capable peers, through meaningful interactions among learners, can impact growth that *precedes* development. The simple theoretical contrast is this: watching what a student can do when she operates independently at play or in completing a task versus watching what a student can do when she has support and can interact frequently with capable peers and a learned adult. According to Vygotsky (1978), "Learning precedes development" (p. 86). He notes the theoretical contrast in this way: "the classics of psychological literature, such as the works by Binet and others, assume that development is always a prerequisite for learning and that if a child's mental functions (intellectual operations) have not matured to the extent that he is capable of learning a particular subject, then no instruction will prove useful" (p. 80). The developmental view protects students within a comfort range of their developmental stage, thereby targeting a lower threshold. In contrast, Vygotsky and other sociocognitive thinkers see learning within a range that in a sense stretches learners beyond their comfort level but still within a supportive environment.

Two influential meta-analyses of studies of writing instruction affirm the Vygotskian perspective that learners benefit from being stretched beyond their comfort zones in order to grow. First, in his influential meta-analysis, Hillocks (1984) scanned thousands of studies, selected those that followed careful empirical controls, and grouped the various projects according to *modes* of instruction and *foci* of instruction. The grouping of studies allowed Hillocks to compare effect sizes across categories of instructional approaches. Simply put, an *effect size* refers to the shift in growth from one point to another. A relatively large effect size suggests substantial growth, while a relatively low effect size suggests little positive effect from instruction. Hillocks reports that instruction in the *environmental* mode (goal-oriented, problem-based, lots of student interaction) had the largest effect size ($d = 0.44$) and *inquiry* had the largest effect size ($d = 0.57$) for focus of instruction, while *free writing* had the next to smallest effect size ($d = 0.16$). Decades later, Graham and Perin's (2007a, 2007b) meta-analysis of studies of writing instruction affirmed these findings, revealing that the largest effect sizes were attained from studies in which students were taught strategies or procedures that were specific to a writing task ($d = 0.82$) and procedures for summarizing ($d = 0.82$) and when the learners had opportunities to collaborate with peers in stages for planning, drafting, reviewing, and revising ($d = 0.75$).

As John Hattie (2009) reports in *Visible Learning*, the effect size is a summary representation of the shift a sample or population experiences over time, as measured in standard deviations. Further, he reports that among the thousands of studies included in his meta-analysis and among over 300,000 effect sizes, 95% of the effects were positive. This does not mean that any intervention or approach to instruction is as effective as any other. Hattie offers as a "hinge point" the effect size of

$d = 0.40$, which is an average of the effect that most samples of students would experience over the course of an academic year. If we accept the proposed hinge point in this way, anything above +0.40 signals some exceptional learning and should get a teacher's attention. From this perspective, the trends that Graham and Perin (2007a, 2007b) and Hillocks (1984, 1986) report should have special resonance for English teachers who have some responsibility to teach writing. In other words, a teacher of English would do well to be mindful of practices that in all probability will result in large effects rather than settling for any positive effect, no matter how small.

At a relatively early stage in Tom's high school teaching experience, the Hillocks meta-analysis had a strong influence. One thing seemed certain: If a teacher were to have a significant impact in his students' development as writers, she or he would have the best chance by focusing on *inquiry* in what Hillocks calls an *environmental* mode. Of course, to do this, any teacher would have to know what an inquiry approach is and what an environmental mode of instruction looks like and feels like. Fortunately, books by some of Hillocks's students provide examples of inquiry in action—for example, Johannessen, Kahn, and Walter's *Designing and Sequencing Pre-writing Activities* and *Writing About Literature*; Smagorinsky, McCann, and Kern's *Explorations: Introductory Activities for Literature and Composition*; Smith's *Reducing Writing Apprehension*; Stern's *Teaching English So It Matters*; and Smagorinsky, Johannessen, Kahn, and McCann's *The Dynamics of Writing Instruction*.

First, a teacher taking an inquiry stance would have specific learning targets in mind. That is, the teacher would presume to set a learning agenda based on her understanding of students' current proficiencies and needs for development. The teacher would analyze carefully the kind of writing that a student would be expected to compose in order to have in mind what students would need to know and be able to do in order to produce such writing. These student needs would likely vary from class to class and from one type of writing to the next. For example, the content of the writing and the procedures for generating text would be different when writing a personal narrative as opposed to writing a critical appraisal of a work of literature. Keeping specific task demands in mind, a teacher would plan carefully the sequence of learning experiences that would likely prepare students for composing in a specific genre, providing practice with the procedures that are appropriate for that genre.

This careful preparation, also known as frontloading or prewriting, marks a contrast with preprocess practices. In his 1981 study of writing in secondary schools, Applebee reports, "In the observational studies, the amount of time devoted to prewriting activities averaged just over three minutes. That included everything from the time the teacher began introducing the topic until the first student began to write" (p. 74). Applebee goes on to report that "those three minutes were spent writing the essay topic on the board, or passing out and reading through a dittoed assignment sheet, followed by student questions about task dimensions: 'How long does it have to be?' 'Can I write in pencil?' 'Do I have to do this?' " (p. 74). The presumption was that students already knew how to write, in some sense, and the teacher merely had to prompt them to produce a composition. Instruction, back in those dark days of 1981 and before, largely took the form of correctives that the teacher marked on students' compositions.

In any inquiry, a question or problem or recognition of an area of doubt triggers a process of investigation. In pursuit of at least some tentative understandings, learners follow logical procedures of investigation. For Hillocks (2006, 2011), the inquiry process would rely on frequent peer interactions throughout several stages, not just during review of what has already been written. The teacher would either provide learners with the data that would support their inquiry or plan a stage for students to access data themselves. The extensive discussions, first led by the teacher and then continued in small and large groups, would involve students in the procedures appropriate for thinking about the problem that a writing task represents and necessary for producing a specific kind of text. The teacher labels the moves that students make in summarizing, analyzing, arguing, explaining, classifying, or narrating, and students reflect in discussion and writing about how they produced the writing they composed.

Here is a simple example of inquiry in action and what Applebee (1986) refers to as a "structured process" for the teaching of writing. The sequence follows the example from Johannessen, Kahn, and Walter (1982) in which they offer a set of scenarios to prompt discussion about the concept of *courageous action*. Johannessen, Kahn, and Walter (2009) also offer a similar activity that focuses on the concept of *hero*. The thinking behind that activity is that in order for students to write an extended definition of an abstract concept, they would need to be able to generate a set of criteria that distinguishes the concept from others with which it could be confused. To learn how to generate criteria, students react to problem-based scenarios, drawing from their prior knowledge to express the rationale behind their judgments. In addition, the writer would need to provide illustrative examples and accompanying explanations to support the criterion statements. The interactions among students are key to immersing the learners in the processes of defining a concept.

Tom recalls preparing high school students to read *King Lear* by exploring their conceptions of *justice*: Is Lear a man "more sinned against than sinning"? If readers decide that Lear got what he deserved or that he was punished beyond the severity of his crimes, they should have a solid basis or critical framework for constructing their decisions. Through discussion, students would be involved in developing the criteria for defining. In other words, they would be working on the procedures necessary in a strategy for defining, ideally with the learners becoming aware of procedures that they can apply in other situations. In addition, the students are developing the critical framework (criteria for defining a concept) that they can apply in discussing and writing about a work of literature. A process of generating the necessary criteria might begin with the whole-class discussion about an initial scenario, like the following:

> In a first-period health class, Mr. Knute Trission, a veteran teacher, discovered Karla Gluko chewing bubble gum. Mr. Trission had announced at the beginning of the term that he would not tolerate anyone bringing food, drink, or candy into the class. Mr. Trission did not like the idea that Karla would violate his classroom discipline policy, and he was especially disturbed that Karla would be chewing sugar-sweetened bubble gum after the class had just finished a unit in which they studied the dangers of consuming too much refined sugar. Mr. Trission insisted that Karla stand up in front of the class while he lectured her about chewing gum in class, noting her lack of thoughtfulness and sensitivity. Furthermore, he predicted that by the time Karla was 21, she would have no teeth. As part of Karla's punishment, Mr. Trission ordered her to write a 10-page report about the dangers of consuming refined sugar, and he would not allow her to return to class until the report was complete. Were Mr. Trission's actions just? Explain.

The following composite of several discussions with several classes illustrates the moves that students typically make in response to the problem. If the writing of an extended definition involves generating criterion statements and supporting each statement with an example, the discussion should allow students to develop skills with these procedures.

> TOM: As we have been discussing, and as we can see in events in the news every day, it is sometimes hard to determine for sure what *justice* is. While we might be quick to say that someone is unjust, even a teacher, we should have a solid standard on which to base our judgment. So, in the situation that we just read, do you judge Mr. Trission to be acting justly?

ALIANA: He is way over the top. He is like way too strict with Karla.

SERGIO: That's too much. What's the big deal about chewing some gum?

NICOLE: He's like a teacher who has his pet peeves and he really doesn't like kids eating or chewing gum in class. That's okay, but his reaction is too big for what she has done.

TOM: But Mr. Trission has alerted that class that he will not tolerate gum chewing in class. At least he warned everyone and he is being consistent in applying his rules.

CARLOS: Yeah, but he went way overboard. He's not supposed to be disrespecting her in front of the whole class. What is that—predicting that she won't have any teeth? That's uncalled for.

TOM: Well, she broke a rule. Shouldn't she get some punishment?

VICTORIA: He might warn her or tell her to spit out the gum. But what he did was way too much for what she did.

TOM: So you want the punishment to be appropriate for the offense? The punishment must fit the "crime," if we can call what Karla did a crime?

VICTORIA: Yeah.

SERGIO: That sounds right. The punishment must fit the crime.

This modeling of a discussion and problem-solving process sets the example for the small group work that follows and helps students to recognize the intellectual "moves" in which they are involved. In carefully organized groups, students would discuss other scenarios, like the two that follow. In the small groups, the students share their judgments, react critically to decisions, offer examples to illustrate what they mean, take into account exceptions, and evaluate multiple possibilities. These moves are all part of the process of generating an extended definition.

During world geography class, as Mr. Strata lectured, Harlan Fleming noisily wadded up a sheet of notebook paper into a ball and sailed it across the room and into the wastebasket next to the teacher's desk. The wad of paper rattled around the metal wastebasket before falling to the bottom. Mr. Strata stopped his lecture and filled out a disciplinary referral form about Harlan. Harlan protested, "You never said we couldn't throw paper away during class." Mr. Strata responded, "You should know by now what kind of behavior is appropriate for class." Harlan went immediately to the dean's office, where he was assigned a 3-day in-school suspension. After Harlan's departure, Mr. Strata told the class, "From now on, if anyone throws a wad of paper across the room, he or she will be sent to the dean's office and will probably be suspended." Were the actions of Mr. Strata and the dean just? Explain.

At the beginning of the school year, several bathrooms were vandalized: graffiti on the walls, wads of wet tissue paper stuck to the ceiling, broken tissue paper dispensers. Mr. Gristmeyer, an English teacher, identified three students who he thought he saw coming out of a washroom at the time that it was vandalized. The three students—Frank Roscoe, Bob Bellamy, and Alejandro Mosca—were brought to the dean's office. Mr. Swift, one of the school's deans, decided that Alejandro was the culprit, noting his record of many discipline problems while attending Floodrock High. When Alejandro protested, Mr. Swift said, "I don't want to hear about it. You've done enough already." Mr. Swift then suspended Alejandro for 3 days and assigned him to a Saturday work detail to help clean the bathrooms. Were Mr. Swift's actions just? Explain.

Typically, with the discussions of such problems, students generate several criterion statements, which they share with their peers in whole-class discussion. Students usually challenge some of each other's claims, inviting examples and accompanying explanations to support the claims. Here are some common statements that derive from small-group and whole-class discussion:

- "The punishment must fit the crime."
- "You can't punish someone for breaking your secret rules."
- "Some rules are obvious and don't have to be explained."
- "You shouldn't prejudge a person about committing a crime."
- "Everyone deserves the right to defend herself."

As the students share, refine, and illustrate these criteria, they are immersed in the process of defining. A next step is for the teacher to draw from the discussions a model of how to construct a body paragraph that expresses a criterion, offers an illustrative or contrasting example, and explains how the example demonstrates the viability of the rule.

This structured process or inquiry sequence introduces a significant problem that typically resonates with adolescents (defining *justice*), taps into students' prior knowledge, provides data (a set of scenarios), allows for extensive student interaction, transforms conversation into composing procedures, and launches students on a subsequent process of drafting and refining. Hillocks (1995) calls the introductory discussions that precede drafting a composition a "gateway activity." When students have a choice for a written response, their options include the writing of an extended definition, the applying of their definition criteria to evaluate a specific case or situation, or the telling of a story about someone who was the victim of injustice. In our experience, even with extensive teacher planning in the overall process, students assume ownership in their writing and value their participation with peers and their contributions to the shared inquiry, which is the desired outcome from both a "natural process" and "structured process" orientation. We judge that the teacher's sponsorship of the line of inquiry, based on her knowledge of students and extensive knowledge of the other components of the curriculum, does not undermine students' commitment to their writing, nor promote artificial voice. Over long teaching careers, we have seen students commit considerable effort to projects for which they might have had limited initial enthusiasm, just as we have applied honest effort or commitment to a variety of writing tasks, even when they were imposed on us. Where we have had difficulty is when we didn't understand the task, couldn't imagine the audience, and lacked sufficient preparation for the effort.

RESEARCH ORIENTATIONS

We understand that our beliefs about what is best for learners drive our practice, and the research we have taken care to study has shaped our beliefs. Among the authorities we have cited in this chapter, some embrace an empirical approach to research by trying to control as many factors as possible to isolate key instructional components that influence students' learning. From such analysis, researchers infer which instructional practices are likely to have a strong positive effect on students' learning to write. Another research orientation relies chiefly on case studies to understand how students develop as writers. The thinkers from these two orientations have often been at odds. For example, in the first edition of *In the Middle,* Nancie Atwell, apparently stung by George Hillocks's unflattering report about the limited effect of a "natural process" approach, reports her school's high-ranking scores on the state's writing assessment. She observes, "so much as far as I'm concerned for George Hillocks' 'findings' concerning the relative efficacy of writing workshop methods" (2014, p. 259).

Those quotation marks around the word *findings* carry great rhetorical weight. Hillocks has had his critics. For example, Langer, Stotsky, Hayes, and Purves (1988) offer careful critiques of his research methods and conclusions. In that set of reactions, Alan Purves et al. contrast Hillocks with Graves, Calkins, and Atwell thus:

Resources for Teachers of Writing

The Company You Keep: People You Should Know

We understand that teachers often operate intuitively, and we know a lot of teachers who have very sound intuitions. At the same time, we judge that we are on shaky ground when we operate only from intuition. In our efforts to become responsible teachers of writing, we have looked to research to help further inform us as to what practices are likely to have the most positive effects on learners— practices that help students to learn the procedures for composing various kinds of texts and practices that respect the learners for the knowledge that they can contribute daily to shared inquiry. Before 1965, the body of research about writing instruction was very thin; but the field has grown much since the 1980s. Again, many researchers, teachers, and English educators can point to the research that impacted them the most, and you will find that the authorities listed below haven't necessarily agreed with each other. The research and expressions of theory represented by the following list suggest possible directions for responsible paths through the territory of writing instruction:

Applebee, A. N., & Langer, J. A. (2013). *Writing instruction that works: Proven methods for middle and high school classrooms.* New York: Teachers College Press.

Atwell, N. (1998). *In the middle: New understandings about writing, reading, and learning.* Portsmouth, NH: Heinemann. (Original work published 1987)

Elbow, P. (1998). *Writing without teachers.* New York: Oxford University Press.

Emig, J. (1971). *The composing processes of twelfth graders* (NCTE Research Report No. 13). Urbana, IL: National Council of Teachers of English.

Gallagher, K. (2011). *Write like this: Teaching real-world writing through modeling and mentor texts.* Portland, ME: Stenhouse.

Graham, S., & Perin, D. (2007). *Writing Next: Effective strategies to improve writing of adolescents in middle and high schools.* New York: Carnegie Corporation.

Graves, D. H. (1983). *Writing: Teachers and children at work.* Portsmouth, NH: Heinemann.

Hillocks, G., Jr. (1986). *Research on written composition: New directions for teaching.* Urbana, IL: ERIC/National Conference on Research in English.

Hillocks, G., Jr. (1995). *Teaching writing as reflective practice.* New York: Teachers College Press.

Johannessen, L. R., Kahn, E., & Walter, C. C. (2009). *Writing about literature* (2nd ed., rev. and updated). Urbana, IL: National Council of Teachers of English.

Macrorie, K. (1970/1996). *Uptaught.* Portsmouth, NH: Heinemann.

Moffett, J. (1983). *Teaching the universe of discourse.* New York: Houghton Mifflin.

Smith, N. B. (2017, May). A principled revolution in the teaching of writing. *English Journal, 106*(6), 70–75.

Much of the research appears to assume that all students are unshaped clay until they come into the clutches of a Svengali or an Atwell. There are case studies of writers, but they usually focus on the writer in the act of writing or pay tribute to the great teacher; they seldom indicate that the writer may be a reader, may have a gender, may have a family, may have a language background, may have a set of attitudes and interests, may have a mind set about writing and school, may have acquired certain beliefs and principles concerning writing. (p. 106)

We can only imagine that Atwell judges that the empirical research orientation (or "comparative," as Purves et al. call it) focuses too much on the practices of the teacher and the quantitative analyses do not sufficiently reveal what teachers might orchestrate to foster students' learning. At the same time, she cites her state's quantitative measures of writing proficiency as evidence of the efficacy of her preferred approach.

We have not seen compelling reasons to dismiss the research methods of Hillocks or Graham and Perin. At the same time, we can see value in observational and case studies of learners to reveal what they do under various conditions for learning. If we look across research orientations and among various authorities to whom we have paid attention over decades, we prefer, like Nicole Boudreau Smith (2017), to seek places where they seem to agree in the best interest of students rather than pick sides in an academic dispute that only cultivates hard feelings and polarization.

POINTS OF CONVERGENCE

It seems almost trite now to say that teachers of English should know how to teach writing as a process. The review in this chapter reports that teachers have thought about *process* in different ways, with some advocating for a natural process of development that allows for expansive student choice and unimpeded development, and others choosing a structured process approach that strategically sets out a sequence of learning experiences to prepare students to complete specific kinds of writing in order to develop a repertoire of ways to respond to situations and problems in writing.

We agree to eschew practices that will encourage students to rely on formulas and to produce predictable writing and artificial language. We judge that it is possible to look closely at any given writing experience—for example, personal narrative, comparison/contrast analysis, persuasive argument—and recognize the demands that the task presents to a particular group of learners at a specific stage in their development. With an understanding of what students need to know and need to be able to do in order to produce a viable piece of writing, a teacher can plan for a sequence of experiences that will allow students to define the genre of writing, access from memory or from other sources the information necessary for the writing, and develop and practice the procedures that are necessary for generating text in the target genre. The sequence of experiences, which require lots of interaction among the learners, would precede the actual drafting of a composition. We judge that a teacher needs to know how to analyze the tasks that she sets before the learners and plan backward to increase the likelihood that all students in a class can complete a task successfully and move on with an awareness of the processes that she or he followed to produce a text.

We understand *process* to mean further that writing is rarely, if ever, automatic. We know from our own attempts that writing involves a lot of planning, attempting, sharing, judging, reflecting, revising, and editing. English teachers need to know how to provide for such a process so that students have sufficient and relevant experience in preparing, drafting and sharing their work, attending to feedback and their own reflections, and refining their work. A teacher should know that in the process, she should provide focused, supportive, and meaningful feedback in order to encourage the development of a particular piece of writing and to bolster the writer's confidence to tackle similar tasks again. An English teacher should know how to prompt students to reflect in writing and discussion about the processes they followed in order to compose a text.

Tom observed a high school history teacher who had prompted his class to write an essay in which the students were to "describe the Louisiana Purchase," which had been the focus of their study for at least two weeks. If the teacher could put himself in the place of the students, he might recognize the specific demands of the task. Obviously, anyone who was to write a meaningful and well-developed composition in response to the prompt would have to know something about the Louisiana Purchase. In addition, the writer would need to know how to access the relevant information stored in memory or recorded somewhere. So, part of a writing teacher's responsibility is to help students understand the subject of their writing, access relevant and accurate data, and command strategies for selecting and sorting information stored in memory. In the case of the history teacher's essay prompt, the learners would also need to know what the teacher wants them to do: Describe the physical limits, location, and geographic features of the land under the Louisiana Purchase? Trace the political, military, social, cultural, and economic forces that led to the transaction? Tell the history of the Louisiana Purchase and trace its impact on the indigenous people and the subsequent benefits to the remaining power groups? In other words, students would find it difficult to complete the task unless they knew what the task was. But even if they knew specifically what the teacher wanted—for example, analysis and critical assessment—they could not produce the appropriate text unless they had developed the kind of procedures necessary for the assignment. A teacher could plan for all of it—the command of the content, the accessing of information, the defining of the genre or writing task, and the development of the generative procedures that will support learners to use the content to produce the genre of writing.

We have done a lot of name-dropping in this chapter—Emig, Graves, Murray, Macrorie, Calkins, Atwell, Daniels, Zemelman, Moffett, Elbow, Gallagher, Hillocks, Smagorinsky, Smith, Johannessen, Kahn, Walter, Applebee, and Langer—and we have neglected many more favorites among teachers of writing. An English teacher should be familiar with several of these names and the approaches to writing instruction that they represent. In our classification, there are three large groups: (1) the traditionalists, who obsess about correctness and promulgate formulas; (2) the developmentalists, who encourage a "natural process" of development that values personal choices and individual voices; and (3) the sociocognitive constructivists, who promote a "structured process" approach that systematically engages learners, usually through peer interaction, in the procedures necessary to produce a variety of genres.

Teachers like to refer to their own personal "styles" of teaching and suggest that a teacher has to teach in a style that is most comfortable to her or him. We appreciate this, if style refers to one's demeanor in the classroom, ways of organizing the classroom environment, and emotiveness of expression. But if style refers to an approach to instruction, then we suggest that some approaches are better than others. For example, while we think that it is important that English teachers have a keen knowledge of how the English language functions, we don't see an approach that focuses on a daily drill in grammar and mechanics as a promising approach to teaching writing. In fact, given decades of research that reveals the futility of such an emphasis (e.g., Britton, Burgess, Martin, McLeod, & Rosen, 1975; Hillocks, 1984), we judge that it would be irresponsible to continue to have students complete grammar worksheets and diagrams in the cause of helping learners to develop as writers. The question of satisfying any teacher's preference or comfort with one "style" over another would not matter, if learners were not impacted by the choice. Hillocks (2009) asks, "Does one method, practice, or paradigm work better for our students than another?" (p. 26). He answers succinctly: "I believe that practices or paradigms make huge differences, not only in student learning but also in student dispositions toward learning" (p. 26). This is not to say that there is one method that we could script for others to follow for guaranteed success in any classroom. We understand that all learning is contextualized, making it fruitless to try to cut one size to fit all. But, as we suggest in this chapter, a substantial body of research reveals practices that are more promising than others—promising in the sense of advancing the learning and achievement of students and in the sense of fostering a positive learning experience in the classroom.

We have known confident teachers who describe their approach as a hybrid of many other approaches. They borrow an activity from this colleague and follow a routine suggested by that blog, or duplicate a handout from a conference and select an appealing exercise from a textbook. We confess that we have been enthusiastic borrowers and lenders, and we have certainly shared much with each other over the years. But we have applied a theoretical filter to anything that others offered to us, recognizing that a set of practices from disparate sources can be wildly inconsistent and philosophically incompatible. Such a filter is hard to come by, requiring the teacher to be familiar with theories of learning and research about the teaching of writing. In the end, an English teacher has the responsibility to be able to describe to others, including his or her students, what he or she plans to do, and why he or she plans to follow this approach.

YOUR THOUGHTS

Even if a teacher has a solid conception of what good writing is, as we discuss in Chapter 3, she would need to do more than describe the standard and direct students to produce writing that conforms to the standard. We understand that when anyone writes, she or he draws from various sources of knowledge to be able to generate coherent texts. We discourage simply assigning writing and relying on feedback at the end of the process as the sole source of instruction. We agree that reliance on the five-paragraph essay and other such formulas do little to foster students' development as writers. But that leaves many other options, presumably to be pursued with consistency and fidelity. What are those options?

- What do you judge to be viable approaches to the teaching of writing?
- What theoretical or research orientation guides your decision about an instructional approach?

- Considering a particular form of writing, what learning activities do you imagine will prepare learners to be able to produce that form? Why would these activities likely have their desired effect?
- To what extent will assessment play an important instructional role in your plan to teach writing?
- To what extent is it possible to advance the concept of "correctness" and insist on writing with precision?
- How can you help learners to write authentically and with a distinctive voice?

5

The Territory of Oral Discourse

When Tom was a school district administrator, he presented to a school board a plan to eliminate a required one-semester speech class and move instead to a broader, varied, and integrated program of oral discourse activities across the curriculum. The proposal to the school board was a product in part of a study of what similar high schools in the area had been doing. The most common practice was to integrate speech activities as an element in all English classes. Instructional leaders in the area high schools affirmed the importance of oral language activities and recognized that the three or four 3-minute speeches common in a required tenth-grade speech class were insufficient to prepare adolescents for the variety of occasions for speaking clearly and confidently and listening actively and critically. Of course, the proposal before the school board brought a succession of complaints, supported by some influential high school alumni who reported that their success in business was predicated on their ability to deliver oral presentations. The arguments derived from a sense that the career and financial success of some local leaders followed from a one-semester class they took in tenth grade.

In the end, the school board approved the proposal for change, presumably because they judged that oral language skills are too important to leave to the fleeting experiences of tenth grade. They also found specious the arguments that when one result (i.e., career success) followed an experience (tenth-grade speech class), it does not follow logically that one thing caused another. We know that aspiring English teachers seldom think of themselves as speech teachers (Tremmel, 2001). At the same time, in surveys that we have administered to student teachers for

8 years, they often report that the teaching of public speaking is one of the areas where they feel least confident. There are occasions when student teachers and licensed teachers are assigned to teach a speech class or to teach speech as an element of the English curriculum. While the one-semester speech class is a time-honored tradition in some school districts, English teachers need to recognize that much of the reading and writing that students do relies on a foundation of spoken language, or as Britton (1983) asserts, "Reading and writing float on a sea of talk" (p. 11). If students are to learn important procedures for reading critically, evaluating arguments judiciously, writing lucidly, and much more, they will benefit from extensive oral language experiences. There is much, then, that teachers of English need to know about oral discourse if they are to do more than assign students to deliver the "Introduction Speech," the "Informative Speech," and the "Persuasive Speech," with or without presentation software.

In this chapter, we discuss what English language arts teachers should know about public speaking and about broader oral discourse activities. We see value in teaching public speaking in itself as a mode of expression. We also know from our own research and experience that ultimately teachers of English need to know how to create supportive classroom environments where students feel safe and confident about expressing themselves and assessing constructively the expressions of others. Attention to the oral discourse in the English classroom means more than being able to assign students to produce three-minute speeches that they reluctantly deliver, sometimes trembling, before their peers. Oral discourse refers more generally to all of the talk in the classroom, and we suggest that a teacher needs to know how to get students talking to each other in a purposeful, civil, and sustained way.

THE RUDIMENTS OF PUBLIC SPEAKING

While we have taught public speaking as part of classes that were labeled either Speech or English and have coached high school debate and judged speech competitions, we are not experts in public speaking. If you have ever heard us at a professional conference, you would know right away that we are not experts. For some sections of this chapter, we rely on the scholarship and counsel from Professors Bryan McCann and Ashley Mack from Louisiana State University (LSU). These experts have taught public speaking in high schools and at universities and have coached speech teams in high school and universities.

First, the teacher is typically the most dominant public speaker in the classroom. We know from the research of Smagorinsky and Fly (1994) that the teacher serves as a powerful model for students' behavior: What the teacher does as a speaker and respondent to other speakers, students tend to imitate. This means that the teacher has to model principled practices as a public speaker. Teachers need to know what elements of public speaking help the speaker to connect with an audience and promote clear communication. While it is too much to ask teachers to be unremittingly dynamic and energetic, teachers can be consistently personable, empathic, and logical. If teachers rely on presentation software or other visual media, they should use them in ways that reflect what teachers expect of students in their own presentations. If a teacher has a standard in mind for judging students as public speakers, she should not only convey that standard to the students but also measure up to the standard every day. Minimally, then, a teacher should speak at a volume to be heard, at a pace that is easy to follow, and with sufficient energy and emphasis to keep students awake.

Teachers need to understand that students come from various rhetorical and vernacular traditions. When we discuss language in detail in Chapter 6, we will review this need in greater detail. This is important to keep in mind in expressing expectations and judging students' speaking based on criteria and professional norms that derive from some traditions that privilege one part of the population over others. Any contemporary classroom in the United States is likely to include students from a variety of backgrounds and, by definition, with various ideas about what constitutes "good" public address. Perhaps for some students the standard for effective public speaking comes from witnessing a dynamic preacher at Sunday service or derives from watching stage or YouTube performers whom the students admire. While these model speakers can convey messages and emotions powerfully, their public speaking practices may not align with the precepts espoused in most public speaking textbooks. So, how does one meet students where they are and instill them with skills that will help them succeed, whether success means functioning as a student; working in a career; interacting with family, friends, and neighbors; or serving as an influential force within a community?

We suggest that a place to start is to observe speakers in action and discuss with learners what elements of the speeches "work" for the students as an audience. We cringe in watching a pervasive commercial for an auto insurance company with a lone speaker in front of the Statue of Liberty enacting the most trite features of novice speech competitors at high school events. In contrast, a class might examine a less conventional speech by Tupac Shakur (e.g., *www.youtube.com/ watch?v=3m2OUSZ5WR8*). While Shakur's speech would have been unlikely to have won him speaker awards at an academic competition (in fact, it would have gotten him suspended from school), there is no denying its persuasive power and its appeal to many students. The idea is not to endorse Shakur's style and dismiss others, but to deliberate about our assessments, leading to a constructed standard of what good public speaking sounds like and looks like.

To draw an idea from Professor Ashley Mack at LSU, teachers need to know about the concept of *methos* and encourage students to embrace their own *methos*. According to Mack (2011), *methos* is a play on Aristotelian *ethos* that emphasizes developing a delivery style that is authentic to oneself (i.e., *me*). Neither teachers nor students become good public speakers by mimicking FDR, Barack Obama, Hillary Clinton, and other noted orators, but by being the best version of themselves. Perhaps this is an important takeaway from Tupac Shakur's speech. He was the only person who could have given that speech. So, the question for teachers and for their students is this: What does the speech that only YOU can give look like? We judge that this is an essential question for all students as public speakers in one way or another to answer. Teachers need to know how to lead students to this question and provide the learners with time and means of reflection to arrive, at least tentatively, at an answer. We have known many students who seem unsure of themselves and very quirky; but when they address a group, they manage to harness the quirks in ways that make for good public speaking. There is no such thing as a born-perfect orator. Successful student speakers take what they already have and find a way to make it work for them when speaking in the classroom and in other contexts.

Lloyd Bitzer's 1968 article "The Rhetorical Situation" has influenced many teachers and scholars in the field of communication. Although his conception of speech acts seems less transformative today, he focused on the ways that rhetoric emerged from a specific demand (exigence), operated within a set of constraints (decorum, etc.), and called on an audience to act. These basic principles can still inform the teacher of public speaking. In turn, the teacher can ask students to think hard about what problem they want to address or solve, how they can do that within the constraints of the situation and the assignment, and who they are trying to motivate to act. As with writing, the audience question is critical because it prevents students from giving generic speeches that don't account for the fact that they're in a room of their peers. In some classes, it would be appropriate for students to survey their classmates and to write audience profiles, prompting their awareness of who their audience actually is. As an extension of this thinking, we would invite students to consider the situation in which it would be important for this specific audience to know what the speaker has to say.

While it is tempting to refer to famous instances of public speaking from the past, it is also important to honor students' frames of reference.

We can easily point to Dr. King's "I Have a Dream" speech and President Obama's "Audacity of Hope" address as admirable examples of public speaking; however, few students find them relevant or stirring today. Some alternatives might be Viola Davis's Emmy-acceptance speech from 2015 or President Obama's Sandy Hook press conference. Students are likely to be moved by Kevin Costner's eulogy for Whitney Houston. The reminder here is that in addition to the power of the teacher as a model public speaker, any teacher can access abundant contemporary examples of speeches that resonate with learners and serve as possibilities to emulate to some degree. Just as Gallagher (2011) makes the case for the use of "mentor texts" to serve as guides for students' own compositions, speeches available to view online are in themselves "texts" and can guide learners in their own production.

The examples above refer to famous speakers addressing an interested audience about a crucial issue at a critical time. While students' situations will have less gravity and historical moment, experience tells us that adolescents today still care passionately about issues that touch their personal lives. English teachers, as teachers of public speaking, can tap into these passions to invite students to address the issues that matter to them and to honor students' choices.

We know from our own classroom experiences as teachers and students that often students approach a public speaking task with dread. Many students see formal public speaking as stuffy and overblown. We have witnessed students whose greatest triumph was *not* fainting straightaway as they delivered a speech, and others who referred mechanically to note cards and delivered in a stiff and uninspired way. Perhaps we exacerbate the students' anxiety by emphasizing the formality of public speaking, especially by the models we choose to share with learners. In contrast, great public speakers are distinctly personable; that is, they have a strong *methos*. Several activities can help to reduce the anxiety and promote the idea of connecting in a natural way with the audience: Have students deliver their speech to a peer while sitting down, or have students walk alongside each other while delivering their speeches. These kinds of activities put learners in situations where they are delivering oratory in traditionally conversational settings.

FOCI FOR SPEAKING

Tom was a debate coach and established a debate team at two high schools. For many students, the lively exchanges supported by relevant research are compelling. Some teachers shy away from debate as regrettably agonistic, breeding competitiveness and resentment. Tom acknowledges that some competitive debate can be cutthroat, but debates can follow a civil and established order, allowing the participants to grapple with controversies about policy in a way that deepens everyone's understanding and allows competitors to remain friendly adversaries rather than mean-spirited enemies.

Much academic writing depends on argument—not in the sense of verbal dueling, but in the Toulmin (1958/2003) (Toulmin, Rieke, & Janik, 1984) sense of informal reasoning. We suggest that teachers need to know much about argument in the sense of logical reasoning, whether the model is based on Toulmin or some other authority, and set a standard for argument. If students are going to engage in debate or express arguments and be judged by a standard for reasoning, they have to move beyond an insistence that anyone's unsubstantiated opinion has as much merit as anyone else's opinion. In competitive debate, one's vehemence, passion, and volume are less likely to win points than a coherent argument in which the speaker supports topical claims with relevant data (e.g., information, expert testimonies, representative examples) and interprets the data. Daily classroom interchanges should forge the expectation that any listener might want to hear the evidence for a claim and want to know how the cited data connects with and necessarily supports the claim. Although it is appropriate for students to embrace and share their opinions, it is also reasonable for an audience to demand the logical bases for the opinions. In addition to requiring evidence and interpretation for claims during daily oral interchanges, teachers can also stage formal debates to encourage the development of argument skills and the ability to grapple with issues in a civil and rational way.

As we have prepared students for public speaking, we have structured that preparation as a process that is similar to the process of writing. Obviously, whether the speech is a narrative about the student's personal experience or an argument for a change in energy, health care, or criminal justice policy, the speaker needs to prepare and practice the remarks. For competitive debaters, it is all about the research. If you were to witness a high school debate tournament, at least in an analog age, you would likely see varsity debaters walking to competition rounds with luggage carriers used to haul their boxes of files and evidence cards, looking for all the world like lawyers arriving in court with their briefs and exhibits. So, for the English teacher as speech teacher, there is a responsibility to know how to prepare learners to research the subjects at the heart of their speeches. This research, as with a written report, requires substantial reading, note-taking, drafting, and refining. That sort of preparation allows the students to produce a text, but the process also requires practice with the delivery of remarks. As Greg Whiteley's fascinating documentary *Resolved* demonstrates, the practice should allow the speaker to communicate clearly with an audience, using the appropriate volume, emphasis, pacing, and visual aids that the situation requires. The practice should build confidence and allow the speaker to convey *intrinsic ethos*—not just looking the part, but knowing the subject, the audience, and the process of communicating well.

Just as with writing, public speaking is an ethical practice (Lucas, 2007, pp. 34–53). The cultures of schools today, with an obsession about college and career readiness, place high stakes on skills for public address. We recognize the value of good communication skills for employment, even for getting through an interview, but they are also central to civic life. People speak publicly on matters of life and death, and speeches themselves can have life-and-death consequences. There are obvious examples when a speaker is persuading a deliberative body about a policy question or when an attorney is pleading with a jury and judge about a criminal case. But there is also the central responsibility to talk as honestly and clearly as one can manage. While there can be clever and proficient propagandists, they ultimately undermine communication by obfuscating, distracting, and misrepresenting. Wander (1984) notes that a "third persona" constitutes people impacted, often harmed, by one's rhetoric. An example might be the speaker who insists that a crime of gun violence could have been prevented if all the people at a crime scene had been equipped with firearms themselves. The speaker reassures various weapon carriers that they are justified in feeling they need protection, but perhaps excites the next mass shooter into arming himself with greater firepower. Part of the knowledge and responsibility of the English teacher as a teacher of public speaking is to help students to envision everyone impacted by the issue they're discussing and to consider how this recognition should affect the way they go about writing their speeches.

KNOWING ABOUT EVERYDAY SPEECH ACTIVITIES

At the opening of this chapter, we reported that Tom once argued before a school board that the high school should drop its one-semester speech requirement in favor of immersive speech activities throughout the curriculum. In part, the argument was based on an understanding that learning in any discipline is socially situated—that students learn much from having opportunities to talk to each other. This idea of learning in a social milieu connects with Vygotsky's (1978) research about how learners learn, and aligns with Bakhtin's (1986) understanding of the dialogic nature of communication and understanding. Applebee and Langer (2013); Applebee, Langer, Nystrand, and Gamoran (2003); Juzwik, Borsheim-Black, Caughlan, and Heintz (2013); and Nystrand

(1997) demonstrate that frequent engagement in authentic discussion supports literacy learning. If, however, a high school is going to eliminate a required speech class, then students will need to have other varied and frequent speaking opportunities, both to learn the content of their subjects and to learn the procedures necessary for writing and for the study of literature. We recognize that this will not be the case if the schools are like the ones that Nystrand and his colleagues studied for his 1997 study, where, on average, students in ninth grade participated in authentic discussion for a mere 15 seconds per class meeting. If that regrettable statistic has not changed, then students are by and large spending their time listening to the teacher or doing quiet seatwork.

Tom recalls that when he was a student in John's literature class at the university, the students engaged in substantial discussions at every class meeting. As Tom remembers, the class met early in the morning and the students were often more prompt than the professor, so the discussions were not always lively. But there was interaction among the students at each meeting. Even as a naive undergraduate, Tom judged that class activities devoted to the discussion of literature were the appropriate mode of learning in an English course. When Tom began teaching, his discussions often fell flat, perhaps because the students were not reading the assigned texts, and perhaps because Tom was not asking the right questions, framing engaging problems, or otherwise preparing the learners to care and to be ready to enter into discussion. For Tom, it has become a kind of preoccupation to learn how to be better at facilitating discussions, and it has become a focus for his scholarship (McCann, 2014; McCann et al., 2015; McCann, Johannessen, et al., 2006).

From observing and interviewing teachers in many schools, Tom has concluded that while the facilitation of discussions might be to a certain extent intuitive to some practitioners, the reliance on authentic discussion as a central element in instruction requires preparation, discipline, solid decision-making in the moment, and reflection. As with most instruction, the students' willingness to participate in discussions will depend on the teachers' approach to fostering a supportive learning environment. There is much to know about making authentic discussion the primary instructional element in the English classroom.

FOSTERING A SUPPORTIVE
ENVIRONMENT FOR ORAL DISCOURSE

Years ago, the *Chicago Tribune Magazine* published a feature story about Vivian Paley, the only kindergarten teacher to win a MacArthur

Grant, the so-called "genius award." In Barbara Mahany's profile, she reports that when one student pushed another student on the way to the music room, Ms. Paley paused to address this rupture in the class's protected sense of inclusion and community the following way: " 'We can't have any happy singing,' Paley says, because the little girl 'feels terrible, and I just want to give her a moment to feel better' " (Mahany, 1995). While teachers are not likely to be drying the tears of adolescents in middle school or high school, Ms. Paley's precept holds true: "We can't have any happy singing" when any member of our class feels like an outcast or disrespected. By "happy singing" we mean here the sense of being part of a community and actually enjoying the experience of the classroom. At a minimum, teachers of English need to know how to foster a classroom environment in which adolescents have the confidence to interact with each other and recognize a sense of agency to advance their own ideas, even when those ideas run counter to the teacher's position and invite opposition from peers.

We have known teachers who have been able to foster a sense of supportive community in a variety of ways, and we don't offer any single approach as the key to making students feel comfortable enough to participate in small-group work and large-group discussions. A teacher we know well in an urban school tells students explicitly every day how much she cares about them and wants the class to have a sense of family while they are in their classroom. We know another teacher who helps students to identify specifically the kinds of interaction behavior they appreciate and the kinds they find offensive or counterproductive, thus establishing the group norms that anyone can invoke to seek improvement in conditions. Most commonly, we have observed teachers who, like Ms. Paley, monitor how students are interacting with each other and intervene quickly to say what was destructive to the common good, how it made the teacher or others feel, and how to improve behavior. Some forms of discussion and debate have their built-in rules and protocols, designed to keep matters civil and productive. Teachers need to be aware of rules for engagement with each other and help learners to be aware of the rules and the rational basis for their use.

PLANNING FOR DISCUSSION

Whether students will be communicating in small groups or discussing something as a whole class, extensive and purposeful discussions rarely occur by chance. We have observed hundreds of teachers in hundreds of classrooms in our roles as supervisors or administrators, and the teachers who have much success in involving many students in extensive discussions have planned with care for the experience. This planning includes the careful grouping of students for small-group work. The planning involves attention to what each student can contribute to the group rather than the liabilities that teachers want to suppress. As Google managers have learned in their long search for the most productive teams (Duhigg, 2016), the magic is not in matching similar or compatible types; instead, the key seems to be that the team members explicitly share their expectations, agree on a standard for working together, and monitor progress based on the adopted norms.

No group or whole-class discussion will function unless the students know exactly what they are supposed to be discussing (Luka, 1983). Part of the planning involves the framing of the problems that will engage learners. Models of teacher evaluation such as the Danielson (2007) framework or Stronge's (2007) sense of the qualities of an effective teacher place an emphasis on knowing how to ask good questions. Other authors (Francis, 2016; Walsh & Sattes, 2015) again place an emphasis on the kinds of questions we pose for learners and the questioning "techniques" teachers use to extend thinking. Nystrand (1997) distinguishes *authentic discussion* as discussion about questions that do not have prespecified answers. The questions that teachers pose to students are important: some questions signal and prompt recitation and others invite wide contributions to address an unknown. But for us, the questions we pose are part of a larger concern about introducing students to problems that they can care about, including the problems related to interpretations of texts.

In order for students to care enough about preparing for and entering into discussions, they have to have a sense that the problems they are exploring are significant to them. As we discuss in Chapters 1 and 2, the teacher's knowledge about literature allows her to frame interpretive problems in ways that students care about. For some teachers, their thinking about a particular problem that resonates with the group of students before them guides the planning for a series of discussions that are part of a shared inquiry, perhaps over weeks of instruction. We offer an example here of one teacher's planning.

Knowing the instructional context is always central. The teacher we have in mind worked with a group of ninth graders in an alternative high school. From her experience with such groups, the teacher knew that the students would be concerned about issues related to friendship and loyalty. Mindful of such interests, the teacher introduced an inquiry-based unit with a problem represented in the case of The Big-Time Lotto.

The Big-Time Lotto

It is common for groups of friends or coworkers to pool their money to invest in lottery tickets. Part of the thinking among these participants is that they will increase their odds of winning if they can buy more tickets as a group than they would have individually. For some, it is fun to share the experience of anticipating the possibility of winning and to compare dreams for using the winnings. With many groups, the weekly investment and the viewing of the lottery drawing is a ritual that bonds friendships and brings coworkers closer. But the following case asks you to think about what is most important—the winning of thousands of dollars or the other less tangible values, like *friendship*, *fidelity*, *integrity*, and *honesty*?

The Story

Five friends who worked together for the W. E. Burrough Excavation Company regularly pooled their money to purchase lottery tickets each week. They took turns each month accepting the responsibility for purchasing the tickets. Everyone pitched in five dollars each week to be able to buy a total of 25 tickets. They thought that buying the tickets in bulk would improve their odds for winning, and they agreed that they would divide the proceeds of any winnings. Last winter they won several free tickets, and in May they won and evenly divided 250 dollars. In early summer, something remarkable happened that tested their friendship.

One of the friends, Tony, did not show up for work on a Monday morning. When the construction manager called Tony's home, his wife reported that he was incapacitated with a backache. In fact, she said his back problems were chronic, causing him to seek the help of a medical specialist in another state. She said that Tony regretted that he would not be able to return to work. He was sorry about the inconvenience, but his health came first.

At first, the other friends—Allie, Chris, Pat, and Sal—thought nothing about another weekend without lottery winnings. That was typical. They were disappointed, however, that their friend would not return to work. After a time, Allie became suspicious about Tony's disappearance, so Allie contacted the State Lottery Office, where she learned that Tony had won the 28 million dollar jackpot. This meant that, after taxes, each member of the lottery-playing group would take away about 2.3 million dollars in winnings.

When Allie and the other coworkers pursued their claim with the State Lottery Office, they learned that Tony claimed that the winning

ticket was one that he had purchased separately from the group purchase, although he did not make photocopies of the separate tickets to
share the group numbers with his coworkers.

Questions for Your Consideration

The central question now is this: *Should Tony share his winnings with
the coworkers with whom he had been playing the lottery?* This central
question connects with other related questions:

- Is there a precedent or a lottery rule that could force Tony to
  share the winnings?
- What principles should apply in determining the distribution of
  the money?
- To what extent should the circumstances in each coworker's life
  influence the distribution?
- To what extent has Tony violated principles of friendship and
  honesty in keeping the winnings secret from his former coworkers?
- If Tony is forced to share the winnings, should he also be punished in some way? What principles would guide the decision to
  punish him and determine the extent of the punishment?

Directions for Discussing the Case

As with many difficult situations we may find ourselves in, it is useful to
start by imagining the thinking from the several perspectives in the case.
The class will discuss the central question in three phases:

1. *Small-group preparation:* With two or three other members of
your class, prepare an argument from the point of view of a single character. Your argument should have the following elements:

- How should the lottery winnings be distributed among the
  members of the group?
- What evidence ("facts" about past practice and current behavior) can you offer to support your conclusion?
- What rules apply to the evidence to allow you to draw your
  conclusion about the distribution of the money (e.g., past practice, State Lottery Guidelines, principles of friendship, fairness,
  decency, etc.)?
- How do other analogous (similar or related) cases help us in
  thinking about the current situation?

Be sure to take notes as you prepare so that you are ready with a coherent argument when the entire class discusses the case.

2. *The Lottery Office Forum:* Enter into a discussion with the whole class in order to listen to the arguments of others and to advance your own position. If everyone is to arrive at a deeper understanding through negotiation, it is important that everyone has a chance to speak without interruption. It is also critical that you are able to connect your contribution to the group discussion by citing the position of someone else with whom you either agree or disagree with to some extent.

3. *Be yourself:* Although you have imagined the case from an assigned point of view, you might not agree with this point of view, or you may have changed your thinking after you have had a chance to hear other thinkers. In this stage of discussion, you will abandon your assigned role and think about the case from your own point of view: How should the winnings be distributed? What should happen to Tony? To what extent is there merit to the arguments of the various characters involved in the case?

Teachers will certainly want to plan carefully for the questions that they will pose to initiate discussions, but the questions alone can be vague abstractions to learners. We judge that students become committed to investigating, discussing, and writing about a problem when it has some flesh and bones on it—that kids can see the problem affecting actual people in recognizable circumstances. The teacher's brief case narrative in part does this. Instead of students trying to think about an existential question (e.g., To what extent must a person be loyal to friends? or Is it possible to forgive someone for violating trust?), the students will grapple with the response to a character's questionable actions and end up thinking about those existential questions in the process. In the end, for the particular group of ninth graders, it becomes less important that they read this specific text or that specific text and more important that, supported by extended discussion, they can think thoroughly about a critical question and read a variety of opinions carefully and write logically and precisely about the problem.

In the planning for the discussion for the case described above, the teacher constructed a set of questions to interrogate a policy issue— linked to a set of related readings about *friendship, loyalty, forgiveness,* and *justice.* Since the related discussions served as a gateway into further inquiry supported by the reading and discussing of several texts, the teacher had to be familiar with a body of literary texts that would extend and complicate students' thinking about the problem. Discussions, then, were not isolated and occasional experiences, but part of an extended conversation that links texts and dialogue.

SCAFFOLDING DISCUSSIONS

If teachers agree with Applebee (1996) that we can envision the English language arts curriculum as extended conversation with the class-mates who are present in the current situation and with contemporary and ancient voices represented in texts, then teachers must know how to plan for linked and layered conversations. In the case of the teacher who invites students to respond to the problem of sharing lottery win-nings, the teacher first recognized that learners had some knowledge and opinions about friendship, loyalty, mercy, and revenge. Building on students' prior knowledge, the teacher used a brief narrative to introduce the problem and organized teams of students to discuss the problem from assigned points of view.

The planned sequence represents one big conversation rather than isolated intellectual events: Friday's discussion depends on Thursday's discussion, Thursday's discussion is not possible without Wednesday's discussion, and so on. In the example of the discussions about distribut-ing the lottery winnings, the small-group preparation positioned stu-dents to be able to contribute to the simulated community meeting, and the simulated meeting exposed several competing points of view, ready-ing students to construct complex arguments that drew support from many sources and accounted for challenges and exceptions. The scaf-folded discussions expanded during explorations of related literature—in this case, literature about mercy, revenge, and justice. See Appendix F (pp. 189–197) for another example of a case- and discussion-based activ-ity that prepares learners for elaborated written responses and serves to prompt complex thinking about themes that would emerge in the related literature that students study in a conceptual unit.

INCLUDING EVERYONE IN DISCUSSIONS

For 23 of the 25 years that Tom taught in high schools, he taught in schools with large populations of non-native speakers of English. For seven years, Tom taught in an alternative school where students were reentering high school after having dropped out. It would be easy to assume a futility in engaging these students—the English learner and the apparently disaffected adolescent—in substantive and extensive dis-cussions. But Tom's experience was otherwise. As Freeman, Freeman, and Mercuri (2002, 2003) and Padron, Waxman, and Rivera (2003) note, English learners, from beginners to long-term learners, benefit from extensive engagement in instructional conversations. Of course, a teacher will need to know much about the learners in order to approach oral discourse activities in a culturally responsive way. Teachers need to learn about the students' cultures and recognize the wealth of knowledge they bring to the classroom, with the emphasis on what students know rather than what they have yet to learn. The conversations would need to be scaffolded carefully to allow students to begin in their native language and then venture into conversations that, over time, expand their experience with English-language use. As with the discussions among native speakers of English, the discussants who use any language will necessarily benefit from practice with language use that immerses learners in procedures important to composition and reading.

Similarly, some teachers in the conventional school setting dismissed the learners in the alternative school as incorrigible—people to be suppressed rather than encouraged to speak up. But Tom remembers rich conversations about George's treatment of Lennie in *Of Mice and Men*, and about Sydney Carton's attempt to reclaim his life through his sacrifice in *A Tale of Two Cities*. After an absence from the alternative school one night, Tom conversed with his substitute about how the lesson plans went. The sub reported giving the students free time to play games on the computers in the classroom rather than follow the lesson plans that called for a discussion of *Of Mice and Men*. The sub explained the change by noting that in her experience, "teens don't like reading books set on ranches." I am not sure how she came to that knowledge, but, to the contrary, I found that students were most eager to read a narrative that invited them to think about friendship, alienation, prejudice, community, revenge, and justice. If students recognized the discussions as genuine and the issues as resonant, they were eager to talk, even allowing for disagreement. In surrendering some control in order to follow the directions that an open discussion took, Tom was able to facilitate meaningful explorations of rich texts and to channel students' oral exchanges into their written responses to a text.

In his 1997 study of classroom discourse, Nystrand notes that on measures of reading and writing achievement, students who frequently engage in authentic discussions outperform their peers who seldom engage in discussions. At the same time, Nystrand reports that students in "honors" classes experience discussions far more frequently than their peers in non-honors classes. There is a cruel irony here: The students who most need to benefit from a powerful instructional experience seldom have the opportunity. In addition, Schultz (2009) reports that learners can be "participants" in discussions in a variety of ways. The apparently diffident learner at the back of the room may not be the most vociferous contributor to discussions and his or her declining to participate must be respected; but the less frequent contributor benefits as well, as long as there is a lively exchange to witness, with competing ideas and a variety of perspectives to ponder.

Tom's most recent research (McCann, Kahn, & Walter, 2018) included observations in a variety of high school classrooms where students discussed a controversy about the teaching of the concept of *white privilege* in social studies classes. The schools included an urban high school, a small-town high school, and two suburban high schools. One teacher was in her second year of teaching and another was in her 29th year. In each situation, across 3 days of discussion in each location, students accounted for more than 50% of the talk in the classroom. This convinces us that students in any instructional setting can and should be included in authentic discussions. Teachers need to know how to engage all learners in oral discourse activities and not dismiss any learners as too disaffected, too introverted, too incorrigible, or too limited in English language proficiency.

PROMOTING CRITICAL THINKING

We found it curious that a major political party offered as part of their state platform to ban critical thinking and higher-order thinking from classroom instruction because higher-order thinking and critical thinking "have the purpose of challenging the student's fixed beliefs and undermining parental authority" (Whittaker, 2012). In contrast, throughout his teaching career, Tom has sought to prompt students to look at problems, including the interpretation of texts, from several points of view and to question established positions. This position is essentially dialogic—that our understandings are not static (i.e., not "fixed beliefs") and one does not really know an "answer" (i.e., an interpretation, a solution, or an explanation) without subjecting it to the scrutiny of others and being able to support a position logically in the face of opposition. In fact, the dynamic of attending to and responding to opposition moves our understandings above the recitation of prejudices and toward positions grounded in reason. We understand that thinkers need to rely on accurate information, but we have to be cautious about what we label as "facts" to be recalled and recited. As Stephen Jay Gould (1981) reminds us, "In science, 'fact' can only mean 'confirmed to such a degree that it would be perverse to withhold provisional assent'" (p. 35). Perhaps the seeming instability of a *fact* is too tenuous for some policymakers, but Gould's position recognizes the necessity for repeated analysis and evaluation, often referred to as "higher-order" thinking skills. Of course, the idea that the "fact" might change, based on new information and/or analysis, is different from "alternative facts," which are more like wishful thinking or denial of data that disputes pre-judgment.

If teachers are to be daring enough to promote critical thinking, then they have to do more than urge students to think analytically and critically about some problem. In fact, teachers need to know how to orchestrate experiences that put students in situations where they have to make critical judgments about their own positions and the positions of others. As Applebee et al. (2003), Juzwik et al. (2013), and McCann (2014) have demonstrated, the active exchanges about issues that matter to adolescents prepare them to read closely and critically and to write extensively.

In the situation described earlier, with a teacher relying on a brief narrative to introduce the problem about the sharing of lottery winnings, the teacher also introduced several perspectives for examining the problem and designed a set of forums to interrogate the issues fully. As part of the preparation, the teacher introduced students to related news stories and reports. It is certainly important that students can read for information and read critically. It is also important that students, and their teachers, experience the collision of competing ideas that challenge preconceived notions, allowing learners to entertain new possibilities and positioning them to find the substantive grounds for their own conclusions. We judge that experiencing the collision of opinions is at the core of critical thinking, which, in turn, is at the heart of any English class.

KNOWING ABOUT OTHER SPEECH ACTIVITIES

Of course, oral discourse activities can take a variety of forms and serve several purposes in an English classroom. We have described above some conventional speech activities—oral presentations, debates, role-playing, and discussions. A glance at an oral communication curriculum can reveal other possibilities, from poetry recitation to dramatic interpretations to original comedy sketches to full-blown stage productions. We invite any teacher of literature to consider the possibility of "putting the work on its feet," whether the literature is a play intended for performance or another work that can be performed in part or as a whole. Several influential authorities can inform a teacher's decisions, but we offer here a couple of relatively simple practices. The examples that require "performance" of scenes from Shakespeare come from John's repertoire of borrowed materials from many teachers of acting and theater (Booth, 2016; Miller, 2001; Spolin, 1986).

Implications for Teacher Development

It is common for teachers of English to see themselves primarily as teachers of literature, and in some instances teachers of grammar. But work with English language arts means experience with the rich, varied, and connected uses of language. English language arts teachers are teachers of reading and writing, but they are also teachers of communication skills more broadly. This means that English teachers need not only to know how to help students become confident and effective public speakers but also how to rely on the extensive discourse in the classroom to support reading, writing, and critical thinking. To this end, we invite teachers of English to plan for a variety of oral language experiences.

- How can you help students to construct for themselves a standard for effective oral communication and to discover a personal *methos* to guide oral expression?

- How can you foster a generally supportive classroom environment that allows students to speak before their peers without fear of ridicule and severe judgment?

- How can you move away from teacher-dominated discourse and encourage frequent, purposeful dialogue among peers?

- How can you help students to follow processes similar to those they use for written composition as they research and construct texts that they rely on for public speaking?

- If the frequent discussions and deliberations in the classroom require argument in the sense of logical units of thought, what model for argument and logic will serve as the standard?

- How can varied speech activities (e.g., speeches, small- and large-group discussions, poetry readings and recitations, scene performances) support other aspects of language arts, and how can you plan strategically for the integration of speaking and listening with other components of the English curriculum?

Shakespeare's plays, with scant stage directions, invite the reader or performer to do the work of imagining the actions, reactions, and movements of the characters. It does not require a seasoned stage director to help students put selected scenes on their feet. We offer two instances. The first example comes from *Romeo and Juliet,* Act I, Scene III, Lines 1–99. This scene introduces Lady Capulet, the character of the Nurse, and Juliet as we get what amounts to some backstory about the relationships among the three through the musings of the Nurse. As the scene opens, Lady Capulet bids her employee, Juliet's Nurse (or Governess), to call her daughter; once Juliet arrives, Lady Capulet dismisses the Nurse, saying that she and Juliet must "talk in secret." However, in the very next line, Lady Capulet asks her to return, with no explanation. At issue is the reason(s) for Lady Capulet's change of mind, and how we, as readers or viewers, learn to see how Shakespeare (and many dramatists) embeds motivation into the dialogue with no further explanation. Imagining players' movement(s) in three-dimensional space is thus a crucial component of learning how to read Shakespeare.

In classroom practice, the teacher asks students to follow a few steps, but the first step (1) involves the whole class taking part in exercises called by the great drama teacher Viola Spolin "Exposure" and "Mirror," involving relatively simple exercises to help students to feel more comfortable on their feet in front of their peers. Once *everyone* in class is up and moving about during these introductory exercises, the teacher asks for three volunteers to read the lines of Lady Capulet, the Nurse, and Juliet. The activity then follows in this way:

1. The three stand before the class and read lines 1–10 aloud, and then sit down.
2. Three more volunteers read the same lines before the class and ask group 1 (above) if they approve.
3. Three more volunteers repeat what group 2 did, and so on, until someone asks why Lady Capulet changed her mind and asked the Nurse to return. If no one has asked the question by the third or fourth trio, the teacher could act puzzled and do the asking.

The speculation about Lady Capulet's motivation could range far and wide, but the crucial elements in this activity are the following: (1) The scene has set in motion a puzzle, one that is not even mentioned in the dialogue but comes about through the movement of the players; (2) the students are not *told* by the teacher that there is a problem but should, by the third or fourth repetition, note (in most cases) that Lady C's change of mind seems odd or unexplained; (3) the students' speculations should be centered on information from the text, but since this scene is done so early in the play, the best that most (who have not previously read or seen the play) can say is a variation of "darned if I know." Unlike the group of political-platform writers who wanted to suppress critical thinking, we judge that it is perfectly all right for students to note a problem but also remain aware that—given the point of their reading in the text—both they and any first-time reader may *not be able* to answer this question. The idea is to raise questions that can guide and inform further reading and to sensitize young readers to detecting critical problems as they read.

The second example comes from a work about reading *Macbeth*. The reunion between Macbeth and Lady Macbeth in Act I offers the opportunity for students to get up and face each other in pairs, following along the lines of the Spolin-type exercises mentioned above. The first student is the blood-encrusted Macbeth; the second is the impatient Lady Macbeth. Students are instructed to pretend they are just like the spousal teams they have seen in their own lives but to make sure that, with permission, these two touch each other during conversations, as if this is usual practice. Touching here is neither erotic nor even so much affectionate, but merely one of the conversational habits of long-married couples. The key movement to be dramatized onstage is the transfer of these images of blood from Macbeth to Lady Macbeth, and back from Lady Macbeth to Macbeth. The teacher selects two "readers" in the audience to speak the lines as players (students) A and B will, one hopes, mime the physical movements the two characters enact so that by the end of the scene, both are (in imagination) bloodstained.

Since the performance in itself reveals much, the teacher does not need to ask the readers to emphasize anything in particular but invites them to stand up and read these lines the best that they can. A next pair then gets up and does the same, asking duo 1 if they approve and (most importantly) why or why not. By duo 3, if students do not seem to enact or recognize the blood transfer physically from one to the other in the very act of their conversations, the teacher may prompt them with appropriate questions. As with the *Romeo and Juliet* scene discussed above, students are asked to keep in mind these images of blood in case they show up again later in the play, as they clearly will (in Act V, Scene I, Lines 35–52) during Lady Macbeth's famous "Out, damned spot" speech.

It has been John's experience that later in the unit on *Macbeth*, the teacher asks the same duos as above to get up and recite Lady Macbeth's famous soliloquy—only she says it not alone, but with Macbeth himself reciting the speech in unison with her. As above, the pairs are to speak facing each other and again invent some possible ways that a married couple might share some common anxiety. Perhaps using as a point of reference a long-married couple with whom they are familiar, the duos are to recite the lines in unison although they are moving and/or behaving differently.

The activity invites some key questions: Why does Lady Macbeth move from being so aggressive to displaying intense guilt? What does one make of these two scenes for Macbeth: His being so unsure of his purpose in Act II, Scene II to his putting on and taking off his armor in Act V, Scene III, Lines 36–60, when only one short scene separates the couple's last two dramatic enactments? See also Appendix G (pp. 198–202) for a related sample learning activity that focuses on the opening scenes of *Macbeth*.

Tom can recall several occasions when he converted scenes from novels into play scripts for students to perform. These occasions involved scenes when the envisioning of the characters' movements and reactions seemed key to interpreting the work as a whole. One example, perhaps for middle school students or ninth graders, comes from *Of Mice and Men*. A particularly promising scene comes from Chapter 4, when Lennie wanders into Crooks' room in the barn. The conversation is tense at the beginning and evolves into more comfortable exchanges. Then Candy appears, and it seems for a moment that Crooks could be included in their dream of a place of their own. But George enters the scene to bring them back to the reality of exclusion and isolation. The scene evolves and the mood shifts, which readers and viewers can appreciate from viewing and hearing it.

The second example comes from Chapter 9 of *Wuthering Heights*, with Heathcliff in the shadows listening to a conversation between Nelly Dean and Cathy, and leaving the scene before Cathy finishes her remarks. While Cathy reveals to Nelly, and unknowingly to Heathcliff, that she intends to marry Edgar Linton, after Heathcliff slips away, she reveals that her marriage actually involves sacrificing her need to always be with Heathcliff in order to help him to advance in a society that seems bent on oppressing him.

In either case, with the pdf of the text readily available online, it is a simple matter of converting the narrative into a script. The first task for the performance is for the team of performers to agree on the "spine" of the work—what it is essentially about. This task in itself invites some lively conversation. While a class of readers can interpret a text in a variety of ways, the creative contributors to a coherent performance must agree on a core interpretation. This sense of the spine then asks each performer to judge how his or her actions and delivery will contribute to this shared vision. After a little rehearsal and the use of simple props, the students can perform the scene for their classmates' edification and assessment.

Mature novels supply several such scenes that can be divided across teams in a class. The performance cannot help but project an interpretation, which prompts further discussion as the audience and the performers weigh the merits of the interpretation.

These simple examples attest that there are many opportunities for oral presentations and creative performances. Some teachers invite their students to perform choral readings, vernacular rewritings of famous poems, or the slam performance of original poems. The idea here is that English teachers need to know the importance of purposeful peer interactions and dialogic discourse. There are many possibilities that require some preparation and the consistent cultivation of a supportive environment that encourages students to take the risks involved with performance or presentation before peers.

POINTS OF CONVERGENCE

We both take distinctly different approaches to discussion and to other speech activities in the classroom. Tom is likely to introduce some complex contemporary problem to stimulate dialogue, while John will rely on the problems inherent in interpreting literary texts as the springboard for discussion. Our primary responsibilities as teachers of English have not been to teach public speaking, but we see a need for English teachers to know how to foster a supportive classroom environment and to prepare learners to be able to speak in front of their peers and to listen actively and critically to other speakers. We hope teachers provide more opportunities for classroom talk besides the three or four conventional speeches that a class can grind its way through in a semester. Instead, we see frequent conversations among students as an essential element in students learning to read closely and critically and to write extensively, logically, and coherently.

Much of the literature that students read in middle school and high school can come alive when portions of it are performed, as seems obvious from so many film adaptations of works of literature that have become standards in schools. John has had broad experience in preparing students for in-class dramatic performances, yet even Tom has had occasions to transform scenes from fiction into simple scripts and to select scenes from works of Shakespeare, Lorraine Hansberry, Tennessee Williams, and August Wilson for students to perform for their peers in order to envision the action and connect it to students' general understanding and judgment about the work. Without becoming drama teachers, all English teachers can learn some fundamentals about performance that can enliven a class.

YOUR THOUGHTS

Perhaps teachers of English do not think of themselves as speech teachers. In fact, Tremmel (2001) reports that English teachers think of themselves primarily as teachers of literature. But we understand that various forms of oral discourse serve the ends of literacy learning. While learning to speak clearly and coherently and to listen carefully and critically are part of literacy learning, we judge that a rich and supportive environment for speaking, especially for interactions among peers, helps students to learn procedures that transfer to their writing and to their critical reading. At the same time, teacher preparation seldom prepares teachers to be teachers of public speaking. What do English teachers need to know if teaching various forms of oral expression is part of their responsibility?

- What place does oral expression have in the conventional English classroom?
- How can online discussions extend oral exchanges in the classroom?
- How can various kinds of oral expression prepare learners for subsequent reading and writing?
- Most classrooms are dominated by the teacher talking, in a frontal mode of teaching (Goodlad, 2004). How can a teacher change the nature of classroom discourse?
- If teachers are not trained as speech teachers or acting coaches, how can they draw from the preparation they did have in order to foster public speaking and dramatic performance?

6

The Territory of Language

What Do We Teach
When We Teach Language?

We can both recall experiences when our preservice teachers came to us after a visit to a host school where a cooperating teacher asked the novice to teach a lesson "about prepositions" or a lesson "about agreement." While we are famously sympathetic, we typically asked why someone would want to teach a lesson as abstract or as narrowly focused as 40 minutes on prepositions or even 20 minutes examining "agreement" in isolation? Would it be fair and accurate to presume that young learners know nothing or little about these language concepts as formulated by teachers starting instruction at the upper end of skill building? Indeed, in order to develop a keen sense of how the English language works, must any novice begin with knowing only "prepositions" or primarily subject/verb agreement? Shouldn't preservice teachers help learners to distinguish structure words from lexical words? Do experienced teachers really presume that a keen understanding of naming parts of sentences, like prepositions, and/or subject and verb agreement will help learners to become more facile writers and speakers, or more attentive and discerning readers?

As language and learning generalists rather than specialized grammarians ourselves, we appreciate an inherent value in an understanding about language that goes well beyond reciting or honoring someone's quirky prescriptions for language use. As with all English language arts instruction, we insist that language study reflect a purpose that learners can recognize and embrace. Thus, in this chapter, we discuss pedagogical content knowledge about language in three contexts. First, we see value in the study of language as a discipline in itself and note that the language that a person speaks identifies the speaker in many ways, and listeners draw assumptions about the speaker. As Devereaux (2015) observes, the connection between language and identity is important, and false assumptions about "proper" language use can influence false assumptions about identities and the value that people attach to those identities. Next, we consider the importance of knowledge about language as an element in writing instruction and development. It appears commonsensical to us that written language is rather different from the spoken word in many ways, and so novice language learners must acquire working knowledge of both. Third, we also demonstrate that knowledge about language assists the teacher and the learner in the close reading of texts, especially literary texts. And finally, we discuss some of the relationships between these three values and student language habits in reading, writing, and speaking.

Long ago, when John and Tom were junior high students, it was common for the English language arts curriculum to be almost entirely about grammar—naming the parts of speech and diagramming sentences. This instructional model had become such a commonplace that, during World War II, poet Henry Reed (1942) parodied that type of piecemeal education by comparing the "naming of parts" to learning how to fieldstrip a rifle during military training. While, thankfully, the emphases have shifted and broadened much since before World War II and later, in the 1960s and 1970s, English language arts teachers still need to know a good deal about language—because in many ways language defines our identity and can stratify a population. While evaluating students' oral expression and written work, we should also examine our presumptions and prejudices about language and proceed cautiously in inviting others to examine how language works and to command language as needed. As Devereaux (2015) says, we often "unconsciously judge a person's abilities, intellect, and potential based on what language variety she or he speaks. These unconscious beliefs may influence our work together in the classroom" (p. 24). And, whether it is in written discourse or in classroom speaking, we urge teachers to tread lightly in admonishing others based on the assumptions of what Devereaux will label as a "correctionist model" (p. 4).

In this chapter, we acknowledge how limited many English teachers are in their knowledge about the language that they teach. Given these limitations, we insist that prescriptions and correctives about the English language are not only presumptuous, but also fail to advance instructional goals to help learners to be eloquent speakers, facile writers, and careful and insightful readers.

WHY MUST I *WATCH* MY GRAMMAR?

It is fairly common for an English teacher to meet someone new and be greeted with "Uh, oh! I'd better watch my grammar!" Not only does the speaker's attitude toward verbal propriety seem to attach itself to English teachers, but it reflects the belief that there are transcendental categories of proper English. So, given their pedagogical devotion, English teachers have, some think, become the walking repositories of "good English" and the guardians on the lookout for offenders of propriety. It takes a bit of conversation to convince someone that one's spoken and written language should be categorized by social reflectors of one's community rather than as possessing one person's *imprimatur.* We argue that, whatever speech or writing that one's community considers valuable and representative of "one of us" is then "proper English," even though the contents of that label "proper" remain in constant motion and may be temporarily limited to that specific audience.

The shifts and mutability of language are evident in everyday experience. Note the bewildered look on the face of any mid-twenties auditor who listens to her younger teenage sibling speak contemporary middle school or high school slang, current to the student but baffling to the older listener a mere handful of years after her own graduation. Consider the poor English or anthropology major who enrolls in law school, takes a writing class, and becomes shocked that most of his hitherto vaunted writing skills need substantial reworking in this new domain merely to pass the course. The same is true of a law student's speech patterns, the ones he was hitherto told to avoid. Now he must start learning, as one of Hamlet's speeches reflected, the technical jargon of the lawyer: "his quiddities, his quillities, his cases, his tenures, and his tricks" (Act V, Scene I, Lines 98–100). Joe Williams (1999) tells us that apprentices in any such new endeavor experience what is called "cognitive overload . . . condition that predictably degrades their powers of written expression" (p. 25).

A teacher or graduate student might note her new colleagues' speech patterns when beginning a job, or enrolling in a new academic program, and adopt them quickly, but possibly unself-consciously, in order to fit in to the informal conversations and the more structured deliberations. Initiation into the discourse patterns of a community is the stuff of continued human social interaction, and the mastery of its context-specific linguistic "rules"—the differences between "prestige" dialects and the actual linguistic equality among them—is what every English teacher needs to learn and then teach students in classroom situations. Labeling such differences also speaks to the importance of being able to communicate with parents, and is somewhat different from having sufficient knowledge of language to be able to know what to teach students. Therefore, not only must the teacher know such "rules," but must then employ them in instructing students and sometimes in explaining instruction to students' parents. John Hattie (2012) argues wisely that it was "informing the parents about the language of schooling that made a big difference" in getting those parents involved as they "learned how to help their children to attend and engage in learning," by themselves "learning to speak with teachers and school personnel" (p. 165). In other words, the "propriety" and impact of the language depends on the context for the communication.

LANGUAGE, GRAMMAR, AND ENGLISH LANGUAGE ARTS INSTRUCTION

The first problem to avoid is confusing the mastery of verbal social rules spoken in one's favorite organization or affinity group with "proper English," and thinking of it as some sort of transcendent category. Most linguists today avoid speaking of "good English" and talk more of contextualized "appropriate English" as the speaker or writer wants to join his or her discipline or business or social group. It was once assumed that joining the educated elite required countless hours of instruction with the by-now widely discredited practice of drilling to learn all the rules of "school grammar." Whether one called the subject *prescriptive grammar* (based often in the public schools on Warriner's famous [or notorious] gray book), or *school grammar*, or just plain *grammar*, many English scholars and writers now think the workbook exercises that tortured English-speaking teenagers for the whole of the 20th century were "a waste of time" (Atwell, 2016). There are still those teachers who, as the linguist Rei Noguchi (1991) pointed out many years ago, form a "cadre of pro-grammar instructors who place so much emphasis on the mechanical errors that they 'red-ink' student writing to a fatal hemorrhage and thereby destroy student interest in writing and writing improvement" (p. 13). At the other end of the continuum are the "growing number of equally staunch anti-grammar teachers who view mechanical errors as unimportant low-level 'surface' features which detract little from writing quality and which students can easily edit out during the writing process" (p. 13). One should note that this latter group advocated "editing out" problems well before computer spell-check and grammar-check programs came with almost all software writing features. The key phrase is, of course, "easily edit out," assuming that most novice writing students will do just that at 3:00 A.M. for a paper due in class at 8:00 A.M. For those who do, great. Those who do not, or who rely *only* on spell-check, could disappoint their anti-grammar instructors, not to mention their future employers a decade later.

Joe Williams (1999), the famous teacher of stylistics, suggests that both camps need to reconsider their positions:

> You may write well, yet can't distinguish a subject from a verb, or you may understand everything from retained objects to the subjunctive pluperfect progressive, and still write badly. From this apparent contradiction many have concluded that we don't have to understand principles of grammar to write well. Writing well, they believe, has to do with being sincere, or writing how they speak, or finding their authentic voices, or just being born with the knack. Others devoutly believe that they learned to write well only because they studied Latin and diagrammed sentences beyond number. The truth will disconcert those of both persuasions. Nostalgic anecdotes aside, the best evidence suggests that students who spend a lot of time studying grammar improve their writing not one bit. In fact, they seem to get worse. On the other hand, there is good evidence that mature writers can change the way they write once they grasp a principled way of thinking about language, but one that is rather different from the kind of grammar some of us may dimly remember mastering or being mastered by (pp. 14–15)

We agree with Williams, and also with Noguchi (1991), who consider both camps as "misguided and self-defeating" (p. 14), even though "formal grammar instruction, as commonly conceived and practiced, has failed to produce significant writing improvement" (p. 15). Noguchi firmly believes, therefore, that the study of "grammar should be made into a more efficient and useful resource for writing improvement" (p. 32). Aye, there's the rub. Give up the "waste of time" filling out of worksheets, and then what? Do we just skip language instruction altogether and remain content when some writing is so riddled with problems as to be indecipherable? As Mary J. Schleppegrell (2007) insists, more research "is needed that investigates the processes by which preservice teachers come to understand and take up functional ways of talking about language and how these new understandings affect their classroom practice and students' writing development" (p. 127).

Too many in the anti-grammar camp blithely dismiss language study (including grammar), like the literary scholar and critic Stanley

Fish (2011), who tells us that he is always "on the lookout for sentences that take your breath away, for sentences that make you say: 'Isn't that something?' or 'What a sentence!'" (p. 3). He is, however, quick to remind us that one "can know what the eight parts of speech are, and even be able to apply the labels correctly, and still not understand anything about the way a sentence works" (p. 19). And, of course, his implication is that, without knowing how a sentence works, a writer can't readily master how to string a series of sentences into a coherent collection of them, much less to use an understanding of sentence variation to learn how or why to accomplish this. Our response to Fish's truism concerning labeling is, "of course, but that is beside the point." Most linguists, like the influential Gulsat Aygen (2014), remind us that "prescriptive and descriptive linguistics should not be perceived as necessarily contradictory tools" (p. 5); rather, both are not only necessary but are, as we write, being practiced by millions daily. Many English-language practitioners now take part in informal language learning, including "on-line games, internet forums, and blogging, and disciplinary interactions, especially in the sciences and in education, as well as in formal class instruction" (G. Aygen, personal communication, 2016). English has, for better or worse, "become the international language of scholarship, and it's only quite recently that we have seen modest development from English-primary scientific exchanges to include the language of the scientist(s)" (G. Aygen, personal communication, 2016).

LANGUAGE DIALECTS AND PRESUMED STANDARDS

While we understand Stanley Fish's claim, the English teacher must be aware that in this 21st century in almost all the public schools and even in most of the private schools, many students are non-native speakers of English, clustering in greater or lesser numbers. What must we learn about the structures and intricacies of English to be able to use a "grammatical vocabulary" to help those students who have not had the easy access to English from their families and friends that native speakers have had? In addition, English teachers must also be able to instruct supportively the English speakers whose dialect variants are thought of in some communities as nonstandard African American vernacular, or, worse, substandard. We'll get to an example of the kinds of problems associated with foreign-language and variant-vernacular speakers and writers later in this chapter, but for now, our discussion will suggest a few ideas that center on what every English teacher should know about language acquisition generally and English-language acquisition specifically.

We will begin by listing some observations concerning language study that might help every teacher adjust his or her attitude toward English-language learners, whether native speakers born in the tongue, one might say, or those whose first language is not English but who wish to learn it well so that the novice English speakers converse fluently and gracefully. The linguist Gulsat Aygen (2016) reminds us that "all varieties of a given language are equal in terms of their linguistic capacity and power. A given dialect should not sound, to its listeners, like a merely corrupt (and corrupting) version of 'proper English,' but, 'in terms of linguistic capacity and power,' equal to that of its 'proper' speakers" (G. Aygen, personal communication, 2016).

What is different is the *community* toward which the speaker intends her articulations. This "perceived hierarchy" by laypeople is a misunderstood product of "sociolinguistic bias," and so a dialect speaker's language is just as "correct" in that speaker's community as a variety of English (or what is sometimes called Broadcast Standard English [BSE]) is in other communities. To teach or not to teach BSE (or what to teach in its place?) remains a hot topic in a multicultural, multidialectal United States, with opinions ranging from schools insisting on English-only for all classes to the opinions of one recent teacher-educator who seriously argued that, metaphorically speaking, teaching BSE in minority communities was somehow comparable to watching a young African American student swallowing toilet paper (Pindyck, 2015). Unlike her peers in "a college essay writing class," this young woman "refuses to eat the institution's seemingly clean language and instead devours a material" not meant for that purpose (p. 74). Paralleling BSE with "whiteness," both as a skin color and a code-word for political-social power, Pindyck argues that the "social injustice that hides behind the seemingly innocuous reproduction of what is commonly called 'Standard English' emerges as a double-edged pencil: the simultaneous force-feeding of institutionalized language and the unequal, racially skewed distribution of discipline to student mouths" (p. 74). In certain ways, her opinion is as extreme as those far to the right of her politically, and the essay is labeled as one in a series of "Provocateur Pieces." Her solution? Pindyck advocates following V. Young's arguments against "code-switching" and substituting instead "code-meshing . . . the blending and concurrent use of American-English dialects in formal discursive products" (Young quoted in Pindyck, p. 75). Unfortunately, Pindyck offers nothing to suggest how to abolish the social class differences out of which the need for code-switching and/or code-meshing arises in the first place. One might notice, by the way, that Pindyck's own prose in this essay is quite familiar itself as academic BSE. Furthermore, one should also notice that African American broadcast journalists on MSNBC, CNN, ABC, CBS,

FOX, and the like all speak to their national audiences in BSE, whatever their dialects used at home or to a convention of specific social groups.

There is, however, another side of this debate, a debate likely more connected to political power struggles and less to linguistic science. While an oppressed minority can claim that, in their opinions, their dialect can readily be adapted into the majority language sound system, another group—equally justified in their own opinions—can also demand that the adjustments should be made by the minority. After all, goes this argument, we (the dominant speakers in a given society) already know how to talk to one another. If you (minority folks) want to join in, we would welcome you but you must speak to us so *we* can understand *you*, and not the other way around.

An example of this type of thinking may be seen in political action at the state and local level in recent years. Linguist Jake Grovum (2014) reports that

> to date (2014), *31 states* and many counties and localities have adopted English [only] as their official languages. Oklahoma became the most recent state to do so in 2010, and many cities or counties have as well, such as Carroll County, Maryland in 2013. Just this year, five states—Michigan, New Jersey, Pennsylvania, West Virginia and Wisconsin—saw pushes to enact official-English laws, although none passed. . . . Despite the country's changing demographics, official-English laws have proven popular and lasting, not just in so-called "red" states, but also in the more liberal "blue" ones. Democratic-dominated Illinois, for example, adopted an official-English law in the 1960s.

One may well ask, "Other than for political grandstanding, why would so many states pass laws that are, essentially, unenforceable, even in the schools?" Many think the issues are related to population stratification, immigration, and fears of social changes by economically insecure individuals. Others suggest that these English-only laws reflect regional political power struggles that harken all the way back to before the founding of the Republic (Woodard, 2011). Those concerns are common when BSE speakers encounter people speaking a different language altogether (e.g., Spanish), and often merely speaking a different dialect. Although many states have passed English-only requirements, what is interesting is how much has gotten done absent official policy changes at the state or local level. In its place, Grovum (2014) tells us, has been "'community action,' where demand generates or causes community organizations, markets, to adjust, and sometimes law and policy tends to catch up to that." But those who demand accommodation amid an increasingly diverse state or community could spur a backlash. Grovum

(2014) reports that Amy H. Liu, Anand Sokhey, and two political science colleagues analyzed state language laws, saying that interest in such measures spikes when immigration increases or the immigration issue rises to the top of the national agenda. "I don't think it's a coincidence that these things are packaged," observes Anand Sokhey, a professor at the University of Colorado, Boulder, referring to a focus on immigration and official-English laws. Liu, Sokhey, Kennedy, and Miller (2014) warn that we are likely to see more of these conflicts playing out in the future. Such battles can be typical amid dense populations where people of different values and expectations rub shoulders with one another daily. Liu et al. (2014) go on to say:

> In the US, despite the "melting pot" rhetoric, proficiency in the English language is a "highly resonant symbol of American nationality" for most citizens. Group unity—an important component of national identity—depends on the relationships between members of the in-group. At some level, there is a "desire to keep 'strangers' out" due to the perceived potential for fracturing such individuals could pose to a broader concept of a unified national identity. However, when the immigrant population is sizable, governments are forced to recognize other languages in the public sphere. When this is the case, these policies can generate strong emotional responses, and calls for English-official legislation can garner mass appeal.

LINGUISTIC DIFFERENCES, SOUND REPRODUCTION, AND SOCIAL DIVISIONS

As every English teacher whose instruction encounters multiethnic, multilanguage speakers, the ongoing human considerations of "one of us" versus "the other" may turn on very small sound changes even though most listeners might be hard-pressed to identify exactly what it is that sounds "different." For example, the vowel changes among English speakers in major cities are, according to William Labov (2007), more pronounced now than 100 years ago. At the same time, English speakers of what is often called African American Vernacular English (AAVE), even those living on either coast, are sounding more alike (pp. 344–387). Nonetheless, the English speaker in Boston whose *R*'s in words like *Cuba* and *tuna* sound to a Midwesterner like *Cuber* and *tuner* is still quite comprehensible to someone who grew up in Chicago or Los Angeles and speaks of *car* as *carr*. The problem is, therefore, not so much linguistic comprehensibility—although noisy classrooms make comprehension difficult (Clopper & Brandlow, 2008)—but more the cultural and social attitudes of the one who hears the sounds and, often with a provincial attitude, affixes a value judgment to that speaker (Hogan, 2011, p. 166).

Hence, we agree that English teachers should know distinctions among dialects and language registers and know also the limitations to assumptions about "standard" English. Equipped with such knowledge, English teachers can then empower each student's own language use, whether standard or nonstandard, while, at the same time helping the student's social, economic, and cultural flexibility by giving him or her help in understanding and using well the dialect associated with the standard business and academic worlds in which each might seek education and employment—that is, helping the student's proficiency with code-switching as well as code-meshing. As Devereaux (2015) suggests, English teachers must help students comprehend the shifting language registers in given social settings outside of his or her own local familiarity, while avoiding the denigration of the language features each student arrives with at school, since, for most students (and many teachers), most of what they hear is just "different," and not very specific.

According to Clopper and Pisoni (2004), "results showed that listeners are able to reliably categorize talkers using three broad dialect clusters (New England, South, North/West), but that they have more difficulty categorizing talkers into six smaller regions" (p. 111). It is hardly uncommon for teachers and students to perceive minor differences in pronunciation without knowing precisely what those differences are, phonologically or morphemically, and too often lumping them into broad categories merely labeling utterances as "different." Overall, if one includes those countries and cultures whose citizens are not native speakers of one variety or another of an English dialect, there are over one billion speakers of English! Hence, some authorities recognize BSE as a widely employed variation, "defined by experts to overcome potential miscommunication across all the varieties of spoken English" (Aygen, 2014, p. 3). In other words, this standard is a kind of compromise toward mutual intelligibility among users, rather than a standard derived from class-based inherent rules of propriety.

In that light, one can see that many AAVE advocates of code-meshing argue thus because they believe that BSE is just a different name for linguistic colonization along racial lines. John suggests another way of considering the problem: Which codes get meshed with which? In a world of one billion speakers of English, wouldn't almost any group of non-U.S. English speakers, say millions of English speakers from India, also complain about their dialect being subsumed and their cultural values remaining "colonized" if their dialects were "meshed" with what could also be termed a limited American variety of English?

Although BSE is a widely recognized variation of English in business, academe, and government, we are also aware and advocate that knowledgeable teachers should demonstrate to students that idiolects and dialects enrich literature, film, and all of the language arts. Furthermore, proponents of "code-meshing" need not worry about a firewall between BSE and, for example, AAVE, since such meshing, to one degree or another, is and generally has been a significant feature of English for at least the last several centuries. Unlike the conservative French Academy for Francophone speakers, there is no similar political body in the English-speaking world prescribing the "rules" of appropriate usage. Rather, like fusion foods and dress fashions, linguistic change in English is both continuous and socially spontaneous, and "dialects are not static but dynamic" (Craig, 2015, p. 431).

Since the advent of the Internet, most science, philosophy, economics, and many elements of culture have been conducted in English or readily translated into BSE. Although the content of any intellectual field may be communicated in any of the varieties of any language, English teachers can model for students how to employ the standard model of the languages found in much academic and professional discourse. While members of the scientific communities commonly make use of mathematics, a "universal language," to communicate with one another, they also employ a "standard" version of the major languages of science (English, Russian, German, Japanese, etc.), but primarily English, to avoid ambiguity, establish clarity, and ensure communication across all dialects and idiolects of that specific language (Huttner-Kores, 2015). There are dangers, however, to monolinguistic adaptation in the sciences for non-native speakers, such that English teachers should exhibit some sensitivity to their students' difficulties.

Examples of some of these student problems may be seen in college and high school study of the sciences. The worldwide adaptation of English as the language of science poses some unique problems for non-native speakers in American schools and universities. As teachers insist on student adaptation of English in an American classroom, some students see this demand as an emotion-laden rejection of their own previous identity and an erosion of that very fabric. As Adam Huttner-Kores (2015) observes, the domination of the English language in every area of academic life, even in the sciences, can be troubling:

> As a consequence, the scientific vocabularies of many languages have failed to keep pace with new developments and discoveries. In many languages, the words "quark" and "chromosome," for example, are simply transliterated from English. In a 2007 paper, the University of Melbourne linguist Joe Lo Bianco described the phenomenon of 'domain collapse,' or 'the progressive deterioration

of competence in [a language] in high-level discourses.' In other words, as a language stops adapting to changes in a given field, it can eventually cease to be an effective means of communication in certain contexts altogether.

Hence, every English teacher should know that certain words and concepts used in their classes may be generally unknown in the student's native language. The student is faced with learning not only words and phrases in English, but the very scientific concepts to which such language is attached. Even bright and well-read students who are, however, new to English may not only be struggling with language and dialect issues but also with elements in the world that are unfamiliar even to better-educated adults in that language.

For most English teachers, common problems faced in language teaching will be dialects, pronunciation, and ordinary communication. In general, English instructors must know and be able to explain the differences between prescriptive and descriptive linguistics, not as contradictory approaches to language study but as complementary. While teaching prepositions in the abstract may not be terribly important in the eyes of a Stanley Fish, the native speaker of Spanish who wishes to learn English, must, for example, learn distinctions in English between *in* and *on*. These little two-letter, one-syllable sounds may not seem initially very important, but to the Spanish-speaking English learner, the differences pose what are called "interference problems." If the novice English learner whose native language is Spanish were to tell the native speaker of English that the former intends to "get *on* the car and head *in* the road," he could be causing some confusion as well as some surprising laughter. Furthermore, although *in* is a word usually connected to solid examples of containment, one could also exhort the Spanish speaker not to be "in despair," about learning all of the irregularities in everyday English speech and writing.

We both think that one can teach a conception of conventional academic English, encouraging its use in compositions, but only if we have made clear the facts about the social qualities of language use by conveying in many ways to our English students that we hold no prejudice against their idiolect or dialect. Learners substituting BSE for their own intuitively learned language might see the switching as a tool necessary to navigate both in their own familiar world and also in the wider universe of commerce and academe. Jeff Bezos, the founder of Amazon, demands that his executives write lengthy memos for presentation during senior-level management meetings. Bezos claims, "Full sentences are harder to write [than brief memos]. They have verbs. The paragraphs have topic sentences. There is no way to write a six-page, narratively structured memo and not have clear thinking" (quoted in Zakaria, 2015, p. 74). We suggest that if English teachers are knowledgeable about language, they can help learners to be aware of a power dialect and how its features support the speaker in attaining power in some contexts.

There is some political debate about the relationships among BSE and the testing of speakers who use a substantial number of AAVE features. Craig (2015) reports, for example, that among AAVE speakers, "bidialectalism relates to higher reading achievement scores" and, among adults, "better wages" (p. 432). Conversely, the "more dense the AAVE feature production the lower the standardized reading scores" (p. 439). However, Craig suggests that "the critical variable for dialect speakers learning to read [is] the extent to which a student learns that she or he must style shift in literacy in tasks with expectations" for BSE (p. 439). So, the first step for the teacher is "dialect recognition," prior to any attempts at "correcting" student speech or writing and having students use the "production of standard alternatives to dialectal forms" (p. 441). Then, such familiar teaching techniques as "vocabulary building, sentence construction, and storybook reading" help students with contrastive analysis as they "translate highly frequent features" from AAVE to BSE as the teacher recognizes the "malleability of dialect patterns" and employs these teaching activities while avoiding negative interactions with his or her students (pp. 441–442). We suggest that teachers reinforce the sense that each dialect may be appropriate in a given setting and, even there, may vary for different purposes.

LANGUAGE STUDY AND THE TEACHING OF WRITING

John reminds the reader that Tom has written extensively on teaching writing instruction (cf. Smagorinsky, Johannessen, Kahn, & McCann, 2010) and so agrees with him completely that a speaker's or writer's confidence in his or her language use promotes proficiency. Like acquiring any skill, one doesn't get to a verbal Carnegie Hall unless one practices, practices, practices. By practice, John does not mean using worksheets filled with school-grammar exercises, but *authentic* use of language. Through the many exchanges and ideas mentioned in earlier chapters, the students may then practice sharing and sometimes arguing with one another, freely expressing ideas, opinions, and creative interactions where what they say and how they say it may both be occasions for language instruction. Nonetheless, as mentioned above, we also advocate some basic work in grammar instruction for all students, those who have grown up using English since infancy and those learning it later in life. But we ask the teacher to take care to learn deeply about how language works, well outside of a prescriptive schoolroom grammar, and to

Implications for Teacher Development

Although a stereotype might persist, English teachers today typically do not spend their days drilling students in grammar and usage and demanding the diagramming and parsing of sentences. Nevertheless, we suggest that teachers of English language arts still need to know much about language. Since language use is at the heart of English language arts, teachers need to know much about how language works. This knowledge can support principled efforts to teach writing, literature study, and oral communication. To this end, we urge teachers to be knowledgeable about the following elements in language study:

- Contrast the differences between *prescriptive* and *descriptive* grammars.

- Consult a reliable *descriptive* grammar and set instructional goals around key concepts that you discover.

- Become familiar with the body of research about the limited impact that formal grammar instruction has on improving the quality of students' writing.

- Study the complex grammar that distinguishes various dialects and the "rules" of production that guide their use.

- Recognize how variants in language use define identity and note how promoting some dialects as "standard" or "proper" but diminishing others as nonstandard often can reduce learners' pride in their own identity.

- Note how the assumptions you might make about the relative prestige of various dialects and the language you use in front of students might suggest to them that you are a representative of an oppressive class.

- Identify, on some logical basis, high-priority grammar and usage concepts— that is, the limited number of concepts that you judge crucial to writing and to reading complex texts closely.

keep in mind, as Smith and Wilhelm (2007), Williams (1999), and Williams and Columb (2010) suggest, when "rules" are actually rules—that is, practices that advance clarity and cohesion. If the teacher of English is to teach students about grammar and usage, she should have in mind a limited number of the high-priority concepts to teach and know why they deserve to be considered high priority.

Thus, mastering any language still requires some attention to that language's rule-making and auditory expectations. Noam Chomsky is famous for, among other work, posing questions about the differences between what he calls well-formed and ill-formed English sentences. For example: Native speakers of English intuitively distinguish the following sentence 1 as well-formed and sentence 2 as ill-formed: (1) Tom walked to school in a hurry; (2) Tom in hurry to walked a school. Some basic knowledge of the differences between the two sentences, including

understanding of English subjects, adverbs, infinitive verbal constructions, and word order—using whatever linguistic descriptors the student
can comprehend—will help the young English speaker to understand
both how to generate such language and how to identify its major components in his or her own prose.

Every teacher should be aware, however, of the differences between
well-formed sentences in AAVE and well-formed sentences in BSE,
although both types are "well-formed" inside their own dialect choices.
Smitherman describes, for example, the usage in AAVE that she calls a
"double subject" (1985, p. 561). In a sentence like "The boy who left, he
my friend," the doubling of the subject "boy" and pronoun "he" is not a
"double subject as such, [but rather] the repetition of the subject in some
other form is used in Black English (sic) for emphasis," a feature that is
"not a mandatory one, so you may hear it sometimes, other times not at
all. . . . The repetition of subject is simply another" option, as multiple
options are also true of "White English speakers" (p. 561).

An interesting example of determining whether (or not) an English sentence is "grammatical," that is, it does "work in a rule-governed
way," systematically, may be seen in the teaching suggestions of Rei
Noguchi (1991). John is a fan of Noguchi, who offers English teachers a relatively simple method for helping native speakers unfamiliar
with beginning grammatical terminology and their uses to label and
understand basic "parts of speech" by employing an intuitively derived
pattern-recognition system. Rather than memorizing uncontextualized
technical labels, Noguchi proposes that students be taught to operation-
alize language test patterns. Most obviously, Noguchi suggests when
teaching the "grammar" of English sentences to a native speaker, the
teacher is to begin by noting that, in English, a personal pronoun "is a
word that can take the place of a noun, noun phrase, or something that
functions as either" (p. 45). This "fact is important since it means teachers can use pronoun substitution as an operational test for nouns and
sentence subjects (and *vice versa*)." If a personal pronoun can do this—
"appropriately substitute for a word or group of words"—that word (or
group) is "functioning as a noun, regardless of its form" (p. 45). In this
way, the teacher then relies on the average middle school or high school
English learners' implicit and intuitive knowledge of English to help
define the subject of a given sentence. Noguchi claims that locating the
subject of a sentence "is a valuable skill since several kinds of common
stylistic problems require identification of subjects," such as when trying
to understand problems "in subject-verb agreement, unnecessary shifts
in person, overuse of non-agent subjects" and so on (p. 46).

But as a composition teacher, Tom wonders why it is important to
be able to name the parts of a sentence. In at least one instance it may

come in handy. Tom encourages students to write as often as possible in active voice, with the intention to promote clarity and concision. Passive constructions inevitably complicate writing unnecessarily; their ability to obfuscate make them popular tools of propagandists. In practice, in modeling the use of active voice, Tom suggests that the subject of the sentence should be the agent doing the action of the verb. This suggests that the verb will convey an action and the subject will proceed the verb in the word order. This relatively simple language may still seem too technical for students, especially if a description is not accompanied by the actual modeling of the construction of a sentence in active voice. The models can offer a contrast. Consider these three sentences:

1. The determination was made by the class that the teacher would treat everyone to pizza (passive construction with the agent of the action *made* buried as an object of a preposition).
2. It was determined that the teacher would treat everyone to pizza (passive construction with the "real" agent of the action *determined* unknown).
3. The teacher determined to treat everyone to pizza (active voice).

Typically, students recognize the relative merits of the active construction in making the sentence more concise and clear, in the sense that it is less puzzling who is doing what for whom.

John would argue further for incorporating at least some of Noguchi's ideas into students' understanding of how well-formed English sentences are made. Noguchi (1991) argues that all native speakers of English carry "intuitive linguistic knowledge" in their heads, and these "can be used to define, for example, the notion of the subject of a sentence" (p. 46). Noguchi suggests looking at declarative sentences and their corresponding tag and yes-no questions.

For example, see the comparisons among the subjects of the sentences below. What appears to be major surface-feature differences as "subjects of the sentences" are, in fact, structurally the same.

1. Jim and Sue can dance the tango.
2. Jim and Sue can dance the tango, can't they?
3. Can Jim and Sue dance the tango?

Readers note quickly that the word following the verbal contraction *can't*, in sentence 2 refers to a compound subject, and sentence 3 has merely inverted the compound subject, Jim and Sue, to follow the verb *can*. "Hence forming the corresponding tag and yes-no questions from the original declarative sentences offers a way of identifying sentences

operationally," rather than delivering the sense of "subject identification" factually by lecture and requiring students to accept those materials
as a given. Hence, a priori defining "a noun as a person, place, or thing"
is a very different mental activity than "doing" the Noguchi operation
above and noticing that the agents of all three sentences remain Jim and
Sue, regardless of how the surface of the language is transformed.

Teachers often talk about an obligation to teach students about parts
of speech and other labels for grammar and usage in order to share with
students a common vocabulary for talking about stylistic issues. But we
suggest what while a teacher of English needs to know much about the
English language, in making her instructional plans, she should focus on
those concepts that actually have an impact on students' writing. Knowing the distinction between active and passive voice is one. Placing an
adjective phrase or clause next to the nominal that it modifies is another.
Promoting cohesion through the use of pronoun references, synonyms,
and transitional phrases is another. But even these few concepts will be
of little use to the student as an emerging writer if the teacher does not
model the intellectual moves and the stylistic choices.

Warriner's popular *English Grammar and Composition*, first published in 1946 and still in use, has reduced the study of language or
"grammar" to the recall of prescriptive rules. By contrast, Aygen (2014)
offers revealing examples and common sense explanations and usage
tips that promote clarity of expression. By using a text as reliable as
Aygen's *English Grammar* as a resource, and by continued writing and
speaking with students from day to day, the English language teacher
may combine qualities of both approaches. Similarly, Constance Weaver
(1996, 1998) and Smith and Wilhelm (2007) dispel common misconceptions about the idea of "correctness," and offer ways that teachers can
teach concepts about grammar and usage in the context of writing and
reading. In brief, learning any language requires the learner of English
to employ a combination of intuitive manipulation of linguistic elements
and the time-honored memorization of some specific instances where
almost everyone trips up in the heat of writing and/or speaking in a
hurry.

We have focused above on a few concepts that we judge to be essential for an English teacher who intends to help students refine their writing skills and read complex texts closely. When Tom studied grammar
in high school, Warriner was the authority of the day, and instruction
involved memorizing dozens of rules and postulates and completing
"exercises" to practice choosing the correct word or editing to add missing elements. Of course, as we have already noted—along with scholars
such as Noam Chomsky, Rei Noguchi, and many others—most middle school and high school students who are native speakers of English
come to school with intuitive knowledge about well-formed sentences,

an inherent knowledge about how to generate English sentences. There is no need, then, to treat students as empty vessels who need to be filled from the bottom with hundreds of rules and variations. Instead, we judge, and invite the reader to judge, the value of what can be called high-priority concepts, like Noguchi's use of intuitive subject-verb characteristics of well-formed English sentences. These would be the critical grammar and usage concepts that most students need to know in order to write clearly and read closely. This effort to identify high-priority concepts goes beyond noting one's pet peeves (e.g., "I hate it when someone begins a sentence with *irregardless.*") and requires a teacher to be able to say what "rules" of grammar and usage are actually "rules" and to identify the concepts that will ultimately support clear and flexible expression.

KNOWING LANGUAGE IN SERVICE
OF THE STUDY OF LITERATURE

In this section, we show how knowledge about language allows a teacher to model the construction of meaning from a complex text. As Tremmel (2001) points out, most teachers of English see themselves as teachers of literature, so they have an obligation to know how to show how language works in the texts they ask students to read. The possibilities for working with the variety of texts in schools are too numerous to represent here. John focuses on one example from *To Kill a Mockingbird*, a text that many middle school and high school students are still required to read. Here is an explanation from a literary text illustrating the attitudes of even educated people during the early 1960s, attitudes that students today should see as contrastive to language study in the 21st century. Devereaux (2015) says that the "three important challenges to the right/wrong paradigm of language" include assuming that "not all secondary students come to school speaking and writing in 'standard' English," but nonetheless, "students and teachers come to the classroom with clear opinions about language variations." Unfortunately, many of these "students may not understand or appreciate the dialectically diverse texts we bring to the classroom" (p. 2).

John has used in his classrooms an example of a skillful writer illustrating "dialectically diverse texts" in a scene from Harper Lee's *To Kill a Mockingbird* (Lee, 1962). Here Lee not only presents place-bound dialects but time-related ones as well, employing three distinct language variations: an AAVE Southern dialect mixing with informal English; a 6-year-old, albeit somewhat precocious, child's imitation of the Southern informal English of her elders; and that same person's older adult voice using far more sophisticated language choices. Lee wraps these language choices into a brief lesson in identity and manners for a 6-year-old girl. The first voice is that of the character of Scout, the 6-year-old, who learns the Southern expectation of hospitality at home via child language usage when her brother Jem invites a poor boy her age named Walter Cunningham over for lunch. Scout's older and retrospective narrative voice explains how the girl's "involvement in Walter's dietary affairs" came about (p. 27). During lunch, Scout notices that Walter's pouring a large amount of sweet molasses over his meat and vegetables and complains that the semi-starved boy has "gone and drowned his dinner in syrup." This announcement was made much to the embarrassment of the children's African American housekeeper, and mother figure, Calpurnia, and so Scout's much older retrospective narrator tells us that she "requested my presence in the kitchen. [Calpurnia] was furious and when she was furious Calpurnia's grammar became erratic. When in tranquility, her grammar was good as anybody's in Maycomb. Atticus said that was because Calpurnia had more education than most colored folks" (p. 29).

In the kitchen, Lee (1962) has the conversation continue in the dialectically diverse interchanges between Calpurnia and the six-year-old Scout. Calpurnia states: "There's some folks who don't eat like us . . . but you ain't called on to contradict 'em at the table when they don't. That boy's yo' company and if he wants to eat up the table cloth you let him, you hear?" Scout responds: "He ain't company, Cal, he's just a Cunningham. . . . " Calpurnia then gives the child a lesson in etiquette that is part language, part manners, and part expectations of Southern identity: "Hush your mouth. Don't matter who they are, anybody sets foot in this house's yo' comp'ny, and don't you let me catch you remarkin' on their ways like you was so high and mighty! Yo' folks might be better'n the Cunninghams, but it don't count for nuthin' the way you're disgracing 'em—if you can't act fit to eat at the table you can just set here and eat in the kitchen." Looking back over the years, the retrospective narrative voice summarizes by saying that "Calpurnia sent me through the swinging door to the dining room with a stinging smack. I retrieved my plate and finished dinner in the kitchen, thankful, though, that I was spared the humiliation of facing them again" (p. 29). The reader is told about Calpurnia's "erratic grammar," although most would now call it code-switching and dialect-change issues. Her "grammar," however, communicates just fine as she code-switches back and forth from "you" to "yo" and "yo" to "you're," with each switch emphasizing emotional intensity rather than a consistent dialect; even to a six-year-old, the message was very clear.

What we have illustrated immediately above could be termed "close reading" of the language of the text, and although the text under analysis was taken from a novel, the same process could be employed as students read a scene from a play or a lyric poem. As Barbara Herrnstein Smith (2015) points out in a recent address to a group of literary scholars:

> Full-dress close readings, now as ever, can be showy or strained. They can also be dim, thin, derivative or pedestrian and, when motivated by a history of injury, sulky or venomous. But, now as ever, they can offer those who hear or read them potentially illuminating engagements with regions of language, thought and experience not otherwise commonly encountered. (Smith, 2016, p. 70)

As teachers model the close reading of texts—"informational," literary, graphic, digital—they need to know a great deal about how language works in order to reveal overtly to students how someone can notice features of texts, reflect on them, and construct meaning. See Appendix H (pp. 203–206) for a sample learning activity that emphasizes close attention to language as a way to "open" the reading of a novel.

POINTS OF CONVERGENCE

John and Tom agree here more than in any other chapters in this book. Both strongly recommend that all writers and speakers of English learn and employ at least two or three dialect patterns: what has been labeled as BSE, whatever dialect they were used to hearing at home, and the dialect of the immediate community feeding the school. Just because, for example, an AAVE speaker hears (or does not hear) the zero copula (*be*) at home, she still needs to learn that (1) it's a regularly used choice at home; (2) it appears to be an arbitrary choice for non-native AAVE speakers; and (3) it remains entirely appropriate in some situations and places while inappropriate in others, as Smitherman (1985) affirms.

Although we agree that the study of language is a worthy discipline in itself, we also note that for most middle school and high school English teachers, the study of language tends toward the specifics of grammar and usage, as those are typically connected to the teaching of writing and the study of literature. As we have shown above, a lesson "about prepositions" or "about agreement" should be in a particular context and have a particular utility if students are to see that some knowledge about prepositions or agreement or other language concepts can help the learners in their attempts to write compositions and in their effort to construct meaning from a variety of texts.

We are cautious about correcting grammar and usage, recognizing how closely language is tied to identity and knowing that presumed "rules" for correctness are simply a matter of agreement among a power elite and often violated by the guardians of correctness themselves. At the same time, we can see that the teacher's deep understanding about language can help her or him to model how to compose sentences and paragraphs that are clear, concise, and cohesive and to show how mature readers construct meaning from complex texts.

YOUR THOUGHTS

Some of our critics will think that we are rather lazy and permissive in not safeguarding "proper" usage. Perhaps it seems contradictory to insist that teachers need to know much about language and not insist that students honor a perceived standard. In the end, we see value in the study of language in more of a descriptive than prescriptive way; we recognize that knowledge about how language works will serve a teacher in modeling how to write with grace and clarity and how to read closely and critically. We may be the exceptions, and we invite the reader to judge what is especially important to know about language.

- What do you see as priority concepts for teachers to teach and learners to know about grammar and usage?
- What concepts about the English language should a teacher know and teach, just as a matter of knowing how language works?
- How does knowledge about language impact other areas of English language arts—specifically oral discourse, written composition, and the study of literature?
- If the study of language does not stand by itself as a focus for English study, how might such study integrate with the teaching of writing and the study of literature?
- Relative to the other areas of English language arts—that is, reading, writing, speaking, and listening—what proportion of time should the study of grammar and usage take up in the English classroom?
- If it is possible for an English teacher to proceed, conscientiously, in teaching without a substantial knowledge of the language, what would such an effort look like?

7

What English Teachers
Should Know

On rare occasions, we have encountered a preservice teacher who maintains that he or she would be happy to follow the school district's imposed curriculum script, or rely on the teacher's edition of an anthology or textbook to guide the goals and activities in the English classroom. In this view, as these rare students have reported, the candidate is just happy to have a job and receive a paycheck for completing the tasks that a supervisor has directed him or her to do. The assigned work requires the kind of knowledge that a technician would need—how to write the current learning target on the board, how to assign tasks or move through a PowerPoint presentation, how to distribute or collect papers efficiently, how to score tests and maintain records, and even how to suppress unruly behavior; in other words, the teacher-as-technician must know the "tricks of the trade," as if the "tricks" represented the body and soul of the endeavor to teach about literature, writing, language, and oral communication.

We also occasionally encounter preservice teachers who recall a favorite English teacher whose mode of instruction involved students reading only their preferred texts and writing the occasional journal entry to "respond" to their reading. The teacher candidate recalls the pleasure of being able to read several titles in the same genre, while setting aside many significant authors and titles; indeed, they recall that reading challenging texts, including Shakespeare, proved anathema, and writing instruction was almost nonexistent. When the teacher always allowed students the freedom to choose their reading and writing, and trusted, Rousseau-like, in a natural developmental process in learning to read literature and to write, the teacher need not be a content expert, but merely a facilitator for the students' self-directed personal development.

As we argue in the preceding chapters, neither of these instructional positions—the technician following someone else's script nor the laissez-faire developmentalist—requires particular expertise in either content or pedagogy. Expertise must include the pedagogical content knowledge necessary to influence students' learning by deciding on learning goals, constructing coherent units of instruction that follow an inquiry path, selecting and designing meaningful instructional activities, and planning aligned assessments. In contrast to laissez-faire facilitators and Gradgrind-type technicians, any teacher of English, we maintain, needs to know a great deal about literature, writing, oral discourse, and language in order to provide students with meaningful learning experiences that allow students to view their disciplined learning as a unified whole. Pedagogical content knowledge guides the teacher in framing essential questions, in connecting a body of literature and discussions, and in making decisions from moment to moment during the dynamic interplay that distinguishes invigorating English language arts instruction.

PEDAGOGICAL CONTENT KNOWLEDGE FOR THE TEACHING OF ENGLISH

We do not want to suggest that *pedagogical content knowledge* refers largely to the command of a body of information that a teacher can attempt to transmit to learners. While we have benefited from the lectures of particularly knowledgeable experts, we see this as an untenable position for middle school and high school teachers, especially at the beginning of their careers. We have known university professors who express skepticism about involving students in extensive discussions about their interpretations and assessments of literature. In these rare instances, a professor wonders why he should tolerate the fumbling efforts of novices when he is the one who possesses the expertise to share. For example, the professor of Romantic English poetry who wrote her dissertation about Wordsworth's *The Prelude* and has subsequently published articles and monographs about Wordsworth and other Romantic poets finds it intolerable to listen to students grope their way through Wordsworth, like listening to "old Triton blowing his horn." In this situation, the professor's position is essentially monologic, "a sordid boon," suggesting that only the single voice of the expert is necessary and nothing is to be gained from the misguided attempts and awkward collisions among less knowledgeable fledglings. We don't think of pedagogical content knowledge as the expertise that a scholar *conveys* for the students to absorb. Instead, we see pedagogical content knowledge as the combination of disciplinary knowledge and, crucially, also an understanding of how learners learn coupled with how instructional practices in the field can support these learners. In this view, disciplinary knowledge includes the content of a subject but also the particular issues, vocabulary, modes of expression, conceptions of research, formats for discussion and writing, and analytical procedures that distinguish the field.

For Shulman (1987), the "missing paradigm" is one that brings together both the content knowledge and the knowledge about teaching that inform choices about what and how to study within that body of content: "A second kind of content knowledge is pedagogical knowledge, which goes beyond knowledge of subject matter per se to the dimension of subject matter knowledge for teaching. I still speak of content knowledge here, but of the particular form of content knowledge that embodies the aspects of content most germane to its teachability" (p. 9). As we have suggested in the previous chapters, pedagogy amounts to much more than "tricks of the trade." The interplay between knowledge of content and knowledge of teaching requires that the teacher knows students well—for example, knows the presence or absence of relevant background knowledge, knows their various registers and dialects for speaking and writing, knows what is likely to capture their interests, knows how they are likely to interact, knows their various talents and enthusiasms, knows the difficulties and sensitivities in their lives, and so forth. While drawing from a deep knowledge of content within a discipline, the teacher also needs to know how learners learn, which would reveal an awareness of the social and dialogic nature of learning and knowing. This knowledge about learners and learning guides a teacher in organizing a line of inquiry and a sequence of connected experiences. Pedagogical knowledge informs practice in the moment as the teacher poses questions, fields questions, responds to contributions, quickens the pace, retraces instructional territory, slows the pace, and monitors understanding. The complexity of these pedagogical decisions and instructional moves is too great to represent here, but certainly pedagogy means more than transmitting information and keeping kids in line.

MANY POINTS OF CONVERGENCE

We don't want to retrace our differences and distinctions and recreate the exchanges we have reported in the previous chapters, and we will not try the reader's patience by recounting in detail what English teachers need to know in order to teach English in a principled way. Instead, we offer a summary of our summaries, to say as succinctly as possible what teachers need to know about literature, writing, oral discourse, and language.

The Territory of Literature

To begin, we disagree about the specific titles and authors a teacher should have read: where Tom is eclectic, John is more of a traditionalist. However, we do agree that an English teacher should read broadly, and in doing so, encourage students to expand their own knowledge base and literacy experiences. We judge that teachers should be familiar with long respected and influential authors as well as more contemporary yet important writers. We judge that teachers should read a variety of genres and look for both the conventional print versions of expression and more recent varieties of video, audio, film, graphic, and digital expressions. Without specifying the titles that every English teacher should read, we are confident that no teacher will be well prepared to teach English if she has read only a steady diet of vampire narratives, teen-level dystopian fantasies, or other genres of fiction with controlled and simplified vocabularies and syntactical minimalism.

Just as we have been compelled from time to time to turn our own and our students' attention to the literature that speaks to important historical and perennial social and cultural issues, we know also that teachers will find it necessary to expose students to the literature that examines critical contemporary issues. We understand that older literature has lasted in part because it has reflected the experiences of a people from a particular place and time. And the fascinating thing about good literature is that it often speaks across the years and even centuries. In the early weeks of the year 2017, for example, dystopian fiction by Aldous Huxley (*Brave New World,* 1932), George Orwell (*Nineteen Eighty-Four,* 1949), and Yevgeny Zamyatin (*We,* 1924) suddenly became overwhelmingly popular again, dozens of years after their initial popular appeal. At some point, teachers should try to help students see that each should be able to recognize that a literary work hitherto unknown to him or her might speak to that person's own time and experience. Again, this requires that a teacher knows students well and expands his or her reading to include works that reflect the social and cultural experiences of the students.

We understand that the reading and discussing of literature can serve a therapeutic function for students as they see characters in a constructed world experience conflicts and tensions that the students might also grapple with. Through the imagined experience, learners can judge the merits of the decisions of characters and reflect on their own actions and means for coping. Sometimes the young adult literature that draws young readers in can seem predictable and formulaic, yet the predictability serves readers' expectations. Teachers should be at least familiar with the genres that their students are reading and should provide them with opportunities to read the texts that they will consume with pleasure and enthusiasm.

If criticism involves interpretation, analysis, and commentary, rather than characterizing the worth of a text, then we agree with A. O. Scott (2016) that "the business of criticism is argument" (p. 215). The shared argument is necessary only when a speaker or writer recognizes that there is doubt, opposition, or "conflict," as G. Graff (1992) puts it. As Graff (2009) would insist, there is no need to share one's thoughts about *To Kill a Mockingbird* if there is a universal subjectivity that tells us that Atticus is an exemplary character and the novel rightfully condemns injustice of any kind. But if any opposing voice, like Gladwell (2009) or Giraldi (2015), upsets prevailing assumptions, then there is reason to take a position and show how one's close examination of a text reveals how a reader could construct a certain meaning and judge its merits. Or, as Graff (2009) puts it, "After all, we would have no reason to make persuasive arguments to begin with unless we were provoked by the arguments and beliefs of others" (p. 8). This necessary awareness of conflict or the collision of adverse positions to prompt responses and to give significance to one's essaying suggests that the well-prepared English teacher not only knows the literature well, but also is familiar with a critical tradition that allows the teacher to frame problems to prompt a class's dialogue and shared inquiry. Controversies about *Huckleberry Finn* or *To Kill a Mockingbird* spur reflective reading to scrutinize these familiar works even more closely and join the conversation that now seems to have elevated significance.

The Territory of Writing

We began our discussions about what English teachers need to know about writing by suggesting that these teachers need to have a strong sense of what good writing is. The simple logic is that if a teacher embraces an obligation to help learners to become better writers, that teacher presumably knows the target toward which she or he is guiding his or her students. If he or she has not already had numerous occasions to do so, the teacher should engage in conversations with colleagues about what distinguishes good writing, even when the standard might shift from genre to genre. If the standard shifts from context to context and genre to genre, the teacher should have in mind at least a standard for the kind of writing that she is asking students to produce in school.

We understand that some self-proclaimed educational consultants have made a cottage industry from developing rubrics and suggesting that students will become better writers simply by following the prescriptions that the descriptors in the rubric suggest. Even if learners apply the rubrics to their peer reviews and their reflections on their own writing, there is a big difference between being aware of a quality standard and being aware of thinking processes and composing procedures that enable the writer to produce quality texts. While it makes sense to us that learners should be aware of a quality standard for writing, we judge that a knowledgeable teacher can orchestrate learning activities to help students define the standard for themselves. An activity might be as simple as examining a set of short texts and discussing them with peers to express the qualities that allow a reader to say why one text strikes the reader as better than another. This kind of inquiry-based activity offers some promise that students will be able to internalize a standard.

We suggest that a deep understanding of what constitutes good writing should constrain the English teacher in making rash judgments about "correctness," "standard usage," and "proper grammar." Writing instruction needs to be much more than assigning writing tasks and then "correcting" the students' efforts. While we all benefit from editors and other thoughtful readers, we see little positive impact on learning when a teacher marks up a paper at the end of a process and allows no opportunity for the writer to use the reader's comments to improve efforts.

We caution that rubrics or other expressions of a quality standard can themselves be constraints that prompt students to produce predictable, formulaic, and sometimes dishonest writing. The five-paragraph essay still appears to hold a firm grip on middle school and high school teachers and learners. While we understand the simplicity of the form seems to serve students to organize and cohere at a certain developmental level, the form does not represent ultimately what strong academic writers do. So, instead of looking to a simple form as a definition of a standard, teachers should look closely at what academic writers actually do.

It is almost a cliché now for an English teacher to say that he or she teaches writing as a *process*. A common conception of a writing process is that it has distinct stages—prewriting (or envisioning), writing (vision), and rewriting (revision). Hillocks (1984, 1986) makes a distinction between "natural process" and what Applebee (1986) termed "structured process." A "natural process" relies on learners' self-directed and supportive efforts, assuming that they will naturally develop as writers if the teacher doesn't get in the way to direct the emerging writer down a path of artificial and stilted expression. Atwell (1987/1998), Calkins (1986), Graves (1983), and others associated with this approach would rely on "workshops," frequent journal writing, teacher-and-learner conferences, and peer reviews. With a "structured process," or inquiry approach, a teacher plans and orchestrates learning experiences that attend to the knowledge domains that impact the writer's production of a text, helping to build background knowledge, to become familiar with particular forms and genres, to support efforts to tap into prior knowledge, and to practice the procedures that are necessary for thinking through matters thoroughly and for producing texts.

We recognize, as Breuch (2002a, 2002b), Olson (1999), Russell (1999) and others have suggested, that to discuss *the* writing process is to imply that there is one universal process that all competent writers follow. Writing is a complex cognitive act, and various kinds of writing, situated in various contexts and communities, follow a variety of processes. If a process-oriented pedagogy is possible, it would take into account who the writers are and what demands a particular written expression intended for a certain community of thinkers makes on the writer. We judge that, equipped with knowledge about learners and about a particular form and audience for writing, an English teacher can tailor writing instruction to help learners to learn flexible procedures for writing and to successfully meet the demands of a current task.

Teachers should know how to adjust instruction for a given group of students and for a specific kind of writing. In many cases, that instruction will require substantial front-loading to help students tap prior knowledge and define a particular genre. As we discuss in Chapters 4 and 5, teachers also need to know how to plan, facilitate, and connect discussions that allow students to practice the procedures that transfer to writing—like summarizing, narrating, defining, classifying, analyzing, and arguing. The interactions among peers allow them to learn many procedures—from handling dialogue to documenting their research.

We judge that an assign-and-assess approach to writing instruction simply doesn't serve students well. But we think that English teachers need to know much about the assessment of writing, beginning with knowledge about a quality standard. Feedback at the *end* of a process does little to help the writer develop a piece of writing and develop as a writer. Teachers or peers need to provide feedback at various stages in a writing process, just as we have experienced such help from indulgent colleagues and supportive editors throughout the production of this book. We have sent multiple drafts to one another and have reacted to each with some thoughtfulness. Sometimes we have thought, "Well, not really," and then rewritten whole paragraphs; at other times we have cut or revised elements of individual paragraphs and sentences and even single words; still other times we have said YES! and returned drafts unchanged along with "looks good" here or there, as one form of collaborative writing goes. As Diederich (1974) pointed out long ago, assessment that is focused, respectful, and supportive is more likely to influence growth than assessment that is vague, demeaning, and pessimistic. English teachers need to know how to respond respectfully and supportively to students to help them develop their writing and develop as writers.

The Territory of Oral Discourse

As we have noted in Chapter 5, even if English teachers have not been assigned to teach courses or units in public speaking, listening and speaking among peers should be a key element in the instructional plan. We can think of many occasions for public speaking in an English class. These opportunities could involve students' introducing themselves to their peers; sharing what they have researched about historical and biographical contexts for the literature that they study; and reporting their reactions and assessments to current events, among many other possibilities. Structured or informal debates or deliberations can help students to judge the merits of policy positions and to explore the thematic implications of works of literature. A common view of a literature class would reveal students engaged with each other in advancing and evaluating various interpretations of works of literature, although the research of Juzwik et al. (2013), McCann (2014), and Nystrand (1997) suggests that such discussions rarely move beyond the level of recitation. Teachers need to know how to prompt and facilitate the authentic discussions about the interpretation of literature and about other critical questions. While such teacher actions seem intuitive, they need to be learned through practice and reflection.

We can also envision opportunities for students to role-play and to enact scenes from literature. Although we are not suggesting that English teachers need to become acting coaches, we insist that they can and should know enough to structure occasions for students to present scenes that allow for envisioning and to showcase the way readers see characters and imagine their actions. Once the teacher has demonstrated, for example, how to read lines in a Shakespeare drama—as contrasted with silently reading most narratives in novels or stories— then the actual physical movement on an imagined stage, along with the comparable text language of the scene, can open up for students a world of interpretations that they can then present to their classmates and instructors on their own. We suggest that the teacher encourage even unconventional or provocative interpretations, since that analysis will need to be demonstrated "onstage" in a way that verbal opinions alone will not always offer as convincing hypotheses.

Most importantly, we see authentic, purposeful discussions as essential to any English classroom, whether these discussions extend into online forums or not. We know that all students, whether the most active participant or the most reluctant contributor, benefit from the rich dialogues that teachers can support in each class. Through discussion, students learn important procedures for constructing meaning from complex texts and for writing a variety of compositions. If learners need to learn the intellectual moves that are necessary for interpreting texts and producing essays and narratives, we wonder how they will learn these procedures if they do not have opportunities to practice. We are confident that learners learn little from some authority *telling* them how to read and how to write. Instead, students need to immerse themselves in the procedures that the acts of reading and writing require.

We understand from observing classes in dozens of schools—from fifth grade to university level, from "remedial" classes to "honors" courses, from affluent communities to high-poverty areas—that students can assume much of the responsibility for the purposeful talk in a classroom, especially when that talk represents the exploration of ideas and practice with literacy procedures. While conversation and discussion seem "natural" and intuitive, teachers need to know how to initiate, sustain, and expand discussions. We know from watching highly effective teachers that they have developed skills that guide them in planning for discussions, initiating discussions, reacting to discussions from moment to moment, and connecting discussions across multiple class meetings and many weeks.

We know that highly effective English teachers keep specific goals in mind as they plan and facilitate discussions. If a teacher expects a class to be able to support an interpretation of a text by citing passages and explaining how they constructed meaning from them, then the teacher poses interpretive problems and follows through with probing questions to prompt students to practice the procedures that the learning goal requires. Similarly, a teacher can help students to evaluate policy questions (e.g., from Chapter 5, What is a fair way to distribute lottery winnings across a group of "friends"?) by organizing discussion forums that allow students to examine the problem from multiple points of view. With the specific learning goals in mind, a knowledgeable teacher can assess the presence or absence of the procedures that are required and can adjust the activities and ask the appropriate questions to bring actions into alignment with goals. As we have seen on rare occasions, teachers can show students what they say during discussions as a way to label the intellectual moves and as a means for students to assess their own thinking, represented in action, as they engaged with peers.

To encourage students to do any of these things—discuss, debate, perform scenes, role-play, read aloud, and the like—teachers need to know how to establish a supportive classroom environment. As Vivian Paley might say, we can't sing happy songs or discuss civilly or perform scenes from Shakespeare if we fear ridicule and derision. While Paley worked with kindergarten students, the same spirit applies in middle school and high school: Students are not going to contribute actively and enthusiastically if they feel threatened by ridicule and harsh criticism.

Through setting expectations, modeling expectations, monitoring behavior, celebrating positive behavior, affirming a sense of community, and many more supportive behaviors, an English teacher can establish the kind of environment where it is possible to experience the collision of adverse opinions without embarrassing classmates, driving reluctant participants into a shell, or inflaming tempers. If the English curriculum is one big conversation, then there must be willing participants and the teacher will need to know how to encourage participation, with word and example.

The Territory of Language

We have noted how English teachers must become conversant in the basics of language study, not to become mini-linguistic experts, but to understand, for example, the connections between one's spoken and written language and identity. While North American speakers usually are not as instantly identifiable along class lines as many are in British-speaking societies, there are still regional, racial, and class markers that teachers must become aware of in order to prepare their charges for the worlds they'll encounter after their formal education (Woodard 2011). And since there is no "English academy" comparable to the *Académie française*, founded by Cardinal Richelieu, trying to insure with modest success the "purity" of spoken and written French, we recognize that language and linguistic "rules" are dynamic and unstable and "linguistic change in English is both continuous and socially spontaneous" (Craig, 2015, p. 431). Descriptive linguistic scholars track, empirically, the movements and changes of languages inside small groups, within large densely populated cities, and textually, even from one historic period to another (Labov, 2007; Leach & Short, 2007).

Partly because language is thus evolving within even a group devoted to "standards" and verbal familiarity, we agree with Rei Noguchi that "formal grammar, as commonly conceived and practiced, has failed to produce significant writing improvement" (p. 15). However, even if a grammatical drill is often considered unhelpful, that does not mean that teachers should ignore language instruction all together. Our colleague and linguistics scholar Guslat Aygen suggests with us that "both prescriptive and descriptive linguistics should not be perceived as necessarily contradictory tools" (personal communication, 2016). Rather, both are not only necessary but are, as we write, being practiced by millions daily. Many English practitioners are now involved with informal language learning as they master computer programming, science research, and even popular culture found in TV programs and films.

The linguistically educated teacher will know that dialect variations and accents are as common as the many ethnic conclaves in American cities and in rural farmland villages all over North America. Given that widespread verbal phenomena, teachers must learn to respect the languages of every student she teaches and to learn the distinctions among dialects and language registers, while also remaining aware of the limitations and social appropriateness of "standard" English. Midwestern-trained teachers working in Brooklyn, NY, for example, may smile respectfully when a service station attendant called Oil tries to sell them a quart of earl, and no native of Brooklyn looks twice or is in the least surprised when asked there by someone with a full bladder for the location of the "terlet." The same sentence in a Chicago gas station would get a response of "Who's this guy Oil, and what for heaven's sake is earl?" Likewise, the teacher's task in a mostly African American community may not automatically become pushing students to learn code-switching (speaking one way on Wall Street and another way in the local community). Teachers might support code-meshing for a majority populace where those working in a business office might learn to integrate a more poetic language code by someone from the neighborhood with the sometimes rather stark formalities of speakers in a brokerage firm. Hence, the idea of an "appropriate language" to employ might itself begin to change as those employees diversify all up and down the social scale.

Linguistic flexibility and acceptance becomes even more important when speakers of languages other than English further integrate all levels of American society. Here, some greater use of "grammar" or usage might take on more importance to native speakers of Spanish who move into largely English-speaking neighborhoods and jobs requiring that they speak English. Spanish speakers must learn the very large differences in meaning between itty-bitty words like *in* and *on*, for example— often referred to as interference issues. Any novice English learner who tells a native English speaker that she intends to "get *on* the car and head *in* the road" will get both a puzzled look and maybe even a laugh. A good-humored English composition teacher will invite the student confusing two prepositions to laugh with the class and not to feel that he is being laughed at. Likewise, the literature teacher needs to model close readings of texts—"informational, literary, graphic, digital"—to help these students understand and then employ language features in texts, reflect upon them, and so construct meanings (Smith, 2015).

FINAL THOUGHTS

As we have noted in our Introduction, the idea of this book, likely in a different form, was the brainchild of George Hillocks, Jr. When he was working on a proposal for the project, he anticipated that such a book would stir some controversy, both because others might react to the presumption that anyone could tell others what they need to know in order to teach English and because some readers might disagree with the pedagogical content that George or any teacher might specify as necessary to know. Furthermore, George hoped that there *would* be controversy, because he knew that controversy spurs conversation and debate, and such conversations advance our understanding. In taking up George's project, we also hope that our presumptions to identify the pedagogical content knowledge for teaching English will provoke many conversations. We judge that such conversations are necessary to encourage reflections on what we teach and why we teach it.

We know that much of what we offer in this book is debatable. In fact, the previous chapters show us debating each other. But we remain confident in saying as one voice that a teacher of English needs to know much about his or her discipline. We tremble at the idea of an English teacher as a technician or automaton who simply follows a script that a curriculum director or publisher has provided. We also recoil from simply telling students to read whatever they want and write whatever they want without the accompanying instruction to help students to become stronger readers and writers. We certainly want students to read enthusiastically and to follow their own passions to guide their reading and writing, but we hope that the shared inquiry experiences and the scaffolded learning in the classroom spurs and supports the independent literacy activities. While we agree with the Goodmans (1979) that learning to read is "natural," we also know that explicit instruction in reading and writing can help students to become more facile, fluent, and flexible readers and writers. We also judge that "natural" does not mean haphazard. Teachers can set learning goals and help students to target their own learning, and teachers need to know a great deal about their discipline in order to do this.

So, what does a teacher of English need to know about reading, writing, speaking, and listening, and about whatever else the reader judges to be elements in English language arts learning? As we have asked at the end of each of the previous chapters, if we have missed the mark in saying what English teachers need to know, what are the alternatives or additions?

Appendix A

What Is the "Business" of Teaching English?

Profiles of English Teachers in Action

The following descriptions profile eight high school English teachers. Although they all work in the same department at the same school, their philosophies about teaching and school and their understanding of the central concepts of their discipline seem to differ markedly. If you were to join this staff and look to one of these teachers as a mentor for your induction into the profession, who would you see as a model? Number the following descriptions in rank order to indicate their *compatibility with your own vision* of the teaching of English. For the ranking, 1 = the most compatible. You might find yourself repeating a number, which is OK. If none of the descriptions fits your vision, write a new description that reveals how you would recommend the teaching of English in a way that is different from the approaches of the other teachers described here.

_____ Camille Esposito teaches eleventh-grade English at Floodrock High School (home of the Braves). The eleventh-grade English curriculum features American literature, and each student has been issued a massive anthology titled *Journeys in American Literature*. The teacher's edition provides abundant support materials, including detailed biographical information about each author and historical notes about the periods of literature. Camille notes that her job as an English teacher is essentially to tell students the story of American literature, from the Pilgrims and Puritans to the contemporary world. Students learn who the important authors and works are, the major literary periods or movements, and the influence of one author on another.

_____ Edward Dunham teaches Advanced Placement English to seniors at Floodrock High School. Edward recalls his favorite professor in graduate school saying, "No one should be teaching English who does not read *The Faerie Queene* every year." The statement impressed Edward with the implication that certain works of literature are just too important to be missed. With the AP class, Edward recognizes his responsibility to familiarize his students with inherently important works of literature. The AP training materials and the lists of literature from past tests provide guidance in identifying the important works. Edward embraces the following statement, which he recently made to his AP class: "A student should not graduate from high school and consider himself or herself an educated person without having read and appreciated Shakespeare's *King Lear.*"

_____ Felix Founteroy teaches sophomores at Floodrock High. The literature component of the curriculum in sophomore English includes an eclectic collection of readings from British and American authors. Felix overtly teaches students how to read the texts that they study, providing experiences that allow students to discover "rules" for reading and interpreting texts. Class discussions focus on critical assessment of the ideas introduced by the authors. Students in Felix's classes write a variety of compositions, including critical analysis of literature. He guides students through stages in writing processes and promotes logic and clarity of expression. Felix hopes that the procedures for reading and writing that students learn in his class transfer to other occasions, in and out of school, when students are expected to read and write.

_____ Carolyn Lupo teaches ninth-grade English at Floodrock High School. In her conversations with local business owners, Carolyn has heard them complain that the writing that they see from Floodrock graduates is filled with grammatical and spelling errors, and their spoken language exhibits careless disregard for the conventions of "standard English." Carolyn is sensitive to this criticism and hopes to improve students' spoken and written language through a steady diet of rigorous exercises in spelling, grammar, and punctuation use. Carolyn also wants students to expand their vocabulary beyond the vernacular of pop culture. She presents regular vocabulary lessons and assigns exercises in a vocabulary workbook. Carolyn expects that the students' expanded vocabulary will support their efforts at reading.

_____ Sean Kim teaches a senior English elective class at Floodrock High. The class is called Multicultural Literature for a Just World. Sean is determined to expand students' knowledge of the world by exposing them to literature from authors who are typically underrepresented in the schools.

The literature selections are by authors from countries outside of the United States and England and usually explore themes about *injustice* and *oppression*. For example, the students recently studied Aime Cesaire's *A Tempest,* a postcolonial variation on Shakespeare's *The Tempest.* Sean hopes that through the study of the literature, students will become sensitive to injustices throughout the world and look to correct injustices in their own community. One requirement of the class is that students complete a community service project that will promote social justice.

_____ Caleb Rittenouer wants to keep his job and someday earn merit pay if the district policy moves in this direction. He understands that his job performance, his "merit," and the quality of the school are judged by how students perform on achievement tests and other standardized assessments. Much of what his students do in learning to write and to read well connect ultimately to preparation for standardized tests. He exposes students frequently to the kind of forced-choice items that they are likely to see on tests. He explicitly teaches students strategies for taking tests well. Caleb judges that these efforts serve students well, because they will be well prepared to take the kind of tests that screen them for postsecondary school admissions and for employment.

_____ Oscar Maretta worries that too often the students in English classes experience a series of disconnected texts and activities. He prefers to engage the learners in his classes by assigning investigations into "big ideas" or "compelling questions." From his experience in working with adolescents for many years, Oscar has concluded that students are especially interested in learning who they are and formulating who they might become. So, for his tenth graders, Oscar has introduced the big question "Who am I?" The students read a series of progressively more challenging texts that explore this question by representing in narratives, poems, and plays some central characters who experience struggles to form a satisfying sense of identity. The unit includes each student's research about who he or she is. The unit involves reading, writing, speaking, listening, and researching, all of which necessarily involve close attention to language. According to Oscar, at any point in the term, each student should be able to see the connection between the current activities and the learning from previous lessons.

_____ Frank Santos wants, above all, students' learning to be meaningful to them. For many years, referring to the learning in English class, students have asked Frank, "What's it all for?" He never had a satisfactory answer until he started listening to his students tell him about what interested and concerned them. Frank now enters the school year with no preconceived notion about what students will study. He knows that he will need to support literacy development, but that leaves many possibilities. If students are particularly troubled by the way that African American and Latino/a teens are treated by authorities in the school and in the community, the class will study the problem through readings, interviews, and documentaries. Students will respond to the problems through stories, poems, plays, films, and arguments. Frank channels such investigations toward the positive steps that each student and the community as a whole can make for improvement. In the end, Frank will tell you that he is teaching English to make a better world—that's what it's all for.

Appendix B

Knowledge about Mode and Form

What Is a *Tragedy*?

Both in ordinary language and in literature study, the word and concept of *tragedy* has taken on an evolving set of meanings over the centuries. To move students away from a more pedestrian sense and misuse of the word *tragedy*, a teacher needs to know much beyond a textbook definition. Aristotle's list of attributes connected to tragedy, "one that has for centuries dominated tragic criticism and is still surprisingly resilient," is an empirical list derived from his watching dozens of ancient Greek dramas (Burian, p. 181). Aristotle's schema begins by emphasizing the hero's (or main character's) *hamartia*, the "tragic flaw of overweening pride, and its punishment" (Burian, p. 181). Some scholars question the idea of "flaw" and prefer instead individual "choice," but either way, the sense of extreme conflict, one that does not admit of compromise or mediation, has been paramount for at least 2,000 years.

Another common pattern includes the idea of the hero's "late learning," or recognition (*anagnorisis*), "after the tragic crisis has already and irrevocably occurred [*peripeteia*]" (Burian, p. 182). Still another Aristotelian attribute is that tragic conflict "ordinarily involves more than a clash of choices freely taken on by human agents." Instead, it includes "such elements as past actions that, whether recognized or not, determine the shape of present choices and even their outcome" (p. 182). Finally, conflict in tragedy is never limited to the "opposition of individuals," but rather always includes the larger society: the "future of the royal house, or the welfare of the community, and even the ordering of human life itself maybe at stake" (p. 182).

As influential as Aristotle's schema of tragedy has been, over the last 400 years, several scholars and theater critics have re-examined the tragic sense in the light of modern and more contemporary life and art. One example has been Raymond Williams's *Modern Tragedy* (1966, rep. 1992), in which he surveys some of the 18th- and 19th-century German scholars (Gotthold E. Lessing, Friedrich Hegel, Fredrik Nietzsche, and several others). Williams claims, for example, that Lessing considers that Shakespearean tragedy is "determined by a very complicated relationship between elements of an inherited order and elements of the new humanism. If the historical idea of [this] development is to be fully understood, we must understand the complicated process of secularization" (p. 150). Rank mattered in the Renaissance, so the death of a nobleman was far more important than a yeoman's. Shakespearean tragedy was itself varied, so in a "revenge tragedy," like *Hamlet,* for example, the fear of civil disorder (the *lex talonis*) following the death of a prince or king came into conflict with the sense that vengeance belongs to God, and so taking matters into one's own hands was a type of blasphemy: "He that revengeth shall find the vengeance of the Lord; and he will surely keep his sins in remembrance" (Ecclesiastes 28:1). "Hence the ravages of revenge appear most clearly in the deterioration of the mind" in a Renaissance culture where mental health depended upon moderation" (Prosser, 1971, p. 5). In *Macbeth,* for example, the deterioration of the Thane's and Lady Macbeth's minds comes from internal sources, from guilt over regicide, and from transgressing their duties to their honored guests.

Finally, in our own time, Williams argues that "when we see death and suffering, when we see mourning and lament, when we see people breaking under their actual loss, we have entered tragedy." In our middle-class culture, we rejected the overwhelming importance of mere rank since the "death of a salesman" was as important and his tragedy could be as real as any prince (and very recently, any princess). Modern tragedy is not what happens to the hero, but what happens through him. The tragic experience lies in the fact that life does not come back, and its meanings are reaffirmed and restored after so much suffering and after so important a death—which gives meaning and importance to life. One of the most influential playwrights, Bertolt Brecht, thought tragedy should not cause the audience member to emotionally identify with the heroic character or his actions, but the play should instead provoke rational self-reflection and a coldly critical look at the action on the stage. Brecht's "historical stories illustrated parallel themes" and ideas to the social problems facing contemporary audiences.

The thumbnail sketch of the evolution of *tragedy* above underscores that the concept of this mode of literature or form of drama continues to evolve for the author and the reader/audience. Rather than just using the word *tragedy* in a loose and popular sense, readers and viewers should keep in mind that human experience is always in motion and that absorbing an artistic experience depends as much on what one might expect as it does on what one actually encounters.

We have found that the following discussion-based activity begins teaching students the process of constructing and refining a conception of literary *tragedy*. The working definition that students derive with their classmates and teacher can serve them well in anticipating the arc of the narrative and in judging the central characters—both in the way the characters strike them as readers and in the way the author expected an audience to recognize characters.

We suggest a three-stage process for discussing the scenarios:

1. The teacher facilitates the discussion about students' judgments of the character in the first scenario. This relatively brief exchange models for the students what they should be doing in the small-group discussions.
2. The teacher organizes students in small groups to talk about the remainder of the scenarios. The idea is to recognize any "rules" or criteria for defining the concept. Consensus is not necessary, and each group might disagree about the criteria.
3. After the small groups have had sufficient time to talk, each team reports their decisions for the class to evaluate. Further conversation is likely to extend from these reports, as students challenge decisions and offer alternative analyses.

The students may not construct a list of criteria that looks like literary orthodoxy, but they will be sharing ways to evaluate the characters and judging appropriate ways to respond to the fates of the characters. Typically students have much to say about the type of character who is the central figure in a tragedy, the pattern of the action, the tone with which the subject is treated, the significance of the harm or downfall for the central character, and the appropriate audience response.

DIRECTIONS FOR STUDENTS

Read each of the following scenarios and determine in each case if the situation is an example of a *tragedy*. Be sure to explain why it is or is not a *tragedy*, based on your understanding of the term. After reading through all the scenarios, you should have a list of criteria for determining what a tragedy is.

1. George Yepesch has been late for his first-period class twelve times in the last three weeks. Mr. Sterne, George's first-period teacher, assured him that the next time he is late for class, he will be sent to the dean's office, where he knows he will be assigned an in-school suspension for 3 days. George rushes to his locker. With 2 minutes until the first-period bell, he can surely get his books from his locker, drop off his coat, and still make it to class on time. This morning, however, George's combination lock won't cooperate. He has had trouble with it many times before. He enters the combination several times, but fails to get the locker open. When the bell rings, George kicks the locker in frustration and breaks his toe.

2. When World War II broke out, Mr. Beemer had three sons. He was very close to his boys. They played ball together; they fished and hunted together; they talked about sports and politics together. He was very proud of his sons, who were good students and excellent athletes. When the United States entered the war, Mr. Beemer's three sons joined the Navy. When Mr. Beemer learned that all three sons were assigned to the same ship, he thought they were fortunate to be together to look out for one another. One day, however, Mr. Beemer received a telegram from the Navy that informed him that his three sons had been killed when their ship sank in the Pacific.

3. Guadalupe had been saving money that she earned from her part-time job to buy an eighty-five-dollar ticket to a concert by a band called Standard Faire. Guadalupe idolized Howard "Bonzo" Wellington, the drummer for the band, and she was happy to pay eighty-five dollars to be near the stage, where she could get a close look at him. Guadalupe had skipped lunch at school and had postponed buying the clothes she wanted and denied herself many other pleasures in order to save the money for this concert. On the night of the concert, as Guadalupe was getting ready, she discovered that she couldn't find the concert ticket. She searched all of her clothes and drawers; she searched all over the house; she even retraced her steps to school to see if she had dropped it on the way. When she realized that it was hopeless, Guadalupe collapsed on her bed and cried uncontrollably.

4. When Wes Mormon's father died, the pain of the loss was eased by the substantial insurance benefit. Mrs. Mormon still worked as the regional manager of a large Midwest bank, and Mr. Mormon had many lucrative investments. Wes was still troubled by the circumstances of his father's death. Mr. Mormon, always a do-it-yourself handyman, decided he would paint the exterior of the house himself. To reach some difficult spots on the side of the house, he had rigged a boatswain's chair, which was to be suspended by a long rope that could be adjusted from time to time. Mr.

Mormon threw the rope over the house and directed Wes to tie it down to something stable. The only thing that Wes could find was the family station wagon, which was parked in the driveway. After Wes tied the rope to the back bumper of the wagon, Mr. Mormon continued painting, secure in his boatswain's chair. Mrs. Mormon, however, knew nothing about the rope. When she pulled out of the driveway in the wagon to go to the store, she catapulted Mr. Mormon over the house and through the neighbor's living room window. Mr. Mormon landed on the neighbor's 100-gallon aquarium, shattering it into a thousand pieces. Mr. Mormon broke his neck and was dead on arrival at the community hospital.

5. The Swarth family lived on the first floor of a two-story frame bungalow in a poor neighborhood of Chicago. On Christmas Eve, Mrs. Swarth was preparing to bake holiday cookies. She ran out of margarine, but she was afraid to go out and leave her four young children alone. She also wanted to avoid bringing the children out into the sub-zero weather. In the end, she decided to leave her children—ages 7 months and 2, 3, and 5 years old—while she walked to the grocery store three blocks away. When she returned from the store, the house was engulfed in flames, with all the children inside.

6. When Kevin Dunghurst was 24, he experienced an eventful year. First his fiancée broke up with him, citing his sports fanaticism and his refusal to attend church with her on days when services conflicted with a Bears game. Next, a tree fell on his brand-new Porsche during a violent storm, bending the car into the shape of a bow tie. Kevin's insurance company determined that the car could be repaired and refused to pay for a replacement. They did, however, raise his insurance rate by 500 dollars per year. A week after the car was demolished, his parents divorced, and his mother came to live with him in his two-bedroom apartment, just until she could "fathom the depths of your father's depravity." He then learned he had advanced gum disease, and all his teeth would have to be pulled out. When things looked their darkest, a burglar broke into Kevin's apartment, beat his mother, killed his cat, and stole all his favorite video games. Then, a month after the burglary, Kevin won 28 million dollars in the Illinois State Lottery.

7. Frank "the Barber" Stanko ruled organized crime in Chicago for 30 years. The Chicago Commission on Crime claims that Stanko, as a "soldier" for the mob, was personally responsible for the slaying of at least 15 men. He had a reputation for being particularly brutal in his executions. After firing six bullets into a victim, for example, he would often take out his knife and cut off a portion of the man's scalp, thus earning him the nickname

"the Barber." As the head of a powerful "family," he probably ordered the slaying of another 50 men, with some innocent bystanders gunned down in the process. The deaths devastated many families, and merchants and other businessmen throughout the city lived in terror of Stanko. At the same time, he was a devoted family man, giving generously of his time, money, and affection. After Stanko died unexpectedly in a plane crash, hundreds of people attended his funeral, and his wife was noticeably distressed.

Appendix C

Practice with Rules of Notice and Rules of Significance

Character Dynamism in
Harry Potter and the Sorcerer's Stone

One challenge in teaching middle school and high school students about prose fiction and literature generally is their understanding of character dynamism: how mimetic characters grow and develop over the course of the text (novel, short story, play). Unfortunately, approaches that involve the use of Venn diagrams or "character charts" reduce the reading of characters to a classification activity and only reinforce a static and one-dimensional look at literary characters rather than guiding students toward the sense of characterological evolution. An alternative would involve demonstration (e.g., following a read-aloud/think-aloud protocol) and practice in doing what mature readers of literature do.

Such guidance in close reading is usually best achieved by helping students understand how a scene in a novel works: showing them how to read closely a few pages of a scene where the character's evolution is best displayed, and noting what the thematic implications are that need further consideration. Often, especially in young adult fiction where the fictional signals are prominently displayed, the analysis of a brief scene can show students the tools to work independently and to learn the processes of literary understanding. While a teacher knows well how a scene works, the job is to help students discover, with a little help from their friends, how a character evolves and how to reflect on the implications of that evolution.

For this sample learning activity, it is useful to keep in mind Rabinowitz's rules of *notice*, of *signification*, of *configuration*, and of *coherence* (or *unity*). We draw on a scene from *Harry Potter and the Sorcerer's Stone*. Novice teachers would be greatly helped by familiarizing themselves with the critical writings of James Phelan (1989), Peter Rabinowitz (1987/1998), Thomas C. Foster (2003), and other theorists, whose thinking about the issues in this appendix provide practical assistance as one plans lessons.

Our sample text comes from a classroom scene in *Harry Potter and the Sorcerer's Stone* (Rowling, 1997, pp. 136–142). The first objective would be to model for students how a mature reader of literature would notice the elements that the author likely expected readers to recognize, specifically these elements:

1. Snape's apparent antipathy—for no obvious reason.
2. Hagrid's contrasting friendliness.
3. Reference to the "grubby little package."
4. Examples of a "forward": Gringotts break-in and where the "grubby little package" may be now; what Hagrid might know about Snape that he didn't want to reveal to Harry.
5. The relationship between the character of Harry and the narrative voice.

In displaying the scene, while reading and verbally thinking out loud for students, the teacher would reveal the scene's dynamics, especially by inviting students to speak out loud the questions that come to mind: Why does Snape attack Harry verbally with knowledge he could not yet know (since it's his first day in the class) and leave Harry confused? Why is Snape so nasty to Harry (the fear of all students with a seemingly irrational, abusive teacher)? Both the reader and the character can only say, puzzled, "darned if I know," at this point in the novel. It is a *temporary puzzle* to be solved! Asking students to *speculate*, randomly, at this point is likely counterproductive (and even frustrating) because the *reader does not yet have enough information* to make even a wild guess. By putting this version of Snape in a static Venn diagram (as merely a "bad teacher") will leave out the information coming about him later in the novel, much less at the end of the seventh novel in the series.

In contrast to the early impressions of Snape, Hagrid is warm and friendly, but very evasive when asked about the incident of a few minutes ago, a natural need by any student for clarification of an unpleasant classroom experience. By using Rabinowitz's rules of significance, we ask ourselves why? Is it important (significant) that we are meant to see these two characters behave in inexplicable ways? Again, perhaps we can only answer "darned if I know"—for now. But, as the reader finds out many pages later, Hagrid's opinions of Professor Snape are more accurate than Harry's at this point in the novel. To further solidify the author's intentions about character evaluation in general, both Ron's and Harry's opinions of Hermione will change as well—as their early (and negative) dynamic leads directly to the scene with the mountain troll, where their friendship is cemented for the rest of the series. In this way, J. K. Rowling has *signaled* to the reader that making snap judgments about Snape could be counterproductive to a full understanding about her character creation during the seven-novel series.

This sample leads to an important teaching principle for the study of literature: since authors oftentimes withhold information from their readers for a variety of reasons, teachers can model both readerly *patience* and awareness of how the rules of *notice* and *signification* are often related in ways that only further reading can answer. While the well-prepared teacher is reading from memory, as Rabinowitz puts it, the first-time reader obviously cannot, and so, like Harry, who didn't know what a "bezoar" was and where to find it, most students will need a literature teacher who can *model patience* as the text and the classroom scene present information that the average student could not know (Hermione is, by definition, hardly a typical student). First-time readers should file away Professor Snape's aggressiveness and Hagrid's evasiveness and seek explanations as they continue to read.

As the narrative progresses, in the context of visiting Hagrid, the characters learn (and the reader *notices* the revelation) a piece of information—the attempted robbery at Gringotts—without knowing at that point how crucial that attempted robbery will be as a clue later in the book. This is, again, information that Rowling deliberately withholds to whet the reader's curiosity. The experienced reader knows to recognize the craft of the writer and models for the learners these moments of discovery.

The questions posed mentally by Harry are what one might call *forwards,* questions the reader will need to turn pages to learn, assuming he or she has already joined the narrative audience. The narrative voice (in "free indirect discourse," as we discuss below) has Harry think to himself "Why does Snape hate me so much?" These *forwards* are the novelist's way of *priming* the reader to want to keep reading. If the novelist does not specifically *prime* the reader in this regard, then the teacher must plant a seed and speculate—perhaps out loud—by modeling how to anticipate the answer that will likely become apparent with further reading.

Stylistically, note the use of *free indirect discourse* in the last sentence of the next to last paragraph on page 142. In effect, the voice and mind of the narrator and the character (Harry) have blended to ask questions about the "grubby little package" that—unknown at the moment to students— will be highly significant later in the novel. It's therefore important to understand that the characters and the narrator in this novel *configure* (form a connected structure) in ways that suggest we can trust this narrative voice. In this first novel in the series, Rowling is really aiming the work at a young adult audience, perhaps 11- to 13-year-old readers, and her stylistic choices confirm our adult sense of a rather controlling yet trustworthy narrator.

Focusing on this seven-page scene helps the first-time reader see that questions raised through scenic analysis set in motion many of the major issues in the rest of the novel and reveal some of the intellectual moves of an active reader of literature. Authors often withhold information—partially or wholly deceptively—so that the reader *will* be surprised, and will keep turning pages to note what has happened. If first-time readers of the novel figure out the text too quickly, or if the clues are too obvious, most will lose interest and either close the book or skim to confirm their previous suspicions. Either way, the emotional and mental connection between the story (and author) and reader is broken or frayed badly.

Although the Harry Potter series contains a mix of genres, one of them is a *bildungsroman* (a novel of initiation into adulthood), and as such, one of our major interests as a reader is to understand Harry's (and Ron's & Hermione's) development over time, especially as they experience a series of episodes that challenge them to operate in increasingly adult ways. We learn that eleven-year-old Harry's primary concern in the first novel is losing points for his House rather than feeling more personally abused (p. 139), and that both he and Ron are "too polite" to turn down Hagrid's "baked goods" (p. 142). Contrast those two bits of information about their politeness with their earlier (and negatively impolite) attitude and behavior toward Hermione (p. 172), and reciprocally, her condescension toward them (p. 156, ff). Their conflicts grow out of a mutual lack of information about each other, and will require a crisis (pp. 172–179) with the "fully-grown mountain troll" before their relationships evolve from mutual antipathy to friendship. As the narrator says at the end of Chapter 10: "There are some things you cannot share without ending up liking each other, and knocking out a twelve-foot mountain troll is one of them" (p. 179).

Appendix D

Applying Rules of Notice
and Signification

We see some value in a teacher modeling for students how to notice text features that prompt the mature reader to anticipate events, to ask questions, and to ponder symbolic and thematic implications. But the modeling is important only to the extent to which the students can imitate the teacher's example and apply the procedures of noting and reflecting on their own and with their classmates.

In this appendix we offer an original short story (by a fictitious author) and a series of supports to prepare learners for the reading. We also recommend directions to engage learners actively in interpretation and assessment. Perhaps the most distinctive part of this example is the inclusion of five critical perspectives for judging the story. We know from experience that when students contend with competing critical views of a work of literature, they have much to contribute to discussions and write more elaborated and focused analyses than if they had no awareness of alternative readings of the work. Confronted by alternative views of the story, the students must evaluate these views and express the support for their own views. Recognizing that all readers do not respond in the same way, and that some responses seem off base, the student can frame a problem that raises the significance of what he or she has to say about the work.

The work with the sample story should follow the teacher's demonstrations in noticing the features of a text and pondering their significance. Many teachers have relied on narrative images, like covers from the *New Yorker,* to discover narrative elements that an attentive reader might notice, drawing from students' contributions to recognize and label the elements that deserve the reader's attention.

We suggest a three-stage sequence for teaching the relatively simple short story that we reproduce here. The first stage involves preparing students to read the text actively and to think critically about the implications. The second stage involves students talking to their peers about their initial impressions of the story, in a way that Gallagher (2004) calls a first-draft reading of the text. The third stage involves students assessing a variety of competing views of the text, consistent with Graff's (1992) idea of "teaching the conflicts" (p. 12).

When we taught literature in high schools, it was difficult to think about the teaching of a single work of literature in isolation. More frequently, we saw the teaching of a single text in connection with a series of conceptually or thematically related texts. The sequence of lessons related to the reading of Graciela Marquez's "A Serious Joke" could introduce a conceptual unit that asks, "Can we dream about a better life?" If students had already worked with visual texts (e.g., *New Yorker* covers) and short constructed texts to recognize rules of *notice* to support an authorial reading of narrative texts, they would likely be in a position to apply these rules of notice to their reading of a short story. A brief introduction to the story could involve a short written response and discussion of a newspaper article about a recent lottery winner. Such discussion activates prior knowledge about state lotteries and students' judgments about the value of lotteries and the potential for any individual to win the lottery to improve his or her economic and social condition. After working with Marquez's "A Serious Joke," students could study Steinbeck's *The Pearl* and the film adaptation of Steinbeck's *The Grapes of Wrath*. The students might also read Lorraine Hansberry's *A Raisin in the Sun,* Ta-Nehisi Coates's article "The Case for Reparations," and several related poems by Langston Hughes.

A quick Internet search will identify several newspaper articles about lottery winners—some whose lives changed for the better and some whose lives became more complicated and miserable. The following questions could prompt a brief written response and open up discussion:

1. If a lottery player won a record jackpot, do you think the same thing could very well *happen to you*? Given your response, would it be a good idea for you and your family to *invest in the lottery*?
2. How is the winner's life likely to change? Will the winner likely be happier, healthier, and more comfortable than she or he is now? How did you make your judgment?

Without revealing much about the plot of the story or the thematic implications, the following questions can invite students to read the story critically: Who, if anyone, is harmed in this story? If someone was harmed, how significant was the harm? We would also ask students to say which characters the author probably wanted readers to like and which she wanted readers to criticize. How did the students figure this out? What details in the story showed what the author thought of the characters? We would display these questions in some way and ask students to jot down answers as they complete their reading of the story. The intention here is to influence students to be active in noticing elements of the narrative and in judging the characters and the author's likely stance about these characters.

A Serious Joke

Graciela Marquez

It had become routine in the Garcia family and among the in-laws to pool money and buy a stack of lottery tickets each Saturday. The responsibility for the purchase of the tickets fell to a different household each week. This week it was Javier Garcia's turn. The fortunate circumstance was that everyone had gathered together at Javier's home to celebrate his daughter Veronica's first Holy Communion, so it would be easy to collect the money. But in the bustle of activity surrounding Veronica's special day, Javier had no opportunity to run to the convenience store to buy the tickets. After celebratory cake and coffee in the late afternoon, the relatives and Javier's wife, Donna, urged Javier to go to the store to buy the tickets. The winning numbers would be announced on television at six o'clock, so he was approaching the deadline and he wouldn't want to miss the opportunity to purchase what might become the winning ticket. Today he felt the financial pinch that comes with hosting a family gathering.

The family had won a modest prize before. By the time it was divided, minus the cost of the tickets, each family walked away with 150 dollars. The meager winnings allowed each family to pay a few bills but did nothing to help them feel more secure or to entertain dreams of better homes in better neighborhoods. Nevertheless, Donna's mother, Yolanda, recalled a poor family who lived down the street from her who had won 28 million dollars. At first they bought a new car and remodeled their home, but eventually they bought a larger home in a swank suburb and travelled on exotic vacations. Yolanda thought, "Why not me?" So it became a position of faith that she would inevitably win a jackpot, making it critically important that the families purchase tickets each week. Although Yolanda knew nothing about the probability of winning, she judged intuitively that the purchase of multiple tickets would increase her chances of winning. She would be happy to share with everyone, as long as there was a big jackpot to share. Each week, Donna tried to temper her mother's exaggerated expectations, feeling her mother's pain with every Saturday night disappointment.

When the lottery drawing was but fifteen minutes away, family members were practically pushing Javier out the door. He seemed to be stalling, as if to tease everyone. "Wait a minute," he said. "I have to get my car keys." Yolanda sat in front of the television and directed Donna to turn to the local station that broadcast the lottery drawing. Javier pulled his brother-in-law Peter aside and told him to write down the winning numbers when they were announced and to call Javier on his cell phone. "What for?" asked Peter. "The deadline will be over. You can't fool anyone."

"Trust me," Javier said. "Just call."

"Would you get outta here," called Yolanda, almost infuriated that Javier was still in the house. "I'm going, I'm going," replied Javier. "The store is just a minute away on Loomis. I'll be right back."

The drawing was still ten minutes away, but Yolanda was shooing away anyone who blocked her view of the television screen. At one point, from her seated position, she swung her purse at three grandchildren who wandered into the living room and positioned themselves between Yolanda and the drawing. Her frustration with the children increased when half the contents of her purse showered onto the carpet. She quickly grabbed for the items—loose change, a lipstick, three ballpoint pens, a package of tissues, her blood pressure medication, and a brochure for a river cruise line.

At the convenience store, Javier waited behind two other customers but had plenty of time to purchase 30 tickets—some with specific numbers deemed lucky because Yolanda or Donna associated them with birthdays and anniversaries, but most were random picks. Then he waited for Peter's call as he thumbed through a newspaper from a wire stand next to the counter.

At the house, Yolanda focused on the drawing. As the numbers were announced, she jotted them down on the back of the cruise line brochure that she had retrieved from the floor. Peter stood behind her and jotted down the numbers on the palm of his hand. "What are you doing?" asked Donna. "Mom is already writing down the numbers."

"I just want to be sure," said Peter. When the television announcer reviewed the numbers, Yolanda looked at what she had written, reading silently, her lips moving as if in prayer.

Peter slipped through the now crowded living room and went to his car. There he called Javier and read aloud the numbers he had written on his hand. "What do you think you are going to do? The ticket will have a time stamp and won't be any good for this week."

"Donna and her mom won't know that when I slip this ticket in with the rest. They're going to think they're millionaires."

"Bad idea, man," responded Peter. "Donna's gonna kill you." Javier laughed.

When Javier got home, he nonchalantly walked over to Yolanda and placed the stack of lottery tickets on the end table next to her chair. Without looking up at Javier, she said, "It's about time. Did you have to go halfway across town for these?" Javier sought out Peter so they could watch together the train of emotions that they had set off toward a cliff. Javier found the wait exhilarating; Peter found it nerve-wracking.

Yolanda slowly and methodically checked each ticket. Since there were now 31 tickets, the process would take a while. At the seventh ticket, Yolanda called out, "One number matches. Two. Three. Four. Four. That's it—only four." This would earn the investors 180 dollars. That at least covered the cost of the tickets and left a little bit extra for each family. But Yolanda wanted more. She plodded on through the stack of tickets. The children played on the living room floor. Family members stood around chatting. The television blared. Javier and Peter watched, as if tracking the spark of a fuse toward a powder keg that would explode in a joyous fury. Almost disheartened but with the resolution of a dreamer, Yolanda selected the next ticket to check. The numbers looked familiar. She called out: "One match. Two matches. Three." Her voice became louder and more shrill. "Four matches!" she shouted. Donna came over to verify. "Five matches!"

Peter whispered, "Uh-oh." Javier smiled, but felt that the room had become suddenly warm.

"Six matches! Oh, my heavens, six matches!" she called. Yolanda grabbed her daughter's two hands, and they both jumped up and down in a celebration dance, calling out, "We're rich! We're rich! We're rich!"

Peter faced Javier. "You're a dead man," he said.

"You, too. You gave me the numbers," Javier replied. "We're both dead."

Everyone but Javier and Peter joined in the celebration. It appeared for the moment that they were all millionaires many times over. Some family members looked stunned, not sure how a pile of money would change their lives, but the dreams that money could buy swirled around the room—cars, homes, jewelry, clothes, vacations, debt relief, and a trip down a European river. Javier tried to turn to leave the room, but Peter caught him by the arm. "When are you going to tell them?"

"I guess now," Javier allowed, like a handcuffed prisoner admitting his guilt before an impatient judge. "Wait a minute," he called out. "Look at the date on the ticket. I bought a ticket for next week."

Donna stared sharply at Javier, having been a victim of his practical jokes on many occasions. "Javier, you didn't."

"What?" asked Yolanda. "I don't understand. What are you saying?"

Donna explained gently, "Mom, he knew the winning numbers but bought the numbers for the next drawing. He knew we would confuse the two."

Still incredulous, Yolanda looked again at the numbers she had written on her brochure and then at the date on the ticket. She began to hyperventilate and looked around to see in the faces of the adults around her the confirmation that she had been duped. Donna began to cry and reached out to her mother, who pushed her away. Yolanda's breath became more regular. She could not look at Javier. Her thoughts were not clear, but she was certain she would not speak to him for a long time. Yolanda slumped into the chair from which she had witnessed the lottery drawing. She deliberately placed the ticket on the pile with the other tickets. The river cruise brochure dropped from her hand to the floor.

We suggest that students should have time in small groups to share their impressions of the story. The postreading experience has two parts: (1) a sharing of impressions about basic elements of the narrative, and (2) a group evaluation of five competing views of the story. The following questions can involve students in explaining how they constructed the meaning from the text. Our questions emphasize an awareness of how the narrative works and asks students to share what they have noticed about the author's craft.

1. Why has Javier played a practical joke on his family? What did he expect to happen? How do you know his intentions and expectations?

2. Why does Peter go along with Javier's joke? What did Peter expect to happen? How do you know what motivates him?

3. Yolanda seems to be the primary victim of Javier's joke. How sympathetic do you think the author is toward Yolanda? How did you figure out what the author thinks of Yolanda?

4. If you think that Javier deserves some sort of punishment and you had it within your power to punish him, what would that punishment be? How would you know if Donna and the author would agree with your proposed punishment, or agree if you decided not to punish him at all?

5. The story ends with the immediate reaction to the practical joke, and the author leaves it to us to imagine what will happen next. If you could follow the characters through the remainder of the weekend, what would happen to them, especially to Javier, Peter, Yolanda, and Donna? How are you able to make these predictions?

To complicate matters a bit, we would also ask students to evaluate five other critical views of the story. We offer five possible views below. A teacher might use the perspectives as is, or devise other possible views of the text. It is possible that one or two of these views would naturally emerge as students discussed the story, but we judge that students would not likely initially express the more gendered and more political views. A key will be to offer distinct possibilities and to include views that are likely to contrast with students' initial judgments.

Mature literature scholars would not likely comment on a work of literature without considering what other commentators have had to say. In fact, it is an awareness of other views—some that seem incomplete, some that disagree markedly with your own position—that prompts the scholar to write about the text. In fact, as Williams (2004) and Graff (1992, 2009) insist, if there were no disagreements (i.e., no "conflicts"), the writer would have nothing more to contribute to the conversation. The recognition of competing views, especially those that contrast with the current reader, allows the current commentator to frame a problem, which elevates the significance of the analysis that she cares to share with others. In fact, based on our many years of teaching and observing scores of other teachers as they taught, we judge that when students know that other readers have read the same text in strikingly different ways, the learners participate more readily in discussions about the text and write more focused, meaningful, and elaborated responses about the text.

In introducing students to the alternative critical perspectives, the teacher might say something like this:

> "Other readers have read the story and have had interpretations that might be different from yours. I am providing you with the views from five different readers. I would like you to read the five perspectives and judge for yourself which of the views most closely aligns with your own. After you have judged for yourself, you will join the other members of your team to share your judgment and to explain how you arrived at your decision. You will want to jot down some notes about what you liked and didn't like about the perspectives."

After the teacher has judged that the students have finished reading the critical perspectives and have written some notes, she can transition into small-group discussion, prompting the teams to address these questions: Which of the five critical perspectives, if any, do you think is most reasonable? If you disagree with any of the interpretations, why do you judge that it doesn't make good sense?

As the teacher circulates among the groups, she can judge if students need clarification about any of the interpretations and can assess when students have shared their judgments and are ready to present their arguments to the rest of the class. The next step in the sequence would involve the whole class sharing the judgments among the various small groups. In listening to the students' evaluations, the teacher can judge the extent to which students are representing the critical perspectives accurately and are offering reasonable judgments, based on references to the features of the text and to the rules of notice and rules of signification. The discussion could extend into another class meeting, and the teacher should listen for evidence that students have followed procedures in arguing an interpretation: summarize, support claims, interpret citations from the text, paraphrase competing views accurately, and evaluate alternative views.

During this oral discourse experience in evaluating critical views and supporting their own judgments, students are practicing the procedures that are important for an elaborated written analysis of the story. A teacher might be content for the moment to hear students' interchanges to detect evidence of their practice with procedures, or the teacher might prompt students at the end of the discussion to write an analysis of the story. Given the preparation for reading and the subsequent grappling with various critical views, a teacher should align the writing prompt with the oral discourse experiences—that is, prompting students to frame a problem, evaluate at least one alternative view, and argue for an interpretation or response that contrasts with the view the student rejects.

FIVE CRITICAL PERSPECTIVES

View 1

Based on my experience, I would say that most often it is men who play practical jokes, especially cruel or hurtful jokes. That is the case in "A Serious Joke." Graciela Marquez, the author, implies criticism of practical jokes and the men who play them. In the story, two men conspire to play the joke on the rest of the family, and they especially hurt two women. Javier and Peter worry about people being mad at them, but what did they expect? They certainly could not have expected everyone to think it was funny to believe they won a fortune and then have it taken away in an instant. They had planned for Javier's wife and mother-in-law to be devastated. In the end, it appears that the author, Graciela Marquez, saw Javier and Peter as representative of a lot of heartless men who direct their cruelties toward women.

View 2

The problem with everyone is that we take ourselves too seriously. In the story "A Serious Joke," Javier is the one fun-loving character, and he wants to show the members of his family how ridiculous they can be. In the end, it is a JOKE! Javier values fun and seeks to surprise others, just as anyone would with the harmless jokes we see at home and in school. If we are honest with ourselves, we will admit that we have all played practical jokes on others or have enjoyed witnessing practical jokes. The joke is only serious when people place too much importance on themselves and don't like to be fooled. I see that in many ways the author expected us to see that Javier and Peter were just trying to have some fun, and Yolanda and Donna were just too serious about themselves.

View 3

Any con man will tell you that you can't fool a person who is not already looking to take advantage of someone else. Javier's goal was to give the greedier members of the family the impression that they had won a big lottery prize and then let them discover that they had won nothing. The joke was that for a moment, family members, especially Javier's mother-in-law, thought that they were fabulously rich. In a sense, at least in their imaginations, they got exactly what they wanted. Yolanda, the primary victim, was most eager to win and to pamper herself. The author probably expected us to see that if Yolanda and other family members were not greedy and placing so much importance on wealth and luxury, then Javier's joke would have had no effect and no one would have been disappointed.

View 4

The author of "A Serious Joke" reveals the destructive behavior of a man who plays a cruel practical joke on family members. The language of the story compares the "joke" to someone setting up a train to go off a cliff. This would be obviously disastrous. In a way, it is like someone who sets off a firecracker behind an unsuspecting person. In those instances, you have to wonder what the perpetrator would expect. He has to know that he is going to do some harm to someone, even though he can't say precisely what that harm would be. It is clear that the author wants the reader to see Javier as the villain, with Peter as his accomplice. The descriptions show Javier planning and anticipating family members' disappointment, especially Yolanda's descent from exhilaration to crushing defeat. When Yolanda sinks into a chair and drops her brochure, it is not certain if her collapse is simply an emotional deflation or a physical collapse. Either way, the author shows us that she wants us to know that Javier is responsible.

View 5

The story illustrates the persistent cruelty of state lotteries. The odds of winning are miniscule. People who are already financially secure never buy lottery tickets, because they already have their money and know that they are not likely to win on a lottery bet. This leaves the working-class people and the very poor people as the primary customers. These are the people who can least afford to be gambling their money. Javier's joke on his mother-in-law might seem cruel, but it is no crueler than the joke that hundreds of thousands of people who buy lottery tickets every week think they have a chance of winning a lot of money and being set for life. The point of the story is that lottery gamblers are inevitably losers, and the lottery agencies and the state governments that profit from the gambles are the big winners. The author wants us to understand that the people behind the lottery are manipulating and exploiting the most economically vulnerable people in the community.

Appendix E

Discovering Rules of Configuration

One area of expertise for the teacher of literature to acquire is a familiarity with common narrative structures, whether in print, or on a screen, or via live action. This familiarity allows a reader or viewer to recognize particular narratives as part of a larger tradition of literature, both in English and in languages worldwide. Hence, experiencing fiction involves a reader in anticipating the progression and development of a narrative, and invites him or her to question any rupture to what may appear to be the typical pattern of a given story line. A reader's knowledge about patterns of narrative development can also be part of the reader's assessment of the quality of a given work, perhaps dismissing some fictions as trite formulas and predictable patterns. We don't recommend that teachers lecture students on common narrative patterns. Instead, we strongly recommend that teachers design collaborative experiences that allow students to discover what they already know about narratives by drawing from their prior knowledge and engaging with a text to predict, question, and judge.

Rabinowitz and Smith (1997) suggest that "configuration . . . is the interpretive activity by which, during the act of reading, a reader assembles the emerging details of a text into larger patterns. It's the application, for instance, of specific strategies that stem from our general recognition of the predictive events" in certain fictions (p. 94). However, when a fictional work (novel, story, play, narrative poem) seems too predictable, we react with a certain boredom, and knowing how people react to the obvious, authors and playwrights disguise and particularize their plot progressions to give readers or viewers a sense of "defamiliarization": they try to make it "strange" to keep their audiences engaged (Shklovsky, 1965, pp. 1–23).

The following inquiry-based activity invites teams of students to confer about where they think a narrative is headed, based on the indicators from the beginning of the tale. As students report their judgments and compare their assessment to similar works of literature, they are able to classify types of narratives and discuss the potential implications of variations and ruptures to the conventional patterns. Rabinowitz tells us of the differences between the teacher's "reading from memory" (she has already completed the work and knows the ending) contrasted with the student who is experiencing a text or performance for the first time. Although we agree with Rabinowitz that any second reading (or rereading) "is essentially a different kind of activity" than a first-time experience (p. 91), we think that teachers can make use of certain types of plot familiarity, suggesting to readers that close attention to a text or film may yield surprises in spite of what appears at first like repetition.

SELECTING A MOVIE

Supposition

With no particular plans for the evening, Araceli and Susan agreed to see a movie together. The question was what movie to see. Susan said that she didn't especially care, even if the movie was intended for a juvenile audience, as long as the film did not have some plot that was *so predictable that she knew within the first 15 minutes* what the action of the narrative would be and the resolution of any apparent conflict. Susan complained that she could not *experience* the narrative if she already knew the direction the narrative was headed in. Araceli suggested that they see the titles of the films showing at the local multiplex and then consult the plot synopses available online at *filmspoilers.com*.

Directions

The synopses of the films appear below. With the other members of a team of three or four classmates, put yourself in Araceli's position:

1. Judge the extent to which you can *predict the direction and outcome* of the narrative.
2. Identify the *details in the synopsis that allow you to make predictions* with some confidence.
3. The details will probably stand out because you have seen similar

patterns and conventions. What similar stories, plays, or films can you *compare the movie* to?

4. Given Araceli's criterion for selecting a film to see, what movie would you *recommend*? Why?

Death at Sea, Rated PG

Synopsis: Industrialist Melvin Pelf invited 12 members of the Enthusiasts Club to sail for a week aboard his yacht the *Gracey Regina*. He insisted that everyone leave all cell phones and other digital devices behind and enjoy the moments at sea. Aboard the yacht, the guests would have luxurious accommodations and be served by a staff of 10; but they would be out of touch with people on the mainland. On the second day of the voyage, one of the guests discovered the dead body of another guest in a storage bin where deck chairs were kept. The first superficial viewing of the body showed no signs of injury, but the death could not have been an accident.

Mr. Pelf insisted that the yacht be anchored and everyone assemble in the dining room. The trip to the mainland would take hours, if not an entire day. Because he knew that the perpetrator of the apparent crime was aboard the yacht, he did not want everyone to reach shore before the crime could be solved. Mr. Pelf judged that one good fortune was the fact that one of his guests was Dr. Stephen Toulouse, a professor of philosophy and logic at Middle Border State University.

The guests, crew, and staff assembled. Dr. Toulouse knew most of the guests well, but he did not know each person's relationship to the deceased. Systematically and subtly, he began his inquiry. . . .

Brother in Name, Rated PG-13

Synopsis: Many years ago, there were two brothers who lived together on a farm near a big town. Their names were Ollie and Orville. Ollie was older. Their father, Rollo the Great, left them a lot of money. But Ollie wouldn't let Orville have any money, and he wouldn't support him in attending college.

Orville appealed to Ollie but he refused to share any of his father's estate. With few options to advance his education and a career, Orville entered a wrestling contest sponsored by the king. The prize was a medal and a substantial amount of money. But when Orville defeated the king's court wrestler, the king refused to surrender the prize and threatened to execute Orville if he remained in the kingdom.

The king's daughter Lucille and her cousin Rosie had observed the wrestling match and were shocked at the king's decree. They wanted to help in some way. Rosie took a gold chain from around her neck and gave it to

Orville, hoping it would bring him good fortune as he made his way into the wilderness. Exiled from the kingdom but warmed by the kindness of Rosie, Orville headed toward the forest. . . .

The Rise and Fall of Hamilton Dane, Rated R

Synopsis: On the day that Hamilton Dane learned that he was appointed executive vice president for Sales for Copenhagen Seafood Industries, he arranged to meet his friends for drinks to celebrate. Hamilton was pleased with the promotion, but he also felt a little unsettled. The president and CEO of Copenhagen Seafood Industries was Hamilton's uncle Claude. As co-owner of the company, Claude had assumed leadership after Hamilton's father, the other co-owner, had died under some mysterious circumstances. Hamilton remained resentful that the charter of the company and his father Reggie's will specified that Claude would assume ownership and serve as president if Reggie were to precede Claude in death.

After an evening of celebratory drinking with his friends, Hamilton made his way home on foot through an unexpected fog in the city. During his walk, Hamilton encountered several panhandlers, including one who looked uncannily similar to his father, Reggie.

When Hamilton awoke the next morning, he recalled his encounter with his father's look-alike. The man had confronted Hamilton, claiming to *be* his father. He insisted that Claude had conspired with Hamilton's mother to poison him and make the death look like a stroke. This ragged Reggie directed Hamilton to have his revenge against both mother and uncle.

Hamilton remained confused, uncertain about his memory and what he had actually witnessed the night before. Was it a dream? Did his senses deceive him in the fog and under the influence of alcohol? How could he ever confirm that the charge against Claude and Hamilton's mother was true? If he was able to confirm the charge, what was he obliged to do . . . ?

No Direction Home, Rated R

Synopsis: It was dusk as Evelyn Barlowe drove across the Pennsylvania countryside. She had apparently missed her turn as she searched for the home of her dear friend from college. As she looked at her cell phone in hopes of using the map function to find her way, she discovered that the battery had run out and she therefore had no phone or GPS capability. She could wander back and forth across the country roads with what little gas remained in her tank, or she could approach a nearby farmhouse to ask the occupants for directions.

As Evelyn parked in the gravel driveway, she noted some sounds of human distress coming from an outbuilding some 50 feet from the home. While the windows of the building were covered with newspapers, the interior appeared to be brightly lit, with occasional flashes of intense illumination. Evelyn hesitated at first, uncertain if she should investigate the sounds of distress, but she proceeded to the front door of the house and rang the bell. She heard dogs barking inside, but no one answered. She rang again and again, sending the dogs into an uproar. Evelyn was inclined to get back in her car, but she knew she didn't have enough gas to allow her to drive across the countryside without direction. Slowly she moved toward the illuminated building, hoping for a friendly reception. . . .

The Power and the Stone, Rated PG

Synopsis: On a mild spring morning many years ago, a child was born in the town of Watermills, the capitol of the tiny nation of Arboria. The parents, Carth and Rusa Heidro—two of the most respected citizens of Arboria, were delighted with their baby boy. They named him Yager and dreamed about the day when he would be a great man in Arboria. Their joy, however, did not last long.

Agorth, the King of Arboria, was a vain and superstitious man. Plans about how to retain his power occupied most of his thoughts. He worried little about attacks from other countries—Arboria, after all, was situated in a mountain range that historically had frustrated many foreign attacks—but he feared revolt from his own people, whom he kept on the verge of starvation in order to use what they produced to satisfy his own avarice. Agorth often consulted his Zethram, the court oracle, to provide him with comforting predictions about his continued reign over Arboria. During the year of Yager's birth, Zethram came to Agorth with a disturbing prediction. Appearing before the king, Zethram untied a cloth bag from his belt, removed a handful of small animal bones from the bag, and threw them on the floor at the feet of the king. Zethram cast a cold stare into Agorth's eyes and announced: "The meaning of the bones is clear. A child is born in this land who will end your reign over Arboria. A male child is born with a circle on his chest. He will grow in power until he brings down your rule." King Agorth called for his ministers of defense and justice. He told them: "Search for a newborn child in this land, a child with a circular mark or medallion on his chest. See that any such child is destroyed."

At dawn a contingent of heavily armed soldiers invaded the Heidro home to find the child whom their informers had identified. But, feeling an overwhelming compassion for the child, a young soldier took the boy to his own parents, a poor peasant couple who lived on the banks of the Green

River. The child, whom the old peasant couple called Zed, remained with the couple for seventeen years, and in that time he thrived and became a masterful swineherd.

One day Zed returned home from a trip to the livestock market to find his home destroyed and his stepparents killed. A mysterious stranger emerged from the shadow of a tree to report who had committed the atrocity and to suggest what Zed needed to do to save others from violence and injustice. Zed judged that he was too young and inadequate to accomplish this task, but the dark stranger recognized his hesitation and said, "Only you can act now, or Arboria will be awash with blood and tears. . . . "

Appendix F

A Case for Discussion
and Written Response

In the chapters of this book, we identify the pedagogical content knowledge that teachers need to internalize in order to support their teaching of English. These discussions emphasize the knowledge and principles that provide a solid foundation to guide instruction. The following example of a lesson sequence suggests how to engage learners in substantial oral discourse that prepares them to produce an elaborated written response to a controversial situation and positions learners to read related texts (and watch films) that explore themes about revenge, mercy, and justice. These themes are common in the literature that students encounter in high school and represent issues that concern them. This blending of an oral language and written language experience is an example of an integrated approach to English language arts instruction, with the speaking and listening activities connected to, and supportive of, the writing of arguments and the reading of literature.

The introduction of a problem that is likely to resonate with teens and the processes of research and discussion are consistent with an *inquiry* approach to writing instruction, as defined by Dean (2010); Graham and

Perin (2007a, 2007b); and Hillocks (1984, 1986). The procedures are also consistent with an approach that Applebee (1986) has labeled a *structured process*. An *inquiry* or *structured process* approach would identify a problem of some consequence to the learners, provide data to support deliberation, and structure opportunities for students to discuss the problem at length. The discussion is key, because it immerses students in the procedures that transfer to their writing and to their judgments about characters' decisions in the literature that students subsequently encounter.

In planning instruction that would make use of the following activity, a teacher would want to project the sequence of discussions and the stages for a process of writing an argument as a response to the case. Discussions would build on themselves: small-group preparation readies students for a simulated meeting; a simulated meeting showcases a variety of viewpoints; a whole-class discussion invites synthesis, comparisons, and evaluations. The extensive classroom interchanges immerse students in procedures that transfer to a written response, but the teacher and students would have to follow through with planning, drafting, reviewing, and revising, as they would with almost any composing effort.

THE QUALITY OF MARCIE

Introduction

The following case invites you to experience the tension between an inclination toward *revenge* and a call for *mercy*. When two people or two groups of people seek to hurt one another or someone connected to the other as retribution for the harms that they have experienced, the cycle of revenge could go on forever, as some infamous feuds like that between the Hatfields and McCoys have illustrated. Such feuds can be destructive for an entire community. Mahatma Gandhi is reputed to have observed, "An eye for an eye only ends up making the whole world blind." Is that kind of idealism practical in everyday life? Is revenge necessary? How can you convince someone to be merciful rather than vengeful? Is *vengeance* the same as *justice*? If there is a difference, how would you make the distinction?

A Note to the Teacher about Academic Language

Depending on the specific group of learners, a teacher might find reason to preview some of the language of the case—both the language of case narrative (content language) and the abstract language in the directions (academic language). We have listed some possibilities below.

Language of the Case	Language in the Directions
confidant	*argument*
exhilaration	*cite evidence*
expired	*clarity*
extremists	*conventional letter*
inflammatory	*edit*
magnitude	*evaluate options*
maimed	*initiate the conversation*
oppression	*interpret the evidence*
platform	*logic*
sponsored	*recognition*
vengeance	*recommend action*
	reiterate
	review the situation
	revise
	summarize the problem
	thoroughness

Case Narrative: A Steep and Swift Decline

Lynn Fiedengeist and Marcie Erbarmen have been residents and activists in their hometown of Unity for years. They have both been concerned about how to end the cycle of street-gang violence in their town. Motivated by their concerns, they both agreed to serve on the Township Youth Commission. In open meetings they have compared the gang violence to the acts of terrorism around the world. With terrorism, political extremists have killed and maimed innocent people, justifying their actions as the necessary vengeance against political powers that have either sponsored or enacted violence and oppression against their families or political parties. In Unity, there are two dominant street gangs, the Insane Assassins and the May Street Maulers. Three years ago, a group of Maulers attacked an Assassin as he traveled home from school, hurting him badly. The Assassins then sought out the attackers and shot at them. The Maulers then shot and killed someone they thought was an Assassin, and then the Assassins attempted to fire upon a group of Maulers who sat on a porch, but shot a child instead. This cycle of revenge and retaliation could go on forever, unless one of the gangs would be willing to break the cycle by suffering the latest insult and injury, even if the gang members had to swallow their pride. As Lynn and Marcie have worked directly and indirectly with the gangs, they have pleaded with them to take the first step by being strong enough and humble enough not to seek revenge, for the good of their families and for the good of the whole community. So impassioned has Lynn been with this work that she ran for political office on a "get tough on crime" platform, and with Marcy's campaign help, she won a seat on the City Council.

While Lynn and Marcie have worked on the Youth Commission, they have moved from being mere acquaintances to becoming fast friends. But their rapidly developing friendship eroded just as quickly as it developed. Perhaps the problems started when Lynn had 50 pink flamingos positioned on Marcie's front lawn to recognize her 50th birthday. While Lynn thought this was funny, Marcie was embarrassed and took offense. In a kind of retaliation, Marcie placed buckets filled with dry ice and dishwashing liquid behind the shrubbery in front of Lynn's house. The combination produced a continuous wave of suds that overwhelmed Lynn's plants and lawn. And so it continued, with each person trying to upstage the other. Most recently, Marcie used a powerful plant killer to burn an obscenity into Lynn's front lawn. Since grass plants connect to each other by their roots, the effect of the herbicide spread, with the unintended consequence that the attack killed most of Lynn's lawn and part of her neighbor's. This outraged Lynn because her house was scheduled to be part of the Unity garden walk this year. Lynn fumed about this assault on her garden and told her neighbor that she was determined to get revenge against Marcie.

A Retaliatory Strike?

Marcie lets her prized Rhodesian ridgeback "Rascal" out into her fenced-in backyard at night before she and her family go to bed. Recently, when she called Rascal to come inside, she noticed what seemed like chocolate smeared on his muzzle. He was panting heavily, as if he had run for miles, and he went into a seizure. Rascal continued to convulse for about five minutes before he expired. The family was shocked and horrified. Marcie's sadness quickly turned to anger, as she suspected that Lynn was behind this attack. Marcie became further convinced when her neighbor reported that she found a large chocolate bar wrapper discarded in her yard. It was a type of dark chocolate, with a fairly high cocoa content. Furthermore, another neighbor reported seeing someone fitting Lynn's description moving around Marcie's yard.

The Plot Continues

On the night when Lynn won election to the City Council, she and members of her campaign celebrated at a local bar and restaurant. In an unguarded moment and feeling the exhilaration of the victory, Lynn drank too much and danced around the bar waving a 9-mm pistol that a police officer friend had confiscated from a gang member that evening. Swept up in a wave of enthusiasm and confidence, Lynn claimed that she would bring down all the gangs. She even pretended that she was shooting at the campaign poster of her political opponent, a former gang member. Marcie captured the moment on video by using her smartphone. Marcie remembered the video and recognized immediately that the sharing of this video online, with appropriately descriptive commentary, would certainly cause Lynn embarrassment, likely cause her to lose her position on the City Council, and possibly trigger criminal prosecution for possession of a handgun without a permit and for using the weapon irresponsibly in a public place. It seemed that Marcie had the power to inflict this damage on Lynn. But this would likely perpetuate the cycle of revenge in a way that Marcie has denounced as a member of the Township Youth Commission.

The Decision: What Should Marcie Do Now?

Should she post the inflammatory video in hopes of causing as much harm to Lynn as possible? Should she endure the loss humbly in hopes that the cycle of revenge and retaliation will stop? Should she patiently wait for law-enforcement authorities to investigate and prosecute, if necessary? Should she bide her time until she has a more significant opportunity to enact revenge in a way that would be comparable in magnitude to the killing of her beloved dog?

Forums for Discussion

In order to have a deep understanding of Marcie's situation and to evaluate her options, it will help to think about the problem from several perspectives. Here are the *stages* for discussion:

Stage 1. Small-Group Preparation

With two or three other students, think about the problem from the point of view of one of the person's listed below (under "Conflicting Advice"). Prepare the argument that this person would offer in a private conference among the group of persons meeting at Marcie's house. (You might want to read a little from the recommended resources to inform your position further.)

Stage 2. An Enacted Private Meeting

Participate in the meeting at Marcie's house. One person will have to initiate the conversation by summarizing the problem and suggesting a course of action. Subsequent speakers will connect their contributions to what previous speakers have said in order to help all participants follow the chain of the conversation.

Stage 3. Large Group Debriefing

After you have heard and evaluated the several perspectives and the advice to Marcie, talk among your classmates about what *you personally think* would be the best plan for Marcie to follow. (Again, you might want to read a little from the recommended resources to inform your position further.)

Conflicting Advice

Marcie knows that she has to be careful about how she proceeds. To help her to think thoroughly about her decision, Marcie seeks advice from the following people, whom she trusts. Friends, neighbors, and family members will meet at Marcie's house to consult about the problem.

Claire Ungewiss, Marcie's neighbor: It would be helpful if Claire could provide a conclusive, positive identification of Lynn giving chocolate to Rascal. She knows Lynn, and judges it was Lynn whom she saw in Marcie's yard, although it *was* dark and she did not witness anyone giving chocolate to the dog.

Brian Stout, a fellow member of the Youth Commission: Brian has been a confidant of Marcie's as she has enacted various pranks on Lynn. He has supported her actions all the way and encourages her now to be more aggressive. Considering the influence that Lynn has in the town, Brian doubts that law enforcement will do anything to punish her.

Peter Symons, a neighbor: Peter cautions that without definite proof against Lynn, it would be wrong to seek any revenge. He would like to see some proof, which he would expect Marcie to turn over to law enforcement and let them handle matters.

Stephanie, Marcie's daughter: Now a teenager, Stephanie remembers bringing Rascal home as a puppy. She has practically grown up with him, and sees him as a member of the family. Stephanie views the act as an assassination of a family member. She wants an aggressive response, without the involvement of law enforcement.

Emma Willard, Marcie's dearest friend: Emma cautions that there seems to be only circumstantial evidence to conclude that Lynn harmed Rascal. She cautions that even if Lynn did feed chocolate to the dog, surely it was only meant as a prank to cause diarrhea or some other less than life-threatening response. Emma suggests that Marcie take Lynn's intentions into account.

Lyle Trocaire, a member of the Youth Commission: Lyle remains resolved that mercy rather than revenge is the proper response to the harms that others cause us. He comes from a faith tradition that encourages him to love his enemy and not to retaliate when he is harmed. He judges it is the more noble action and the better example for the youth in the family and in the community for Marcie to forgive the terrible action and forget about it. Lyle judges that it would be hypocritical for Marcie to seek revenge against Lynn and then expect street-gang members to forgive their rivals who shoot at them.

Research about Revenge and Mercy

Many people in our contemporary world and throughout history have faced conflicts about enacting revenge or exercising mercy. The examples from other cases and the commentary from other thinkers can help you prepare for discussion. Your own research will provide you with examples, and the following few texts can support your efforts.

The Thinking behind Revenge

Pamela Gerloff. "The Psychology of Revenge: Why We Should Stop Celebrating Osama Bin Laden's Death." *Huffington Post,* May 2, 2011.

George Orwell. "Reflection on Gandhi." In *Shooting an Elephant, and Other Essays.* Penguin, 2003, pp. 347–357.

Unlawful and Dangerous Revenge

Erica Goode. "Victims Push Laws to End Online Revenge Posts." *New York Times,* September 23, 2013.

Perceived Value of Revenge

Bryan Robinson. "Why Revenge Is Bad and Good." ABC News, November 13, 2013.

Infamous Example of Vengeance

Hatfields and McCoys: See Wikipedia and related online sources to learn about one infamous feud.

A Cycle of Retaliation

John Buntin. "What Does It Take to Stop Crips and Bloods from Killing Each Other? *New York Times,* July 10, 2013.

Related Reading

The essential problem that Marcie faces—whether to seek revenge or extend mercy and forgiveness—is a problem that many characters in literature face. You and your classmates might want to consider your thinking about this contemporary problem when you judge the behavior of characters in other circumstances in one or more of the following works of literature:

- *Medea*
- *Antigone*
- *Hamlet*
- *Othello*
- *The Count of Monte Cristo*
- *Song of Solomon*
- *Native Son*
- "The Cask of Amontillado"

Written Response to the Case

Imagine that you are a friend and confidant to Marcie and she seeks your advice. She knows that you participated in the recent discussion in her home to seek a solution to her problems with Lynn and to help her decide what she should do. Write to her now to advise her about a course of action. Since she does not want to leave a digital trail about anything incriminating about her and you, Marcie has asked that you write her a conventional letter, which she can keep private, that will *review the situation, evaluate the many options,* and *recommend the best course of action.* It is appropriate for your letter to have the following features:

- A brief account of the recent events, recognition of the dilemma that Marcie faces, and a general recommendation about the course of action she should follow.
- A systematic review and evaluation of the recommendations from friends, neighbors, and family members, especially if they do not all agree with your position.
- An argument for the course of action that you recommend, citing evidence and the principles you apply to interpret the evidence.
- A conclusion to reiterate a position and to offer encouragement.

As you work on developing your letter, share it with another reader to get the reader's impressions of the letter's clarity, logic, and thoroughness. Your reader might have questions about the composition and suggestions for refinement. Use your best judgment in relying on these comments to revise and edit your work.

Process Notes for the Teacher

The series of discussions and the reading of the case narrative and related articles will give students much to say about Marcie's dilemma. When students deliberate together about how to respond to the problem, they will practice several important procedures: for example, summary, narrative, analysis, synthesis, and argument. All of this is the *preparation* for writing an elaborated composition. There is much that a teacher can do to facilitate the process of writing a response. Here are some possibilities:

- Model how to *plan a response,* through a formal outline, a numbered list, or a graphic representation.
- Model how to *introduce a discussion,* by writing in front of the students, "thinking out loud," and drawing on students' suggestions.
- Allow time for students to do *their own planning.*
- Allow students time to *draft* a response.
- Schedule opportunities for peers to *review* each other's work, and/or for the teacher to *confer* with individual students.
- Encourage the *use of feedback* to guide editing and revision for a "publishable" version of the written response.

Note: In schools that provide students with sufficient access to technology in order to support writing instruction, teachers should consider ways that students might shape their written response to the controversy in a way that is distinct for a digital platform. We refer the reader to the work of Kristen Turner and Troy Hicks (2016), who remind writers about considerations like the graphic design of a blog on a web page, with the writer's argument supported with links to various kinds of data, including images, films, and music.

Appendix G

Drawing on Knowledge about Drama

Reading a Shakespeare Play as Performance

A teacher's knowledge about literature will include knowledge about the historical, political, and cultural milieu in which the work was produced, and knowledge about the conventions of the specific genre that a teacher proposes for students to study. We recommend here an approach to teaching students how to read a Shakespeare play. While drawing on knowledge about the political backdrop of Shakespeare's world and the predispositions of his Elizabethan audience, a teacher can stage the opening scenes to slow down the reading and help students to envision movement in order to interpret that movement and to note patterns of imagery that invite the reader/audience to think critically about the implications of those patterns. In other words, we want readers new to Shakespeare to pay close attention not only to language, but also to movement and staging—to see how characters' nonverbal actions contribute directly to the meanings that one can derive from the work. The opening scenes from *Macbeth* and a selected scene from later in the play will serve to illustrate for staging, and we offer as a rule in reading Shakespeare that a slow reading and staging of the opening scenes will equip readers with procedures for enjoying the balance of the play and thinking about how he envisioned a performance.

To prepare for the "staging" of the opening scenes, a teacher would have to assign students to teams (e.g., the performers in scene i) and to individual parts. We suggest a three-stage sequence: (1) allow time for the team to practice reading their lines to accomplish an acceptable level of fluency and to get on their feet and practice saying their lines as a group of interacting players; (2) prompt the players to perform, using a space that will allow for the switching back and forth between scenes and their settings; (3) invite reflection on what the movements reveal. As a result of their performance experience, your students are likely to learn to do the following:

- Speak Shakespeare's early modern English fluently, making appropriate internal translations from the playwright's language to one's own.
- Comprehend rare words and unusual syntax during the activity of decoding an unfamiliar language variation.
- Translate the words on the page into imagined movements by the actors on stage—learn to move more easily "up and down the snakes and ladders of abstraction," going from the printed word and image to the voice and action of the actor/character to the larger thematic, mimetic, and aesthetic implications of what is being perceived by the audience.
- Note and understand allusions to texts, characters, and fictional situations from other literary sources, works written both before and after Shakespeare's time (i.e., recognize intertextuality).
- Collaborate with partners in producing a dramatic performance for everyone to enjoy.
- Contribute to in-class discussions to share perspectives, pose questions, and conjecture about subsequent actions and likely meanings.

In introducing *Macbeth*, a teacher would likely serve students well by concentrating close attention to the first four scenes of the play, moving between a desolate setting on a misty heath and a more populated scene on the edge of a recent battle. In an excellent book on Shakespeare's *Macbeth*, Gary Wills (1996) asks about the central problem of dramatizing the play: "If *Macbeth* is such a great tragedy, why do performances of it so often fail?" (p. 3). Wills suggests that some adaptations (e.g., Verdi's opera, or Kurosawa's *Throne of Blood*) have been more successful than others, and many performers and directors consider the work almost unplayable as a whole and unteachable. The great film director Orson Welles was convinced that the play fell into two distinct parts: "No Macbeth can play the first *and* second half. . . . I've never seen that problem successfully bridged. Certainly I didn't" (Welles & Bogdanovich, pp. 216–217, cited in Wills, 1996, p. 6, n. 11). Wills goes on to say more about the consequences of this sort of play structure, accusing many directors of

> front-loading [the play] . . . to sheer away any larger social context for the protagonists' struggling. . . . The result is a lopsided play, dead

in the most embarrassing places, toward the end, where the action should accelerate and interest be intensified. A front-loaded play is a back-crippled play. That is the real curse [of the Scottish play]. (p. 6)

The big question, then, for teachers, is how to make the whole play interesting to read for first-time readers. Although a staple of many high school English classes, *Macbeth* is not exactly high on most teenagers' preferred casual reading list, even for readers who otherwise love Shakespeare. Wills offers some historical background for the play, which can be helpful as students think about how they will perform scenes. We summarize here, but we caution against a teacher *lecturing* students on this bit of history; instead, a teacher might gloss selected passages as needed or ask students to read about this background on their own.

SOME BACKGROUND OF THE PLAY

What is important for first-time readers to understand is that witches are central to the plays of 1606 (i.e., *Macbeth*) and that they have a political role. Witchcraft was part of the ideology of the gunpowder treason of Catholics and was denounced by English Protestants as "diabolic." In their political view, Guy Fawkes's Gunpowder Plot's hatching took place at a Black Mass, where hell's aid was secured by sacrilegious oaths and rites. In the play, witches prompt Macbeth to regicide—the very sin toward which the devil guided the plotters through their oaths at a Black Mass.

We first see Macbeth enter directly from battle: bloody, dirty, and exhausted. In the Elizabethan worldview, battlefields were magnets for witches: the exploitation of dead bodies for occult purposes was called *necromancy*, prophecy by way of the dead. Hence, witchcraft was not just a matter of private concern . . . but also a factor in affairs of state. Most of the major conspiracies against King James I involved witchcraft; Macbeth conjures witches who are acting as subordinates to their superior, Hecate, who has a "court" of attendant spirits with her. In necromancy, the conjurer (Macbeth) gets binding powers to force answers from the devil—in return for selling his soul to Old Scratch via "the formal act of witchcraft involved in his participation at the necromantic rites" (Wills, 1996, p. 46). Security for Macbeth means upholding the bond, "enacted by a compact with the Devil" (Wills, 1996, pp. 35–48).

What this means to the reader and the performer of the play is to pay as great attention to the images conjured up during movements on stage as to the movements *per se*. To this end, we want to put the play "on its feet" in the three-stage sequence we note above. As we suggest in Chapter 5, even before acting the selected scenes from *Macbeth*, students will benefit from brief Spolin-like exercises to warm to the idea of acting and to gain some confidence in performing before their peers.

We focus on the first four scenes, with two sets of actors: (1) the witches with Banquo and Macbeth, and (2) Duncan and his many attendants and messengers. In Scenes III and IV, there is interplay between the two groups, as messengers seek Macbeth and as Banquo and Macbeth are reunited with their king. There are plenty of parts to go around, but a teacher will want to select judiciously the students who can read the extensive parts of Macbeth, Banquo, and Duncan. Initially, students should read their parts to become familiar with the language and to pay special attention to the movement suggested by the player or by the speech of other characters in the scene. This means that the students will need to read the whole scene and not just their individual parts, even those who don't have spoken lines, for they are all acting in the scenes. After the students have read their parts and have "rehearsed" a bit in their groups, it is time to enact the scenes, perhaps across two class meetings.

Entering into the performances of the first four scenes of the play, we pose two ongoing questions: Why do seemingly normal (and perhaps admirable) human beings do terrible things? How is it possible that matters can be both fair and foul? For the beginning reader of Shakespeare, we judge that these questions invite the consideration of the play as the "simultaneous expression of multiple points of view," as one of our university professors once observed. When we address these questions after the students have experienced their performance of the opening scenes, we expect that the learners will question some actions: Why does Macbeth start at hearing the witches' pronouncement of good fortune for him? Why does Macbeth seem wrapped in his own thoughts as Banquo addresses the witches? How do you account for Macbeth's strong reaction when he is greeted as Thane of Cawdor? What general precept does Duncan offer when he observes, "There's no art to find the mind's conception in the face" (Shakespeare, Act I, Scene IV, Lines 13–14)? What does Macbeth (and Shakespeare) reveal through his asides during Scenes II and IV? These questions invite speculation and not the recitation of prespecified answers. The performance of the opening scenes supports the inquiry into these questions, perhaps in a way that reading alone would not allow. As a result of the work with these opening scenes and the related discussion, the students can proceed, perhaps haltingly, through the subsequent scenes, noting the recurrence of the "fair is foul" image and questioning what motivates Macbeth's actions across the balance of the play. It is the language and the complex view of human behavior and the complicated interrogation of ideas that account in part for the enduring attraction to Shakespeare's plays.

After this initial work with performance, students can put other selected scenes on their feet. For example, later in the ongoing reading and discussing of *Macbeth*, the teacher might ask a duo to stand before the class and recite Lady Macbeth's famous soliloquy—only she says it not alone (for the purpose of this game and not being worried about plot contradictions), but with Macbeth himself reciting the speech in unison with her. As with the *Macbeth* example in Chapter 5, the pairs are to speak facing each other and, again, are to invent some possible ways that a married couple might share and reveal some common anxiety. Perhaps using as inspiration an old married couple with whom they are familiar (no names mentioned), the duos are to recite the lines in unison although moving and/or behaving differently.

Key questions the teacher may again offer the class rather cryptically: Why does Lady Macbeth move from being so aggressive to displaying so intense a guilt level? What does one make of these two scenes for Macbeth: his being so unsure of his purpose in Act II, Scene II, to his putting on and taking off his armor in Act V, Scene III, Lines 36–60, when only one short scene separates the couple's last two dramatic enactments?

Appendix H

Using Language Analysis
to "Open" a Novel

When novice teachers begin to work with an often-taught text like Orwell's *Animal Farm* (1946/1954), they soon learn that the text may be read on a variety of levels, ranging from simple animal stories to debates concerning post-war military power tensions. Along that continuum, the play with language in *Animal Farm* is one commonality all levels may share. Since the author of such famous essays as "Politics and the English Language," "Such, Such were the joys," and "Why I Write" was fascinated with language and its political uses, a close look at *Animal Farm* illustrates how students' playing with the novel's language is often a great way to get readers to engage with problem solving in fiction and so develop a better understanding of how imaginative writing works even in a simple allegory. This work with a literary text provides an opportunity to embed close work with language to recognize how choices in the use of language carry ethical as well as political implications, as language can be used to clarify or obfuscate, to stir others to positive action or to manipulate and exploit victims.

A body of commentary about Orwell and his work invites this question: Was Orwell really a "socialist," in the scary sense that the term reverberated for most Americans during the Cold War (1946–1989), or was he allied more with the devotees of muscular anti-communism? There is plentiful evidence for each political faction to claim him for its own, as each did. Appeals to empirical evidence get a bit more complicated since readers in the 21st century now know that, according to Orwell's biographer Gordon Bowker (2004), Mrs. Sonia Orwell, Orwell's widow, sold the rights for a film version of *Animal Farm* (in cartoon form) to one Howard Hunt, a CIA operative (later of Watergate infamy). Since she was "politically naïve" and her understanding of Orwell's artistic intentions may have been somewhat limited then (she and Orwell had been married only for a few weeks before he died), she unwittingly sold the film rights to a partisan producer and so lost any ability to insist on Orwell's exact language. As Bowker reminds us, once the rights were sold, Mrs. Orwell's "control of any resulting script and film would have been out of her hands" (2004, pp. 421–422):

> The takeover of film rights of Orwell's last two books [including *Nineteen Eighty-Four*] produced movies tailored to ideological ends. In the cartoon version of *Animal Farm* the banquet at which the pigs become indistinguishable from their human oppressors was changed. Orwell's pessimistic intention was thereby obscured and the message that the tyrannical Stalinist pigs are no different from the cruel capitalist farmers was lost. (2004, p. 422)

Hence, "empirical evidence" in literary study may itself remain subject to some debate, so perhaps the most helpful sources for answers come from the author's words themselves. For students who depend on the film interpretation of a work of literature, there remains the question of the film producer's and director's fidelity to the original *language* of the work, when much depends on the nuances in the language choices and shifts.

In judging the "real" partisan allegiance of a decidedly political writer like Orwell or judging implications of the work, we suggest paying close attention to the very beginning of the novel, what one might call "the opener," and watching for little details of language that often illustrate the writer's larger purposes. For complex works of literature, we advise that often it is worth an investment in instructional time to read slowly and aloud the opening page or two to model for students how a mature reader notices features and reflects on their purpose. In this case, the teacher can model what she notices about the shifts in the language of the narrator and the characters. For example, *Animal Farm* opens with the habitual bedtime routine of a farmer who, significantly, was "too drunk to remember to shut the popholes" (1946/1954, p. 1). Why he was drunk will be revealed shortly, but the focal point moves in the very next paragraph to the animals who were "a stirring and a fluttering all through the farm buildings." One could speculate already that Mr. Jones's drunken carelessness might have something to do with the restlessness among the animals. Thus far, Orwell uses his well-known "plain style" with simple language and sentences containing multiple short clauses. Then, in the third sentence of *Animal Farm*'s second paragraph, Orwell appears to violate his own dictum in "Politics and the English Language," published in the same year as the novella, where he reminds us in his listing of writing habits to "never use the passive voice where you can use the active" (Politics, 1954, p. 176). In the novella, the narrator says: "It had been agreed that they should all meet in the big barn as soon as Mr. Jones was safely out of the way" (p. 15).

A puzzled but informed reader might wonder why Orwell used the passive voice here in fiction when, in an essay published in the same year, he "ruled" against its use. One could look outside the text for more recent clarification, consulting a reliable resource like Williams's *Style: Lessons in Clarity and Grace*. In it, one could read Williams's suggestion in Chapter 4 that "the passive is often the better choice" (2010, p. 61). Why? Speaking of the typically missing agency in passive constructions, Williams argues that, at times, we "don't say who does an action, because we don't know or readers won't care" (p. 61). This may not likely be a good reason at the opening of *Animal Farm* because we've just been introduced to the characters and might well care about who they are and their motives. Williams's second reason emphasizes smooth movement from sentence to sentence, but again, this analysis may not be very helpful because Orwell's plain style already feels smooth and readable. However, Williams's third reason does give us pause: "Would the active or passive give readers a more consistent and appropriate point of view?" (p. 62). And here Williams's question helps us understand Orwell's fictional intentions better.

Given the fabliau nature of this work, three important questions apply: By which convention would an author have animals speak any humanlike language? Which language *would* the several animals speak? Would the goats, pigs, horses, and cows all talk in the same dialect, or would Orwell just prefer to keep this mimetic detail general and vague? Interestingly, the reader quickly learns that both the narrative voice and all the animals speak a variation of British English; hence, the passive voice, "It had agreed that they should meet," bypasses these problems in an entirely plausible way, and the first beast-fable difficulty has been solved. Right? Well, the problem has generated further questions, as is often the case in ill-formed problems set like literary criticism.

What if there are language and dialect differences among the animals, and how are they used for good fictional purposes? How would Orwell play with language to create what has been called the greatest political satire since Swift's *Gulliver's Travels*? While there are all sorts of sentences in the novella that make use of "it" constructions and passive voice, the reader notices rather quickly that as soon as the pigs assert control over the other animals, the passive voice constructions seem always to relate to power differences among the members of Animal Farm. Look, for example, at the strong, active-voice, compound sentence that ends Chapter 1, the chapter ending with old Major's powerful exhortation, followed by their hopeful singing of "Beasts of England": "The birds jumped on to their perches, the animals settled down in the straw, and the whole farm was asleep in a moment" (p. 24).

In the second chapter, after the Rebellion, the animals rejoice in their newfound freedom, and one of the first things they do is milk the long-suffering cows. As they wonder what to do with this "frothing creamy milk," Napoleon cries, "Never mind the milk, comrades," and "placing himself in front of the buckets," he shouts, "Forward comrades! The hay is waiting" and they all "trooped down to the hayfield to begin the harvest." However, "when they came back in the evening, it was noticed that the milk had disappeared" (p. 34). Contrast the last sentence in Chapter 1, with that in Chapter 2, and Napoleon's rather disingenuous "Among us animals let there be perfect unity, perfect comradeship in the struggle" (p. 21). The sentence ending Chapter 2 exemplifies the initial break in the democratic tradition espoused by old Major, as Napoleon's exhortations divide intention from truth.

At the end of Chapter 3, the "mystery of where the milk went to was soon cleared up." It was "mixed every day into the pig's mash," along with the windfall apples. When questioned about how only they got milk and apples, the pig Squealer, "skipping from side to side," was "sent to make the necessary explanations to the others." He claimed that the food was brain food, the pigs were brainworkers, and the "whole management and organization of this farm depend on us [pigs]." If they failed their duty, "Jones would come back." All the animals were completely certain that they did not want Jones back, so in the last sentence of Chapter 3, "it was agreed without further argument that the milk and the windfall apples . . . should be reserved for the pigs alone" (pp. 42–43). Hence, the uses of passive voice sentences and "it" constructions as the novella progresses all illustrate Orwell's language is used in evolutionary ways: first for simple problem solving (animal speech), and second, for contrast between the strong declaratives employed when the animals all felt hope for their futures versus the agentless passive sentences constructed by the pig-fascists that represented a faux populism in order to gain power.

Later in *Animal Farm*, the passive-voiced sentences regularly become the pigs' necessary aids in consolidating power. At the end of Chapter 7, following Napoleon's murderous purge trials and executions, the animals all feel that "it was not for this" sort of terror that they had "built the windmill and faced the bullets of Jones's gun" (p. 86). Huddling together for emotional warmth, they begin singing "Beasts of England," but slowly and mournfully. At that moment, Squealer shows up, "attended by two dogs," perhaps from Napoleon's Praetorian guard, and then animals are told "it was forbidden to sing" the old revolutionary anthem. Their protests are in vain since the revolution is "now completed [because the] execution of the traitors . . . was [its] final act." "So, beasts of England was heard no more" (p. 86).

This brief look at Orwell's language when beginning classroom work with *Animal Farm* serves as an example of how many aspects of teaching English intersect. The close look at language informs the reading of the text, allowing for the construction of subtle and not-so-subtle symbolic meanings and the recognition of elements of writing style and syntax that in turn can help influence how students write their own compositions.

References

Applebee, A. N. (1981). *Writing in the secondary schools.* Urbana, IL: National Council of Teachers of English.

Applebee, A. N. (1986). Problems in process approaches: Toward a reconceptualization of process instruction. In A. R. Petrosky & D. Bartholomae (Eds.), *The teaching of writing: 85th yearbook of the National Society for the Study of Education* (pp. 95–113). Chicago: University of Chicago Press.

Applebee, A. N. (1993). *Literature in the secondary schools.* Urbana, IL: National Council of Teachers of English.

Applebee, A. N. (1996). *Curriculum as conversation: Transforming traditions of teaching and learning.* Chicago: University of Chicago Press.

Applebee, A. N., & Langer, J. A. (2013). *Writing instruction that works: Proven methods for middle and high school classrooms.* New York: Teachers College Press.

Applebee, A. N., Langer, J. A., Nystrand, M., & Gamoran, A. (2003). Discussion-based approaches to developing understanding: Classroom instruction and student performance in middle and high school English. *American Educational Research Journal, 40*(3), 685–730.

Appleman, D. (2014). *Critical encounters in secondary English: Teaching literary theory to adolescents* (3rd ed.). New York: Teachers College Press.

Arnold, M. (2008). *Culture and anarchy: An essay on political and social criticism.* Fairford, UK: Echo Library. (Original work published 1869)

Atwell, N. (1998). *In the middle: New understandings about writing, reading, and learning.* Portsmouth, NH: Heinemann. (Original work published 1987)

Atwell, N. (2007). *The reading zone: How to help kids become skilled, passionate, habitual, critical readers.* New York: Scholastic.

Atwell, N. (2014). *In the middle: A lifetime of learning about writing, reading, and adolescents.* Portsmouth, NH: Heinemann.

Aygen, G. (2014). *English grammar: A descriptive linguistic approach.* Dubuque, IA: Kendall Hunt.

Bailin, A., & Grafstein, A. (2016). *Readability: Text and context.* London: Palgrave Macmillan.

Bakhtin, M. (1986). *Speech genres and other late essays.* Austin: University of Texas Press.

Beers, K. (2002). *When kids can't read: What teachers can do: A guide for teachers, 6–12.* Portsmouth, NH: Heinemann.

Beers, K., & Probst, R. E. (2013). *Notice and note: Strategies for close reading.* Portsmouth, NH: Heinemann.

Bieler, D., & Burns, L. D. (2017). The critical centrality of social justice in English teacher education. In H. Hallman (Ed.), *Innovations in English language arts teacher education* (pp. 147–163). Bingley, UK: Emerald.

Bitzer. L. F. (1968). The rhetorical situation. *Philosophy and Rhetoric, 1*(1), 1–14.

Blum, L. (2012). Five things high school students should know about race. *Harvard Educational Letter, 28*(6), 1–2.

Booth, S. (2016). On the aesthetic significance of non-signifying signification in *Romeo and Juliet.* In *Close reading without readings: Essays on Shakespeare and others* (pp. 117–141). Madison, NJ: Fairleigh Dickinson University Press.

Bowker, G. (2004). *George Orwell.* London: Abacus Press.

Bransford, J., & Johnson, M. (1972). Contextual prerequisites for understanding: Some investigations of comprehension and recall. *Journal of Verbal Learning and Verbal Behavior, 11*(6), 717–726.

Brecht, B. (1977). *Brecht on theatre: The development of an aesthetic* (13th ed.) (Ed. & Trans., J. Willett). New York: Hill & Wang.

Breuch, L. M. K. (2002a). Post-process 'pedagogy': A philosophical exercise. *Journal of Advanced Composition, 22*(1), 119–150.

Breuch, L. M. K. (2002b). Thinking critically about technological literacy: Developing a framework to guide computer pedagogy in technical communication. *Technical Communication Quarterly 11*(3), 267–288.

Britton, J. (1983). Writing and the story of the world. In B. M. Kroll & C. G. Wells (Eds.), *Explorations in the development of writing: Theory, research, and practice* (pp. 3–30). New York: Wiley.

Britton, J., Burgess, A., Martin, N., McLeod A., & Rosen, R. (1975). *The development of writing abilities, 11–18.* London: Macmillan Education for the Schools Council.

Brookhart, S. M. (2013). Assessing creativity. *Educational Leadership, 70*(5), 28–34.

Brottman, M. (2011, October 23). Tackling texts alone. *Chronicle of Higher Education.* Retrieved from *www.academia.edu/8230426/_tackling_texts_alone_*

Burian, P. (1997). Myth into muthos: The shaping of tragic plot. In P. E. Easterling (Ed.), *Cambridge companion to Greek tragedy* (pp. 178–208). Cambridge, UK: Cambridge University Press.

Burke, J. (2010). *What's the big idea?: Question-driven units to motivate reading, writing, and thinking.* Portsmouth, NH: Heinemann.

Burke, J. (2012). *The English teacher's companion, fourth edition: A completely new guide to classroom, curriculum, and the profession*. Portsmouth, NH: Heinemann.

Calkins, L. M. (1986). *The art of teaching writing*. Portsmouth, NH: Heinemann.

Calkins, L. M., & Graves, D. H. (1980). Research update: Children learn the writer's craft. *Language Arts, 57*(2), 207–213.

Carr, N. (2010). *The shallows: What the internet is doing to our brains*. New York: Norton.

Chandler, R. (1950). *The Big Sleep*. New York: Knopf. (Original work published 1939)

Christenbury, L. (2006). *Making the journey: Being and becoming a teacher of English language arts* (3rd ed.). Portsmouth, NH: Heinemann.

Christenbury, L., & Lindblom, K. (2016). *Making the journey (3rd ed.): Being and becoming a teacher of English language arts*. Portsmouth, NH: Heinemann.

Clopper, C. G., & Bradlow. A. R. (2008). Perception of dialect variation in noise: Intelligibility and classification. *Language and Speech, 51*(3), 175–198.

Clopper, C. G., & Pisoni, D. B. (2004). Some acoustic cues for the perceptual categorization of American English regional dialects. *Journal of Phonology, 32*(1), 111–140.

Colby, S. A., & Lyon, A. F. (2004). Heightening awareness about the importance of using multicultural literature. *Multicultural Education, 11*(3), 24–28.

Coplan, A. (2004). Empathetic engagement with narrative fictions. *Journal of Aesthetic and Arts Criticism, 62*(2), 141–152.

Court, F. (1992). *Institutionalizing English literature: The culture and politics of literary study, 1750–1900*. Stanford, CA: Stanford University Press.

Craig, H. K. (2015). African-American English and its link to reading achievement. In A. Pollatsek & R. Treiman (Eds.), *Oxford handbook of reading* (pp. 431–446). New York: Oxford University Press.

Csikszentmihalyi, M. (1996). *Creativity: Flow and the psychology of discovery and invention*. New York: HarperCollins.

Culham, R. (2003). *6 + 1 traits of writing: The complete guide, grades 3 & up: Everything you need to teach and assess student writing with this powerful model*. New York: Scholastic.

Culham, R. (2010). *Traits of writing: The complete guide for middle school*. New York: Scholastic.

Daniels, H. (2002). *Literature circles: Voice and choice in book clubs and reading groups*. Portland, ME: Stenhouse.

Daniels, H., & Bizar, M. (1998). *Methods that matter: Six structures for best practice classrooms*. York, ME: Stenhouse.

Daniels, H., & Zemelman, S. (1988). *A community of writers: Teaching writing in the junior and senior high school*. Portsmouth, NH: Heinemann.

Danielson, C. (2007). *Enhancing professional practice: A framework for teaching* (2nd ed.). Alexandria, VA: Association for Supervision and Curriculum Development.

Davis, P. (2013). *Reading and the reader*. New York: Oxford University Press.

Dean, D. (2008a). *Bringing grammar to life*. Urbana, IL: National Council of Teachers of English.

Dean, D. (2008b). *Genre theory: Teaching, writing, and being.* Newark, DE: International Reading Association.

Dean, D. (2010). *What works in writing instruction: Research and practices.* Urbana, IL: National Council of Teachers of English.

DeMott, R. (1989). *Working days: The journals of The Grapes of Wrath.* New York: Viking.

DeStigter, T. (2015). On the ascendance of argument: A critique of the assumptions of academe's dominant form. *Research in the Teaching of English, 50*(1), 11–34.

Devereaux, M. (2015) *Teaching about dialect variations in secondary English classrooms.* New York: Routledge.

Diederich, P. B. (1974). *Measuring growth in English.* Urbana, IL: National Council of Teachers of English.

Downing, D., Harkin, P., & Sosnoski, J. (1994). Configurations of lore: The changing relations of theory, research, and pedagogy. In D. Downing (Ed.), *Changing classroom practices* (pp. 3–34). Urbana, IL: National Council of Teachers of English).

Duhigg, C. (2016, February 25). What Google learned from its quest to build the perfect team. *New York Times Magazine.* Retrieved from *www.nytimes.com/2016/02/28/magazine/what-google-learned-from-its-quest-to-build-the-perfect-team.html*

Elbow, P. (2007). Reconsiderations: Voice in writing again: Embracing contraries. *College English, 70*(2), 168–188.

Elbow, P. (2012). *Vernacular eloquence: What speech can bring to writing.* New York: Oxford University Press.

Eliot, G. (2007). *Silas Marner.* New York: Signet Classics. (Original work published 1862)

Emig, J. (1971). *The composing processes of twelfth graders* (NCTE Research Report No. 13). Urbana, IL: National Council of Teachers of English.

Engage/NY: Differences between Horatian and Juvenalian satire. Understand tone, ironic or straight. Web 2014. Retrieved from *www.engageny.org/resource/grade-12-ela-distinguishing-between-horatian-and-juvenalian-satire-rl11-126-sl11-124*

Fish, S. (2011). *How to write a sentence, and how to read one.* New York: HarperCollins.

Fisher, D., Frey, N., & Lapp, D. (2012). Building and activating students' background knowledge: It's what they already know that counts. *Middle School Journal, 43*(3), 22–31.

Flower, L., & Hayes, J. R. (1981). A cognitive process theory of writing. *College Composition and Communication, 32*(4), 365–387.

Follett, W. (1998). *Modern American usage: A guide* (E. Wensberg, rev.). New York: Hill & Wang. (Original work published 1966)

Foster, T. C. (2003). *How to read literature like a professor.* New York: Quill.

Foucault, M. (1972). *The archaeology of knowledge.* New York: Pantheon.

Fowler, H. W. (2015). *Fowler's dictionary of American usage* (4th ed., J. Butterfield, Ed.). New York: Oxford University Press. (Original work published 1926)

Francis, E. M. (2016). *Now that's a good question!: How to promote cognitive rigor through classroom questioning.* Alexandria, VA: Association for Supervision and Curriculum Development.

Freeman, Y., Freeman, D., & Mercuri, S. (2002). *Closing the achievement gap: How to reach limited-formal-schooling and long-term English learners.* Portsmouth, NH: Heinemann.

Freeman, Y., Freeman, D., & Mercuri, S. (2003). Helping middle and high school age English language learners achieve academic success. *NABE Journal of Research and Practice, 1*(1), 110–122.

Frye, N. (2000). *Anatomy of criticism: Four bibliographic essays.* Princeton, NJ: Princeton University Press. (Original work published 1957)

Gallagher, K. (2004). *Deeper reading: Comprehending challenging texts, 4–12.* Portland, ME: Stenhouse.

Gallagher, K. (2009). *Readicide: How schools are killing reading and what you can do about it.* Portland, ME: Stenhouse.

Gallagher, K. (2011). *Write like this: Teaching real-world writing through modeling and mentor texts.* Portland, ME: Stenhouse.

Gallagher, K. (2014). Making the most of mentor texts. *Educational Leadership, 71*(7), 28–33.

Gallagher, K. (2015). *In the best interest of students: Staying true to what works in the ELA classroom.* Portland, ME: Stenhouse.

Gardner, J. (1991). *The art of fiction: Notes on craft for young writers.* New York: Vintage Press.

Gee, J. P. (2001). Literacy, discourse, and linguistics: Introduction, and what is literacy? In E. Cushman, E. R. Kintgen, B. M. Knoll, & M. Rose (Eds.), *Literacy: A critical sourcebook* (pp. 525–544). New York: Bedford.

Giraldi, W. (2015, July 15). Just how good is *To Kill a Mockingbird? The New Republic.* Retrieved from *https://newrepublic.com/article/122306/just-how-good-kill-mockingbird*

Gladwell, M. (2009, August 10). The courthouse ring: Atticus Finch and the limits of Southern liberalism. *New Yorker,* pp. 26–32.

Goodlad, J. I. (2004). *A place called school* (2nd ed.). New York: McGraw-Hill.

Goodman, K., & Goodman, Y. M. (1979). Learning to read is natural. In L. B. Resnick & P. A. Weaver (Eds.), *Theory and practice of early reading* (pp. 137–155). Hillsdale, NJ: Erlbaum.

Gould, S. J. (1981). Evolution as fact and theory. *Discover, 2,* 34–37.

Graff, G. (1989). *Professing literature: An institutional history.* Chicago: University of Chicago Press.

Graff, G. (1992). *Beyond the culture wars: How teaching the conflicts can revitalize American education.* New York: Norton.

Graff, G. (2003). *Clueless in academe: How schooling obscures the life of the mind.* New Haven, CT: Yale University Press.

Graff, G. (2008). "How 'bout that Wordsworth!" *MLA Newsletter, 40*(4), 3–4.

Graff, G. (2009). The unbearable pointlessness of literature writing assignments. *The Common Review, 8*(2), 6–12.

Graff, G., Birkenstein, C., & Durst, D. (2009). *They say, I say, with readings.* New York: Norton.

Graham, S., & Perin, D. (2007a). What we know, what we still need to know: Teaching adolescents to write. *Scientific Studies of Reading, 1532-799X, 11*(4), 313–335.

Graham, S., & Perin, D. (2007b). *Writing Next: Effective strategies to improve writing of adolescents in middle and high schools.* New York: Carnegie Corporation.

Graves, D. H. (1980). Research update: A new look at writing research. *Language Arts, 57*(8), 913–919.

Graves, D. H. (1983). *Writing: Teachers and children at work.* Portsmouth, NH: Heinemann.

Green, E. (2014). *Building a better teacher: How teaching works.* New York: Norton.

Grossman, P. L. (1989). A study in contrast: Sources of pedagogical content knowledge for secondary English. *Journal of Teacher Education, 30*(5), 24–31.

Grossman, P. L., & Shulman, L. S. (1994). Knowing, believing, and the teaching of English. In T. Shanahan (Ed.), *Teachers thinking, teachers knowing: Reflections on literacy and language education* (pp. 3–22). Urbana, IL: National Council of Teachers of English.

Grossman, P. L., Smagorinsky, P., & Valencia, S. (1999). Appropriating tools for teaching English: A theoretical framework for research on learning to teach. *American Journal of Education, 108,* 1–29.

Grovum, J. (2014, August 8). The English-only debate heats up again. *Governing: The states and localities.* Retrieved from *www.governing.com/news/headlines/the-english-only-debate-heats-up-again.html*

Guillory, J. (1993). *Cultural capital: The problem of literary canon formation.* Chicago: University of Chicago Press.

Gustav Freytag. *Freytag's pyramid.* Retrieved from *www.britannica.com/biography/gustav-freytag*

Harris, V. J., & Willis, A. I. (2003). Multiculturalism, literature, and curriculum issues. In J. Flood, D. Lapp, J. R. Squire, & J. M. Jensen (Eds.), *The handbook of research on teaching the language arts* (2nd ed., pp. 825–834). Mahwah, NJ: Erlbaum.

Hattie, J. (2012). *Visible learning: A synthesis of over 800 meta-analyses relating to achievement.* New York: Routledge.

Hattie, J. (2012). *Visible learning for teachers: Maximizing impact on learning.* New York: Routledge.

Hayles, N. K. (2012). *How we think: Digital media and contemporary technogenesis.* Chicago: University of Chicago Press.

Hayles, N. K. (2013). Combining close and distant reading: Jonathan Safran Poer's *Tree of Codes* and the aesthetic of bookishness. *PMLA, 128*(1), 226–231.

Heller, S. (2015). Teaching writing, rather than writings. *English Journal, 104*(5), 12–14.

Hicks, T. (2013). *Crafting digital writing: Composing texts across media and genres.* Portsmouth, NH: Heinemann.

Hillocks, G., Jr. (1984). What works in teaching composition: A meta-analysis of experimental treatment studies. *American Journal of Education, 93*(1), 133–170.

Hillocks, G., Jr. (1986). *Research on written composition: New directions for teaching.* Urbana, IL: National Conference on Research in English.

Hillocks, G., Jr. (1995). *Teaching writing as reflective practice.* New York: Teachers College Press.

Hillocks, G., Jr. (2002). *The testing trap: How state writing assessments control learning.* New York: Teachers College Press.

Hillocks, G., Jr. (2003). How state assessments lead to vacuous thinking and writing. *Journal of Writing Assessment, 1*(1), 5–21.

Hillocks, G., Jr. (2005). The focus on form vs. content in teaching writing. *Research in the Teaching of English, 40*(2), 238–248.

Hillocks, G., Jr. (2006). *Narrative writing: Learning a new model for teaching.* Portsmouth, NH: Heinemann.

Hillocks, G., Jr. (2009). Some practices and approaches are clearly better than others and we had better not ignore the differences. *English Journal, 98*(6), 23–29.

Hillocks, G., Jr. (2011). *Teaching argument writing, grades 6–12: Supporting claims with relevant evidence and clear reasoning.* Portsmouth, NH: Heinemann.

Hillocks, G., Jr. (2016). The territory of literature. *English Education, 48*(2), 109–126.

Hillocks, G., Jr., McCabe, B., & McCampbell, J. (1971). *The dynamics of English instruction, grades 7–12.* New York: Random House.

Hirsch, E. D. (1988). *Cultural literacy: What every American needs to know.* New York: Vintage Books.

Hogan, P. C. (2011). Science, literature, and cultural colonialism. *Scientific Study of Literature, 1*(1), 165–172.

Hunt, T. J., & Hunt, B. (2005). Learning by teaching multicultural literature. *English Journal, 94*(3), 76–81.

Huttner-Kores, A. (2015, August 21). The hidden bias of science's universal language. *The Atlantic.* Retrieved from *www.theatlantic.com/science/archive/2015/08/english-universal-language-science-research/400919*

Johannessen, L., Kahn, E., & Walter. C. C. (1982). *Designing and sequencing pre-writing activities.* Urbana, IL: National Council of Teachers of English.

Johannessen, L. R., Kahn, E., & Walter, C. C. (2009). *Writing about literature* (2nd ed., rev. and updated). Urbana, IL: National Council of Teachers of English.

Johnson, T. S., Thompson, L., Smagorinsky, P., & Fry, P. G. (2003). Learning to teach the five-paragraph theme. *Research in the Teaching of English, 38*(2), 136–176.

Joos, M. (1967). *The five clocks: A linguistic excursion into the five styles of English usage.* New York: Harcourt.

Juzwik, M. M., Borsheim-Black, C., Caughlan, S., & Heintz, A. (2013). *Inspiring dialogue: Talking to learn in the English classroom.* New York: Teachers College Press.

Kermode, F. (2013). *An appetite for poetry.* New York: Bloomsbury.

King, S. (2010). *On writing: A memoir of the craft.* New York: Scribner.

Knapp, J. V. (1976). Contract/conference evaluations of freshman composition. *College English, 37,*(7), 647–653.

Knapp, J. V. (1996). Critical reasoning in the interactive classroom: Experiential exercises for teaching George Orwell's *Animal Farm. College Literature, 23*(2), 143–156.

Knapp, J. V. (2000). 'Wandering between two worlds': The MLA and English department follies. *Style, 34*(4), 635–669.

Koestler, A. (1941/2006). *Darkness at noon.* New York: Scribner.

Kohn, A. (2006). Trouble with rubrics. *English Journal, 95*(4), 12–15.

Kohn, A. (2011). *Feel-bad education.* Boston: Beacon Press.

Krashen, S. (2011). *Free voluntary reading.* Santa Barbara, CA: ABC-Clio.

Kynard, C. (2013). *Vernacular insurrections: Race, black protest, and the new century in composition-literacies studies.* Albany: State University of New York Press.

Labov, W. (2007). Transmission and diffusion. *Language, 83,* 344–387.

Langer, J. A. (2001). Beating the odds: Teaching middle and high school students to read and write well. *American Educational Research Journal, 38*(4), 837–880.

Langer, J. A. (2004). *Getting to excellent: How to create better schools.* New York: Teachers College Press.

Langer, J. A., Stotsky, S., Hayes, J., Purves, A. C., Hillocks, G., Jr. (1988). Research on written composition: A response to Hillocks' report. *Research in the Teaching of English, 22*(1), 89–116.

Leach, G., & Short, M. (2007). Style in fiction: New directions for research. *Style, 41*(2), 115–116.

Lee, C. D. (2007). *Culture, literacy, and learning: Taking bloom in the midst of the whirlwind.* New York: Teachers College Press.

Lee, H. (1962). *To kill a mockingbird.* New York: Popular Library.

Liu, H., Sokhey, A. E., Kennedy, J. B., & Miller, A. (2014). Immigrant threat and national salience: Understanding the "English official" movement in the United States. *Research and Politics.* Retrieved from *www.rap.sage-pub.com/content/1/1/2053168014531926*

Lowenthal, D. (1985). *The past is a foreign country.* Cambridge, UK: Cambridge University Press.

Lucas, S. E. (2007). *The art of public speaking* (9th ed., annotated instructor's ed.). New York: McGraw-Hill.

Luka, L. R. (1983). *The conceptualization of instruction by nine high-school English teachers.* Unpublished doctoral dissertation, University of Chicago, Chicago, IL.

Mack, A. N. (2011). Delivering yourself: Expressing meaning in public presentations. In K. Stimpson, A. Battaglia, A. Young, & J. Daly (Eds.), *Professional communication skills* (pp. 313–329). New York: Pearson.

Macrorie, K. (1996). *Uptaught.* Portsmouth, NH: Heinemann. (Original work published 1970)

Macrorie, K. (1986). *Writing to be read.* Portsmouth, NH: Heinemann.

Mahany, B. (1995, June 25). Mrs. Paley's lessons: The only kindergarten teacher to receive a Macarthur Grant has a message for you from her pupils. *Chicago Tribune Magazine*.

McCann, T. M. (1991). If you want my advice. *Classroom Notes Plus*. Urbana, IL: National Council of Teachers of English.

McCann, T. M. (2014). *Transforming talk into text: Argument writing, inquiry, and discussion, grades 6–12*. New York: Teachers College Press.

McCann, T. M., D'Angelo, R., Galas, N., & Greska, M. (2015). *Literacy and history in action: Immersive approaches to disciplinary thinking grades 5–12*. New York: Teachers College Press.

McCann, T. M., & Flanagan, J. M. (2002). A "Tempest" project: Shakespeare and critical conflicts. *English Journal, 92*(1), 29–35.

McCann, T. M., Johannessen, L. R., Kahn, E. A., & Flanagan, J. M. (2006). *Talking in class: Using discussion to enhance teaching and learning*. Urbana, IL: National Council of Teachers of English.

McCann, T. M., Kahn, E. A., & Walter, C. W. (2018). *Discussion pathways to literacy learning*. Urbana, IL: National Council of Teachers of English.

Mencken, H. L. (1988). *Supplement one: The American language* (14th ed.). New York: Knopf.

Milgram, S. (1973). The perils of obedience. *Harper's, 247*,(1483), 62–77.

Miller, B. J. (2001). *Head first acting: A commonsense technique for young actors*. Hanover, NH: Smith and Kraus.

Miller, S., Williamson, P., George, M., King, J., Charest, B., Bieler, B., et al. (2015). Applying the CEE position statement beliefs about social justice in English education to classroom praxis. *English Education, 44*(1), 63–82.

Moffett, J. (1983). *Teaching the universe of discourse*. New York: Houghton Mifflin.

Moje, E. B. (2015). Doing and teaching disciplinary literacy with adolescent learners: A social and cultural enterprise. *Harvard Educational Review, 85*(2), 254–278.

Moss, S. P. (1967). *Composition by logic*. Belmont, CA: Wadsworth.

Murray, D. (2003a). Teaching writing as a process not product. In V. Villanueva (Ed.), *Cross-talk in comp theory* (2nd ed.). Urbana, IL: National Council of Teachers of English.

Murray, D. (2003b). *A writer teaches writing* (rev. 2nd ed.). Boston: Thomson Heinle. (Original work published 1972)

National Council of Teachers of English. (2012). *Standards for initial preparation of teachers of secondary English language arts*. Urbana, IL: Author.

Nell, V. (1988). *Lost in a book: The psychology of reading for pleasure*. New Haven, CT: Yale University Press.

Noguchi, R. R. (1991). *Grammar and the teaching of writing*. Urbana, IL: National Council of Teachers of English.

Nystrand, M. (1997). *Opening dialogue: Understanding the dynamics of language and learning in the English classroom*. New York: Teachers College Press.

Olson, G. A. (1999). Toward a post-process composition: Abandoning the rhetoric of assertion. In T. Kent (Ed.), *Post-process theory: Beyond the writing process paradigm* (pp. 7–15). Carbondale: Southern Illinois University Press.

Orwell, G. (1946/1954). *Animal Farm* (Intro., C. M. Woodhouse). New York: Signet Classic.

Orwell, G. (1954). Politics and the English language. In *A collection of essays by George Orwell* (pp. 156–170). Garden City, NY: Anchor. (Original work published 1946)

Padron, Y. N., Waxman, H. C., & Rivera, H. H. (2003, Spring). Educating Hispanic students: Obstacles and avenues to improved academic achievement. *ERS Spectrum*, pp. 27–39.

Phelan, J. (1989). *Reading people, reading plots*. Chicago: University of Chicago Press.

Pindyck, M. (2015). Provocateur pieces: White abjections: Language and feeling in the urban English classroom. *English Education, 48*(1), 72–81.

Plato. (1973). The symposium. In *The Republic and other works* (pp. 319–365). New York: Anchor.

Prosser, E. (1971). *Hamlet and revenge* (2nd ed.). Palo Alto, CA: Stanford University Press.

Rabinowitz, P. (1998). *Before reading: Narrative conventions and the politics of interpretation*. Columbus: Ohio State University Press. (Original work published 1987)

Rabinowitz, P., & Bancroft, C. (2014). Euclid at the core: Recentering literary education. *Style, 48*(1), 1–34, 94–111.

Rabinowitz, P., & Smith, M. W. (1997). *Authorizing readers: Resistance and respect in the teaching of literature*. New York: Teachers College Press.

Reed, H. (1942, August 8). Naming of Parts. *New Statesman and Nation, 24*(598), 92.

Richardson, B. (2016). Unnatural narrative theory. *Style, 50*(4), 385–405.

Richardson, W. (2013). *Blogs, wikis, podcasts, and other powerful web tools for classrooms* (3rd ed.). Thousand Oaks, CA: Corwin Press.

Rogoff, B. (1990). *Apprenticeship in thinking: Cognitive development in social context*. New York: Oxford University Press.

Romano, T. (2000). *Blending genre, altering style: Writing multigenre papers*. Portsmouth, NH: Boynton/Cook.

Romano, T. (2007). Teaching writing from the inside. In K. Beers, R. E. Probst, & L. Rief (Eds.), *Adolescent literacy: Turning promise into practice* (pp. 167–178). Portsmouth, NH: Heinemann.

Rousseau, J. (1764/1979). *Emile, or on education* (Intro., trans., and notes by A. Bloom). New York: Basic Books.

Rowling, J. K. (1997). *Harry Poter and the sorcerer's stone*. New York: Scholastic.

Russell, D. (1999). Activity theory and process approaches: Writing (power) in school and society. In T. Kent (Ed.), *Post-process theory: Beyond the writing process paradigm* (pp. 80–95). Carbondale: Southern Illinois University Press.

Sager, C. (1973). *Improving the quality of written composition through pupil use of rating scale.* Paper presented at the annual meeting of the National Council of Teachers of English.

Santirocco, M. S. (2016). Introduction: Reassessing Greece and Rome. *Dædalus, 145*(2), 5–19.

Schleppegrell, M. J. (2007). The meaning in grammar. *Research in the Teaching of English, 42*(1), 120–128.

Scholes, R. (1999). *The rise and fall of English.* New Haven, CT: Yale University Press.

Scholes, R. (2001). *The crafty reader.* New Haven, CT: Yale University Press.

Schultz, K. (2009). *Rethinking classroom participation: Listening to silent voices.* New York: Teachers College Press.

Scott, A. O. (2016). *Better living through criticism: How to think about art, pleasure, beauty, and truth.* New York: Penguin Press.

Shakespeare, W. (2003). *Macbeth.* New York: Simon & Schuster.

Shanahan, T. (2013). Letting the text take center stage: How the Common Core State Standards will transform English language arts instruction. *American Educator, 37*(3), 4–11, 43.

Shaughnessy, M. (1979). *Errors and expectations: A guide for the teacher of basic writing.* New York: Oxford University Press.

Shaw, G. B. (1994). *Pygmalion.* New York: Dover. (Original work published 1916)

Shesgreen, S. (2009). Canonizing the canonizer: A short history of *The Norton Anthology of English Literature. Critical Inquiry, 35*(2), 293–318.

Shklovsky, V. (1965). Art as technique. In *Russian formalist criticism: Four essays* (L. T. Lemon & M. J. Reis, Trans.) (pp. 3–24). Lincoln: University of Nebraska Press.

Showalter, E. (2003). *Teaching literature.* Malden, MA: Wiley-Blackwell.

Shulman, L. S. (1987). Knowledge and teaching: Foundations of the new reform. *Harvard Educational Review, 57,* 1–22.

Smagorinsky, P. (2001). *Teaching English through principled practice.* New York: Pearson.

Smagorinsky, P. (2007). *Teaching English by design: How to create and carry out instructional units.* Portsmouth, NH: Heinemann.

Smagorinsky, P. (2009). Is it time to abandon the idea of "best practice" in the teaching of English? *English Journal, 98*(6), 15–22.

Smagorinsky, P., Clayton, C. M., & Johnson, L. L. (2015). Distributed scaffolding in a service-learning course. *Theory Into Practice, 54*(1), 71–78.

Smagorinsky, P., & Fly, P. K. (1994). A new perspective on why small groups do and don't work. *The English Journal, 83*(3), 54–58.

Smagorinsky, P., Johannessen, L. R., Kahn, E., & McCann, T. (2010). *The dynamics of writing instruction.* Portsmouth, NH: Heinemann.

Smagorinsky, P., Johannessen, L. R., Kahn, E., & McCann, T. (2012). *Teaching students to write fictional narratives.* Portsmouth, NH: Heinemann.

Smagorinsky, P., McCann, T., & Kern, S. (1987). *Explorations: Introductory activities for literature and composition, 7–12.* Urbana, IL: National Council of Teachers of English.

Smagorinsky, P., & Smith, M. W. (1992). The nature of knowledge in composition and literary understanding: The question of specificity. *Review of Educational Research, 62*(3), 279–305.

Smith, B. H. (2015, May 6). What was "close reading"?: A century of method in literary studies. *Minnesota Review, 87,* 57–75

Smith, E. E., & Swinney, D. A. (1992). The role of schemas in reading text: A real-time examination. *Discourse Processes, 15,* 303–316.

Smith, M. W. (1984). *Reducing writing apprehension.* Urbana, IL: National Council of Teachers of English.

Smith, M. W., Appleman, D., & Wilhelm, J. D. (2014). *Uncommon core: Where the authors of the standards go wrong about instruction—and how you can get it right.* Thousand Oaks, CA: Corwin Press.

Smith, M. W., & Wilhelm, J. D. (2007). *Getting it right: Fresh approaches to teaching grammar, usage, and correctness.* New York: Scholastic.

Smith, M. W., & Wilhelm, J. D. (2010). *Fresh takes on teaching literary elements.* Urbana, IL: National Council of Teachers of English.

Smith, N. B. (2017). A principled revolution in the teaching of writing. *English Journal, 106*(6), 70–75.

Smitherman, G. (1985). "It bees dat way sometime": Sounds and structure of present-day Black English. In V. P. Clark, P. A. Eschholz, & A. F. Rosa (Eds.), *Language* (4th ed., pp. 552–568). New York: St. Martin's Press.

Sosnoski, J. J. (1994). *Token professionals and master critics: A critique of orthodoxy in literary studies.* Albany: State University of New York Press.

Spenser, E. (1590/2001). *The Faerie Queen.* New York: Longmans.

Spolin, V. (1986). *Theater games for the classroom: First teacher's edition.* Evanston: Northwestern University Press.

Steinbeck, J. (1989). *Working days: The journals of The Grapes of Wrath* (R. DeMott, Ed.). New York: Penguin.

Stern, D. (1995). *Teaching English so it matters.* Thousand Oaks, CA: Corwin Press.

Stodolsky, S., & Grossman, P. L. (1995). The impact of subject matter on curricular activity: An analysis of five academic subjects. *American Educational Research Journal, 32*(2), 227–249.

Stotsky, S. (2010, Fall). Literary study in grades 9, 10, and 11: A national survey. *Forum: A Publication of the ALSCW, 4,* 2–75.

Stronge, J. (2007). *Qualities of effective teachers.* Alexandria, VA: Association for Supervision and Curriculum Development.

Strunk, W., & White, E. B. (1999). *The elements of style* (4th ed.). New York: Longman.

Tatum, A. (2009). *Reading for their life: (Re)building the textual lineages of African American adolescent males.* Portsmouth, NH: Heinemann.

Toulmin, S. E. (1958/2003). *The uses of argument.* Cambridge, UK: Cambridge University Press.

Toulmin, S. E., Rieke, R., & Janik, A. (1984). *An introduction to reasoning.* New York: Pearson.

Tremmel, R. (2001). Seeking a balanced discipline: Writing teacher education in first-year composition and English education. *English Education, 34*(1), 6–30.

Tsur, R. (2010). Poetic conventions as cognitive fossils. *Style, 44*(4), 496–523.

Turner, K. H., & Hicks, T. (2016). *Argument in the real world: Teaching adolescents to read and write digital texts.* Portsmouth, NH: Heinemann.

U.S. Department of Education. (2002). *Meeting the highly qualified teachers challenge: The secretary's annual report on teacher quality,* Washington, DC: Author.

Vermeule, B. (2010). *Why do we care about literary characters?* Baltimore: Johns Hopkins University Press.

Vygotsky, L. S. (1978). Interaction between learning and development. In M. Cole, V. John-Steiner, S. Scribner, & E. Souberman (Eds.), *Mind in society: The development of higher psychological processes* (pp. 79–91). Cambridge, MA: Harvard University Press.

Walsh, J. A., & Sattes, B. D. (2015). *Questioning for classroom discussion: Purposeful speaking, engaged listening, deep thinking.* Alexandria, VA: Association for Supervision and Curriculum Development.

Wander, P. (1984). The third persona: An ideological turn in rhetorical theory. *Central States Speech Journal, 35,* 197–216.

Warriner, J. E. (1946). *English grammar and composition* (6 vols.). New York: Harcourt Press.

Weaver, C. (1996). *Teaching grammar in context.* Portsmouth, NH: Heinemann.

Weaver, C. (1998). *Lessons to share on teaching grammar in context.* Portsmouth, NH: Heinemann.

Weissman, G. (2016). *The writer in the well: On misreading and rewriting literature.* Columbus: Ohio State University Press.

Welles, O., & Bogdanovich, P. (1993). *This is Orson Welles.* New York: Harper Perennial.

Whittaker, R. (2012, June 27). GOP opposes critical thinking: Party platform paints original ideas as a liberal conspiracy. *Austin Advocate.* Retrieved from *www.austinchronicle.com/daily/news/2012-06-27/gop-opposes-critical-thinking*

Wiggins, G. (2012). *On assessing for creativity: Yes you can, and yes you should.* Retrieved from *https://grantwiggins.wordpress.com/2012/02/03/on-assessing-for-creativity-yes-you-can-and-yes-you-should*

Wiggins, G., & McTighe, J. (2005). *Understanding by design* (2nd ed.). Alexandria, VA: Association for Supervision and Curriculum Development.

Wilhelm, J. D., & Smith, M. W. (2014). *Reading unbound: Why kids need to read what they want—and why we should let them.* New York: Scholastic.

Williams, J. M. (1999). *Style: Ten lessons in clarity and grace* (6th ed.). New York: Addison-Wesley.

Williams, J. M. (2004). *Problems into PROBLEMS: A rhetoric of motivation.* Fort Collins, CO: WAC Clearinghouse. Retrieved from *http://wac.colostate.edu/books/williams/williams.pdf*

Williams, J. M. (2010). *Style: Lessons in clarity and grace.* New York: Longman.

Williams, J., & Bizup, J. (2013). *Style: Lessons in clarity and grace* (11th ed.). New York: Longman.

Williams, J., & Columb, G. G. (2010). *Style: Lessons in clarity and grace* (10th ed.). New York: Longman.

Williams, R. (1966). *Modern tragedy.* London: Chatto and Windus.

Wills, G. (1996). *Witches and Jesuits: Shakespeare's Macbeth.* New York: Oxford University Press.

Wilson, P. (1983). *Second hand knowledge: An inquiry into cognitive authority.* Westport, CT: Greenwood Press.

Woodward, C. (2011). *American nations: The history of the eleven rival regional cultures of North America.* New York: Penguin.

Zakaria, F. (2015). *In defense of a liberal education.* New York: Norton.

Zimbardo, P. G. (2007). *The Lucifer effect: Understanding how good people turn evil.* New York: Random House.

Zinsser, W. (2006). *On writing well: The classic guide to nonfiction writing.* New York: Harper.

Index